Contents

Appendices

Introduction

THE 9/11 COMMISSION, IN ITS JULY 2004 REPORT, RECOMMENDED THAT THE UNITED STATES UNIFY ITS "INTELLIGENCE COMMUNITY WITH A NEW NATIONAL INTELLIGENCE DIRECTOR" (NID).[1] FIVE MONTHS LATER, SEEKING "TO UNIFY AND STRENGTHEN THE EFFORTS OF THE INTELLIGENCE COMMUNITY [IC] OF THE UNITED STATES GOVERNMENT," PASSAGE OF THE NATIONAL SECURITY ACT OF 2004 CREATED JUST SUCH A POSITION.[2] WHILE IMPLEMENTING THE RECOMMENDATION REPRESENTS A MAJOR RESTRUCTURING, THE NOTION ITSELF DOES NOT CHARACTERIZE A FRESH APPROACH. ALFRED CUMMING OF THE CONGRESSIONAL RESEARCH SERVICE CLAIMS: "THE COMMISSION'S RECOMMENDATION TO STRENGTHEN MANAGEMENT AUTHORITY OVER THE IC IS THE LATEST CONTRIBUTION TO AN IC STRUCTURAL REFORM DEBATE THAT DATES AT LEAST TO 1955 WHEN ARGUMENTS FOR STRONGER IC AUTHORITY BEGAN TO SURFACE."[3]

THIS DEBATE ENCOMPASSES MORE THAN 20 MAJOR INVESTIGATIONS OF THE IC, ALMOST ALL OF WHICH RECOMMENDED SOME MEASURE OF STRENGTHENING CENTRAL CONTROL OVER THE COMMUNITY. THESE RECOMMENDATIONS RESULTED IN NUMEROUS NATIONAL SECURITY COUNCIL (NSC) DIRECTIVES, EXECUTIVE ORDERS, AND LEGISLATIVE BILLS DESIGNED TO PROVIDE THAT CONTROL. NEVERTHELESS, AFTER 50 YEARS OF SUCH EFFORTS, CONGRESS STILL SAW A REQUIREMENT FOR NEW LEGISLATION. WHY DID PREVIOUS EFFORTS TO CENTRALIZE THE US INTELLIGENCE COMMUNITY FAIL TO PROVIDE THE DESIRED RESULTS? MORE IMPORTANTLY, WILL THE SAME FORCES THAT HAMPERED PREVIOUS EFFORTS CONTINUE TO FRUSTRATE THE NEW NID IN THIS LATEST ATTEMPT TO UNIFY THE IC UNDER A CENTRAL CONTROLLING AUTHORITY?

A PRELIMINARY EXAMINATION OF THE CONFOUNDING FORCES THAT FRUSTRATED PREVIOUS EFFORTS AT ESTABLISHING AND STRENGTHENING CENTRALIZED CONTROL OF US NATIONAL INTELLIGENCE IS WARRANTED, AND SERVES AS THE BASIS FOR IDENTIFYING RELEVANT CAUSAL FACTORS THAT DETERMINE THE LIKELIHOOD OF SUCCESSFUL REFORM. FIVE SUCH FACTORS ARE IDENTIFIED HERE: THE MOTIVE AND ABILITY OF EXISTING INTELLIGENCE ORGANIZATIONS TO RESIST CENTRALIZED CONTROL; THE ASSOCIATION OF CENTRAL DIRECTORS WITH COVERT OPERATIONS; THE TENDENCY TO TIE A CENTRAL DIRECTOR'S AUTHORITY TO HIS/HER ACCESS TO THE PRESIDENT; THE PROLIFERATION OF INTELLIGENCE AGENCIES AND ACTIVITIES; AND THE INCREASING CO-OPTION OF OTHER INTELLIGENCE ORGANIZATION BY THE DEPARTMENT OF DEFENSE (DOD). WHILE THESE MAY NOT BE THE ONLY FACTORS THAT IMPEDE THE ESTABLISHMENT AND PRACTICE OF CENTRALIZED CONTROL, THEIR REPEATED APPEARANCE AND

---

[1] 9/11 COMMISSION. *THE 9/11 COMMISSION REPORT.* (NEW YORK: W.W. NORTON, 2004), 399.

[2] US SENATE. *NATIONAL INTELLIGENCE REFORM ACT OF 2004*, 108TH CONG., 2ND SESS., 2004, S.2845, 13.

[3] ALFRED CUMMING. *THE POSITION OF DIRECTOR OF NATIONAL INTELLIGENCE: ISSUES FOR CONGRESS.* (WASHINGTON DC: CONGRESSIONAL RESEARCH SERVICE, 2004), N.P.

SIGNIFICANCE THROUGH IC HISTORY IS STRIKING. THESE FACTORS MUTUALLY REINFORCE EACH OTHER AND IN SOME CASES OVERLAP; THEIR ORDER OF PRESENTATION DOES NOT SIGNIFY ANY DEGREE OF RELATIVE SIGNIFICANCE OR IMPORTANCE. IN THIS PAPER I SEEK ONLY TO EXAMINE THE PROSPECTS OF THE GOVERNMENT'S ONGOING EFFORT TO EXERT GREATER CENTRAL CONTROL OVER THE IC, AND DO NOT ADDRESS THE DEBATE ON WHETHER OR NOT CENTRALIZED CONTROL OF THE NATIONAL INTELLIGENCE EFFORT IS A DESIRABLE GOAL.

IN CHAPTER 1, I TRACE HOW THESE FACTORS FRUSTRATED WOULD BE REFORMERS FROM WWII UNTIL 2001. IN THE NEXT CHAPTER, I EXAMINE EVENTS SINCE THE TERRORIST ATTACKS OF 9/11 TO PROJECT WHICH, IF ANY, OF THESE FACTORS HAVE BEEN MITIGATED, AND WHICH WILL CONTINUE TO PLAGUE THE NEW NATIONAL INTELLIGENCE DIRECTOR AS HE ATTEMPTS TO ESTABLISH THE PRECEDENTS THAT WILL LIKELY DEFINE THE IC FOR THE FORESEEABLE FUTURE. I CONCLUDE THAT WHILE THE NEW STRUCTURE WILL LESSEN THE IMPACT OF COVERT ACTIONS ON THE NID'S AUTHORITY, THE REMAINING FOUR FACTORS ARE STILL IN FORCE, AND IN THE CASE OF THE DEPARTMENT OF DEFENSE'S PROCLIVITY TO RESIST CONTROL OR CO-OPTION OF INTELLIGENCE FUNCTIONS, BECOMING MORE POWERFUL.

SEVERAL EXCELLENT SURVEYS OF IC REFORM EFFORTS ALREADY EXIST. ONE OF THE MOST SUCCINCT, *THE EVOLUTION OF THE U.S. INTELLIGENCE COMMUNITY – AN HISTORICAL OVERVIEW*, DEVELOPED BY THE ASPIN-BROWN COMMISSION, DETAILS THE HISTORICAL CONTEXT IN WHICH MAJOR REFORM EFFORTS EMERGED. A MORE DETAILED STUDY PREPARED BY THE CONGRESSIONAL RESEARCH SERVICE ENTITLED *PROPOSALS FOR INTELLIGENCE REORGANIZATION 1949-2004*, LINKS THE VARIOUS STUDIES OF THE IC WITH THE RESULTING ACTIONS BY PRESIDENTS AND CONGRESS ALONG WITH A BRIEF ASSESSMENT OF THE EFFECTIVENESS OF SUCH EFFORTS. NEITHER, HOWEVER, SYSTEMATICALLY ATTEMPTS TO DEVELOP COMMON CAUSES FOR THE REPEATED FAILURES OF REFORM EFFORTS.

CURRENT LITERATURE ABOUNDS WITH ASSESSMENTS OF THE 9/11 COMMISSION'S PROPOSALS AND THE NATIONAL INTELLIGENCE REFORM ACT OF 2004. MOST QUESTION WHETHER THE NEW STRUCTURE ENVISIONED IN THE BILL AND LED BY THE NID WILL SUCCEED IN PRODUCING BETTER INTELLIGENCE FOR NATIONAL POLICY MAKERS. WHILE BETTER INTELLIGENCE IS THE KEY ISSUE, THE QUESTION BECOMES MOOT IF THE NID NEVER SUCCEEDS IN WIELDING ANY POWER TO INFLUENCE THE IC. OTHER RECENT ARTICLES QUESTION WHETHER THE NID HAS THE AUTHORITY NEEDED TO BE SUCCESSFUL. MANY OF THESE LATER ARTICLES DISCUSS SIMILARITIES TO PAST REFORM EFFORTS THAT FAILED, PARTICULARLY THE ABILITY OF THE MILITARY AND ITS CONGRESSIONAL PATRONS TO FIGHT CENTRAL CONTROL. WHILE THESE ARTICLES ARE INFORMATIVE, BY FOCUSING ON ONE FACTOR THEY FAIL TO DEMONSTRATE HOW MULTIPLE FACTORS MUTUALLY REINFORCE EACH OTHER TO COMPOUND THE RESISTANCE FACING WOULD BE REFORMERS OF THE IC.

IN THIS PAPER, I USE THE TWO OVERVIEWS MENTIONED ABOVE AS A STARTING POINT, AND WHERE POSSIBLE LOOKED AT THE ORIGINAL REPORTS OF THE VARIOUS COMMISSIONS AND PANELS. WHILE SOME REPORTS ON THE IC REMAIN PARTIALLY CLASSIFIED; THE EBERSTADT REPORT OF 1949, THE SCHLESINGER REPORT OF 1971, THE REPORT OF THE CHURCH COMMITTEE IN 1976, THE 1996

IC21 STUDY BY THE HOUSE'S PERMANENT SELECT COMMITTEE ON INTELLIGENCE, THE 2002 REPORT OF THE JOINT INQUIRY BY BOTH HOUSES OF CONGRESS, AND 2004'S 9/11 COMMISSION REPORT WERE PARTICULARLY ACCESSIBLE AND RELEVANT. LARGE SEGMENTS OF THE EARLIER REPORTS COULD HAVE BEEN INCLUDED IN THE LATER WITHOUT APPEARING OUT OF PLACE. ADDITIONALLY I EXAMINE THE DIRECTIVES, ORDERS, BILLS THAT RESULTED FROM SUCH REPORTS, AS WELL AS BOTH CONTEMPORARY AND HISTORICAL COMMENTARY TO DETECT RECURRING PATTERNS.

FOR THE PRESIDENT'S EYES ONLY BY CHRISTOPHER ANDREW, WAS AN INVALUABLE SOURCE OF HISTORICAL CONTEXT FOR THE VARIOUS REFORM EFFORTS. TWO OTHER SOURCES THAT ARE WORTH PARTICULAR MENTION ARE *U.S. INTELLIGENCE* AND *INTELLIGENCE: FROM SECRETS TO POLICY,* BOTH BY MARK M. LOWENTHAL, WHICH ILLUMINATE THE OFTEN COMPLEX STRUCTURES, MISSIONS, AND PRACTICES OF THE US INTELLIGENCE COMMUNITY. WHILE I TOUCH ON THE TENSION BETWEEN CIVILIAN LEADERSHIP AND MILITARY INTELLIGENCE, THIS TOPIC DESERVES FURTHER STUDY. AN EXCELLENT STARTING POINT IS RICHARD RUSSELL'S "TUG OF WAR: THE CIA'S UNEASY RELATIONSHIP WITH THE MILITARY" IN *SAIS REVIEW, A JOURNAL OF INTERNATIONAL AFFAIRS* AND *FLAWED BY DESIGN* BY AMY ZEGART.

WHETHER OR NOT THIS LATEST EFFORT TO IMPOSE CENTRALIZED CONTROL OVER THE COMMUNITY UNDER A NATIONAL INTELLIGENCE DIRECTOR SUCCEEDS IS MORE THAN JUST AN ACADEMIC QUESTION. WHAT INTELLIGENCE THE US COLLECTS AND HOW SUCH INTELLIGENCE IS ANALYZED AND DISSEMINATED IMPACTS WHAT POLICIES IT PURSUES. WITH ANYWHERE FROM 80 TO 90 PERCENT OF NATIONAL INTELLIGENCE ASSETS CURRENTLY RESIDING WITHIN THE DEPARTMENT OF DEFENSE, THE QUESTION IS NOT SO MUCH WHETHER CENTRALIZED CONTROL OVER THE COMMUNITY WILL SUCCEED AS WHETHER SUCH CONTROL WILL BE CIVILIAN OR MILITARY. IF THE NID IS NOT EMPOWERED TO EFFECTIVELY ESTABLISH PRIORITIES, COORDINATE INFORMATION SHARING, PROMOTE INDEPENDENT AND COMPETITIVE ANALYSIS, AND PRODUCE THE BEST CONSENSUS OF THE IC; THE PENTAGON WILL ASSUME THOSE RESPONSIBILITIES. WHILE THE DoD WOULD OPTIMIZE INTELLIGENCE TO SUPPORT THE WARFIGHTER, THERE IS NO INDICATION THAT THE MILITARY IS EITHER INCLINED OR ABLE TO IMPARTIALLY WEIGHT ITS INTELLIGENCE NEEDS AGAINST THOSE OF THE OTHER INSTRUMENTS OF NATIONAL POWER. IF THE LATEST REFORM ACT FAILS TO ACCOMPLISH ITS GOALS, THE RESULT MAY WELL BE A FUTURE IN WHICH THE NATION FRAMES BOTH ITS CHALLENGES AND ITS RESPONSES TO THEM THROUGH A MILITARY LENS.

CHAPTER 1

HISTORICAL ATTEMPTS TO CENTRALIZE THE
INTELLIGENCE COMMUNITY: WWII TO 9/11

WHILE THE CONGRESSIONAL RESEARCH SERVICE DATES THE STRUCTURAL REFORM DEBATE ON CENTRALIZING CONTROL OVER THE INTELLIGENCE COMMUNITY (IC) TO 1955, THE CONTROVERSY IS AT LEAST A DECADE OLDER.[4] DURING WWII, PRESIDENT ROOSEVELT ESTABLISHED A COORDINATOR OF INTELLIGENCE (COI) TO CENTRALIZE WARTIME INTELLIGENCE. THE COI FELL OUT OF FAVOR, HOWEVER, WHEN PRESIDENT TRUMAN ENTERED OFFICE. FOLLOWING THE WAR, TRUMAN CREATED THE POSITION OF DIRECTOR OF CENTRAL INTELLIGENCE (DCI) TO COORDINATE THE INTELLIGENCE COMMUNITY WITH THE HELP OF A CENTRAL INTELLIGENCE GROUP (CIG). THIS ARRANGEMENT PROVED UNSATISFACTORY, AND THE NATIONAL SECURITY ACT OF 1947 INTRODUCED THE THIRD MAJOR STRUCTURE DESIGNED TO CENTRALIZE AUTHORITY OVER THE IC. THE TITLE OF DCI WAS RETAINED, BUT RESPONSIBILITIES AND AUTHORITIES WERE UPDATED WITH THE CREATION OF THE CENTRAL INTELLIGENCE AGENCY (CIA).

THE BASIC INTELLIGENCE STRUCTURE CREATED IN 1947 STOOD REMARKABLY INTACT FOR 57 YEARS, BUT FAILED TO SATISFY PROPONENTS OF STRONG CENTRAL LEADERSHIP. NUMEROUS COMMISSIONS, PANELS, AND INDEPENDENT GROUPS STUDIED THE INTELLIGENCE COMMUNITY AND NEARLY ALL RECOMMENDED STRENGTHENING CENTRALIZED AUTHORITY. WHETHER THE ISSUE WAS THE NEED TO EMPOWER THE IC WITH REGARD TO AN INTELLIGENCE FAILURE, OR THE NEED TO RESTRAIN THE IC IN LIGHT OF TRANSGRESSIONS, THE PROPOSED SOLUTION WAS THE SAME: GIVE MORE POWER TO THE DCI OR CREATE A DIRECTOR OF NATIONAL INTELLIGENCE (DNI) WITH EXPANDED AUTHORITY OVER THE IC. NATIONAL SECURITY COUNCIL DIRECTIVES, CONGRESSIONAL LEGISLATION, AND EXECUTIVE ORDERS ALL SOUGHT TO ESTABLISH SUCH AUTHORITY, YET CRITICS OF THE SYSTEM STILL "ARGUE THAT THE ABSENCE OF STRONG, CENTRALIZED LEADERSHIP HAS RESULTED IN DIVIDED MANAGEMENT OF INTELLIGENCE CAPABILITIES; LACK OF COMMON STANDARDS AND PRACTICES ACROSS THE FOREIGN-DOMESTIC INTELLIGENCE DIVIDE; STRUCTURAL BARRIERS THAT UNDERMINE THE PERFORMANCE OF JOINT INTELLIGENCE WORK; AND A WEAK CAPACITY TO SET PRIORITIES AND MOVE RESOURCES."[5]

A SURVEY OF REFORM EFFORTS FROM 1940 TO THE END OF THE CENTURY EXPOSES SEVERAL REOCCURRING CAUSES FOR THEIR FAILURE. IN THIS CHAPTER, I EXAMINE FIVE SUCH FACTORS, DISCUSSING HOW THEY FRAMED THE INVESTIGATION, WEAKENED THE IMPACT OF LEGISLATION, OR COMPLICATED THE IMPLEMENTATION OF VARIOUS REFORM EFFORTS. EACH FACTOR IS INTRODUCED AND DISCUSSED IN TURN.

FACTOR 1: THE MOTIVE AND ABILITY OF EXISTING INTELLIGENCE

---

[4] ALFRED CUMMING. *THE POSITION OF DIRECTOR OF NATIONAL INTELLIGENCE: ISSUES FOR CONGRESS* (WASHINGTON DC: CONGRESSIONAL RESEARCH SERVICE, 2004), N.P.
[5] Ibid.

ORGANIZATIONS TO RESIST CENTRALIZED CONTROL

ONE OF THE PRIMARY REASONS THAT THE CIA AND DCI FAILED TO MELD THE WORK OF THE VARIOUS INTELLIGENCE AGENCIES INTO A COORDINATED NATIONAL EFFORT IS THAT THE EXISTING AGENCIES HAVE BOTH THE INCENTIVE AND THE RESOURCES TO RESIST SUCH COORDINATION. AS THOMAS F. TROY, A FORMER CIA OFFICER, OBSERVED, "TO THE UNINVOLVED THE WORD 'COORDINATION' CONNOTED RATIONALITY, EFFICIENCY, AND NECESSITY. TO THE POTENTIAL OBJECTS OF COORDINATION, HOWEVER, TO THE INTELLIGENCE DEPARTMENTS WITH THEIR VESTED INTERESTS – RESPONSIBILITIES, TASKS, BUDGETS, PERSONNEL, OPERATIONS – THE WORD RAISED THE SPECTER OF TYRANNY."[6] THE ATTITUDE OF EXISTING INTELLIGENCE SERVICES OF THE VARIOUS GOVERNMENT DEPARTMENTS TOWARD THE CIA AND DCI HAS RANGED FROM SUSPICION TO OUTRIGHT HOSTILITY. SUCH ANTIPATHY DOES NOT MERELY EXPRESS ITSELF THROUGH RESENTMENT. TO THE CONTRARY, OTHER INTELLIGENCE ORGANIZATIONS ARE IN AN IDEAL POSITION TO RESIST EFFORTS TO EXERT CONTROL OVER THEM.

WHILE THE CIA ENJOYS THE STATURE OF BEING THE SOLE INTELLIGENCE AGENCY THAT REPORTS DIRECTLY TO THE PRESIDENT, INDEPENDENT OF ANY GOVERNMENTAL DEPARTMENT, IT DOES SO AT THE EXPENSE OF A DEPARTMENTAL PATRON IN BUREAUCRATIC POWER STRUGGLES. THE JUSTICE DEPARTMENT DEFENDS THE AUTONOMY OF THE FEDERAL BUREAU OF INVESTIGATION (FBI) AND THE DRUG ENFORCEMENT ADMINISTRATION; THE DEPARTMENTS OF STATE, ENERGY, TREASURY, AND HOMELAND DEFENSE, EACH LOOK AFTER THEIR INTERNAL INTELLIGENCE AGENCIES, AND THE DEPARTMENT OF DEFENSE JEALOUSLY PROTECTS SEVEN SEPARATE INTELLIGENCE AGENCIES.[7] WITHIN THE UNIQUELY AMERICAN FORM OF CONSENSUAL DEMOCRATIC GOVERNMENT, THESE DEPARTMENTS SUCCESSFULLY DILUTED THE BEST EFFORTS OF INTELLIGENCE REFORMERS TO GIVE THE DCI THE AUTHORITY TO COMPEL MORE COOPERATION THAN THE EXISTING AGENCIES WILLINGLY EXTENDED.

THE CIA AND DCI ALSO LACKED THE PATRONAGE THAT OTHER AGENCIES, MOST NOTABLY THOSE IN THE DEPARTMENT OF DEFENSE (DOD), TRADITIONALLY ENJOY IN CONGRESS. THE POWERFUL ARMED SERVICES COMMITTEES IN CONGRESS HAVE HAD TWO REASONS TO BLOCK MOVES TO CENTRALIZE CONTROL OF INTELLIGENCE FUNCTIONS CURRENTLY IN THE DEPARTMENT OF DEFENSE. FIRST, THE MILITARY HAS THE ABILITY TO REPAY LOYALTY WITH PORK BARREL SPENDING AND SECOND, KEEPING INTELLIGENCE FUNDS FLOWING TO THE PENTAGON INCREASES THEIR OWN BUDGETARY AUTHORITY, A KEY MEASUREMENT OF POWER IN WASHINGTON.[8] INTELLIGENCE, ON THE OTHER HAND, HAS LITTLE WITH WHICH TO REWARD CONGRESSIONAL SUPPORT. IT DOES NOT BRING ANY IMMEDIATE AND CONCRETE GOOD TO INDIVIDUAL HOME STATES, ASSOCIATION WITH COVERT ACTIONS CAN SULLY

---

[6] Thomas F. Troy, *Donovan and the CIA: A History of the Establishment of the Central Intelligence Agency* (University Publications of America, Inc., Frederick, Maryland, 1981), 357.

[7] Stan A. Taylor and David Goldman, "Intelligence Reform: Will More Agencies, Money, and Personnel Help?," *Intelligence and National Security*, Vol.19, No.3, (Autumn 2004): 421.

[8] Mark M. Lowenthal, *Intelligence From Secrets to Policy*, Second Edition, (Washington DC: CQ Press, 2003), 36.

POLITICAL REPUTATIONS, AND DUE TO ITS INHERENT SECRECY, SUCCESSES RELATED TO NATIONAL SECURITY GENERALLY CANNOT BE GRANDSTANDED FOR POLITICAL GAIN.[9]

UNTIL 1976, NO CONGRESSIONAL COMMITTEE HAD SPECIFIC RESPONSIBILITIES FOR NATIONAL INTELLIGENCE. EVEN FOLLOWING THE CREATION OF THE SENATE SELECT COMMITTEE ON INTELLIGENCE, THE DCI DID NOT GAIN A POWERFUL ALLY IN CONGRESS. THE INTELLIGENCE COMMITTEE'S PRIMARY RESPONSIBILITY WAS RESTRAINING THE IC, NOT PROMOTING IT. THE POWER OF THE PURSE STILL BELONGED TO THE DoD, AS THE DEFENSE SUBCOMMITTEE OF THE APPROPRIATIONS COMMITTEES MADE APPROPRIATIONS FOR THE CIA TO THE SECRETARY OF DEFENSE, WHO THEN TRANSFERRED THE CIA'S MONEY TO THE DCI.[10] FOLLOWING A PUBLICIZED INTELLIGENCE FAILURE THERE IS POLITICAL GAIN TO BE HAD FOR INVESTIGATING AND POINTING OUT THE WEAKNESSES OF THE SYSTEM, BUT LESS FOR THE DIFFICULT WORK OF LEGISLATING CHANGE AFTER NATIONAL INTEREST HAS WANED. AS A RESULT, MOST REFORMS TO THE INTELLIGENCE COMMUNITY HAVE COME THROUGH THE LESS AUTHORITATIVE PRESIDENTIAL DIRECTIVE, OR HAVE AMOUNTED TO WATERED DOWN CONGRESSIONAL ACTIONS THAT ONLY ADDRESS THE NON-CONTROVERSIAL PERIPHERY OF INTELLIGENCE ISSUES.

WELL BEFORE THE NATIONAL SECURITY ACT OF 1947 CREATED THE CIA AND POSITION OF DCI, THE EXISTING INTELLIGENCE ELEMENTS OF THE VARIOUS DEPARTMENTS VIGOROUSLY RESISTED ANY ATTEMPTS TO CREATE A BODY TO OVERSEE AND COORDINATE THEIR EFFORTS. IN 1940, WILLIAM, "WILD BILL" DONOVAN, A VETERAN OF WWI, CONDUCTED A FACT-FINDING TRIP TO BRITAIN ON BEHALF OF PRESIDENT ROOSEVELT, AND CONCLUDED THE CENTRALIZED BRITISH INTELLIGENCE ORGANIZATION HELD POTENTIAL VALUE FOR THE US.[11] EVEN BEFORE DONOVAN FOUND A RECEPTIVE AUDIENCE FOR HIS PROPOSALS, HE RUFFLED FEATHERS WITHIN THE ESTABLISHED INTELLIGENCE ORGANIZATIONS. BRIG GEN MILES, THE G-2 (INTELLIGENCE OFFICER) OF THE MILITARY INTELLIGENCE DIVISION (MID), WROTE GENERAL GEORGE C. MARSHALL, THE ARMY'S CHIEF OF STAFF, WARNING THAT DONOVAN WAS ADVOCATING A "SUPER AGENCY CONTROLLING *ALL* INTELLIGENCE" AND THAT SUCH AN AGENCY WOULD "COLLECT, COLLATE, AND POSSIBLY EVALUATE ALL MILITARY INTELLIGENCE WHICH WE NOW GATHER."[12] MILES WENT ON TO ASSERT, "FROM THE POINT OF VIEW OF THE WAR DEPARTMENT, SUCH A MOVE WOULD APPEAR TO BE VERY DISADVANTAGEOUS, IF NOT CALAMITOUS."

THIS CONCERN WAS NOT LIMITED TO THE ARMY. AFTER RECEIVING DONOVAN'S PROPOSAL FOR A COORDINATOR OF INTELLIGENCE, FRANKLIN DELANO ROOSEVELT ASKED THE ARMY, NAVY, AND FBI TO CONFER ON THE ROLE OF A "COORDINATOR OF INTELLIGENCE ON THE NATIONAL LEVEL." BRIG. GEN. MILES OF THE ARMY, CAPT KIRK (CHIEF OF ONI [OFFICE OF NAVAL INTELLIGENCE]), AND J. EDGAR

---

[9] AMY ZEGART, *FLAWED BY DESIGN* (STANFORD, CALIFORNIA: STANFORD UNIVERSITY PRESS, 1999), 214.
[10] 9/11 Commission, *The 9/11 Commission Report* (New York: W.W. Norton, 2004), 410.
[11] TROY, *DONOVAN AND THE CIA: A HISTORY OF THE ESTABLISHMENT OF THE CENTRAL INTELLIGENCE AGENCY*
   (FREDERICK, MARYLAND: UNIVERSITY PUBLICATIONS OF AMERICA, INC., 1981), 32-33.
[12] Ibid., p. 42.

HOOVER OF THE FBI CONCLUDED A COORDINATOR WAS "A GREAT COMPLICATION," IF NOT A "SERIOUS DETRIMENT TO THE NATIONAL SERVICE, WHILE OFFERING ONLY NEGLIGIBLE ADVANTAGES."[13]

WHEN ROOSEVELT GAVE THE TITLE COORDINATOR OF INTELLIGENCE (COI) TO DONOVAN, AND LATER CREATED THE OFFICE OF STRATEGIC SERVICES (OSS), THE ESTABLISHED ORGANIZATIONS USED THEIR BUREAUCRATIC CLOUT TO SHIELD THEIR PRIMARY INTERESTS FROM THESE CENTRALIZING AUTHORITIES. HOOVER, "FEARING A LOSS OF AUTHORITY TO THE NEW COORDINATOR, SECURED THE PRESIDENT'S COMMITMENT THAT THE BUREAU'S PRIMACY IN SOUTH AMERICA WOULD NOT CHANGE."[14] THE BUDGET BUREAU LARGELY SUCCEEDED IN STRIPPING OSS OF ANY RESPONSIBILITY FOR ECONOMIC INTELLIGENCE.[15] REAR ADMIRAL TRAIN, CHIEF OF ONI FROM 1942 TO 1943, LATER ADMITTED THAT G-2 AND ONI WERE FEARFUL OF OSS "WANDERING INTO THE SERVICE INTELLIGENCE FIELD" AND REFUSED TO GIVE OSS OPERATIONAL INTELLIGENCE, AND EVEN REQUESTED STUDIES BY OSS JUST TO KEEP IT "OCCUPIED AND OUT OF THE WAY OF THE ARMY AND NAVY."[16] THUS BEGAN A HOSTILE WORKING RELATIONSHIP BETWEEN THE INDEPENDENT OSS AND THE ORIGINAL INTELLIGENCE SERVICES THAT CONTINUED AS THE OSS EVOLVED INTO THE CENTRAL INTELLIGENCE GROUP AND ULTIMATELY THE CENTRAL INTELLIGENCE AGENCY.

FROM THE CIA'S INCEPTION, THE ESTABLISHED INTELLIGENCE ORGANIZATIONS MADE CLEAR THAT COOPERATION BETWEEN AGENCIES WOULD OCCUR ON THEIR TERMS. IF THE CIA WAS TO BE, AS PROPOSED, THE GOVERNMENT'S FOCAL POINT FOR THE GATHERING AND EVALUATION OF INTELLIGENCE, THE CIA NEEDED ACCESS TO ALL INFORMATION COLLECTED BY OTHER AGENCIES.[17] THE FBI REQUIRED WRITTEN NOTICE BEFORE GIVING THE CIA ACCESS TO ITS FILES AND EVEN THEN COOPERATED ONLY WHEN ACCESS WAS "ESSENTIAL TO THE NATIONAL SECURITY."[18] THE SECRETARY OF STATE INITIALLY REFUSED TO SHARE STATE DEPARTMENT CABLES FOR INCORPORATION IN THE PRESIDENT'S DAILY BRIEFING, "ON THE GROUNDS THAT IT WAS HIS RESPONSIBILITY ALONE TO INFORM THE PRESIDENT OF THE CABLES' CONTENTS."[19] THE MILITARY REFUSED TO SHARE ELECTRONIC SIGNALS INTELLIGENCE (SIGINT) ON THE GROUNDS OF SECURITY CONCERNS, RESULTING IN EARLY CIA ANALYSTS PREPARING DAILY SUMMARIES FOR THE PRESIDENT WITHOUT ACCESS TO ONE OF THE NATION'S BEST SOURCES OF INTELLIGENCE.[20] THE MILITARY ALSO "REFUSED TO PROVIDE WHAT THEY REGARDED AS OPERATIONAL

---

[13] Ibid, p. 49/51.

[14] ASPIN-BROWN COMMISSION. "THE EVOLUTION OF THE U.S. INTELLIGENCE COMMUNITY – AN HISTORICAL
OVERVIEW." IN *STRATEGIC INTELLIGENCE: WINDOWS INTO A SECRET WORLD*, ED. LOCH K. JOHNSON ET AL. LOS
ANGELES, (CALIFORNIA: ROXBURY PUBLISHING COMPANY, 2004), 7.

[15] Troy, *Donovan and the CIA*, 100.

[16] Ibid., 170.

[17] Aspin-Brown Commission, *The Evolution of the U.S. Intelligence Community*, 10.

[18] Ibid.

[19] Andrew, *For the President's Eyes Only* (New York: HarperCollins Publishers, 1995), 165.

[20] Ibid., 166.

DOCUMENTS FOR INCLUSION" IN THE CIA PRODUCTS."[21] AS ONE EDITOR OF THE CIA'S DAILY SUMMARY
COMPLAINED:

> UNDER THIS GUISE, THEY HAVE WITHHELD FROM CIA SUCH SENSITIVE MATERIALS AS
> GENERAL MCARTHUR'S REPORTS FROM TOKYO, GENERAL CLAY'S REPORTS FROM
> BERLIN, ADMIRAL STRUBLE'S REPORTS FROM THE SEVENTH FLEET . . . ETC. CIA DOES
> NOT RECEIVE REPORTS MADE TO THE JOINT CHIEFS, MANY OF WHICH, BECAUSE OF
> THEIR ORIGIN AND THEIR SUBJECT MUST BE WORTHY OF THE PRESIDENT'S
> ATTENTION.[22]

TRUMAN, WHO HARBORED HIS OWN MISGIVINGS OF A POWERFUL CENTRALIZED INTELLIGENCE
ORGANIZATION, WAS NOT INCLINED TO FIGHT FOR THE CIA'S STATUS IN ITS CHARTER LEGISLATION, THE
NATIONAL SECURITY ACT OF 1947. HIS PRIMARILY GOAL FOR THAT ACT WAS TO UNIFY THE MILITARY
SERVICES. TO GAIN MILITARY APPROVAL OF THE ACT, TRUMAN ACCEPTED DEMANDS FOR LIMITS ON THE
ROLE OF THE CIA. IN THE END, ALTHOUGH THE ACT CHARGED THE CIA WITH "COORDINATING THE
INTELLIGENCE ACTIVITIES OF THE SEVERAL GOVERNMENT DEPARTMENTS AND AGENCIES," IT "PROVIDED
NO LANGUAGE COMPELLING THESE VARIOUS AGENCIES TO COOPERATE." INSTEAD IT EXPLICITLY STATED
THAT SUCH AGENCIES "SHALL CONTINUE TO COLLECT, EVALUATE, CORRELATE, AND DISSEMINATE
DEPARTMENTAL INTELLIGENCE." ADDITIONALLY, THE ACT PLACED THE CIA "UNDER THE DIRECTION OF
THE NATIONAL SECURITY COUNCIL," WHICH INCLUDED THE SECRETARIES OF STATE AND DEFENSE, AND
THE THREE MILITARY SERVICES, EFFECTIVELY PLACING THE CIA "BENEATH THE VERY AGENCIES IT WAS
SUPPOSED TO COORDINATE."[23] THUS, THE LEGISLATION STRUCTURALLY CREATED THE TENSION, LACK OF
COORDINATION, AND DUPLICATION OF EFFORT THAT BECAME THE SUBJECT OF STUDIES FOR THE NEXT
FIFTY YEARS.

IN JANUARY OF 1948, PRESIDENT TRUMAN COMMISSIONED ALLEN W. DULLES, WILLIAM H.
JACKSON, AND MATTHIAS F. CORREA TO CONDUCT THE FIRST STUDY OF THE CIA AND ITS RELATIONSHIP
WITH OTHER AGENCIES.[24] THE RESULTING DULLES-JACKSON-CORREA REPORT, GIVEN TO THE NSC IN
JANUARY OF 1948, CONCLUDED THAT THE CIA WAS FAILING TO MEET ITS MANDATES TO COORDINATE
THE VARIOUS INTELLIGENCE AGENCIES AND TO PRODUCE "NATIONAL INTELLIGENCE."[25] IT FAULTED THE
CIA FOR NOT DRAWING ON THE WORK OF OTHER AGENCIES IN PREPARING ESTIMATES. IN THE VIEW OF
THE REPORT, "NATIONAL INTELLIGENCE, EXPRESSED IN THE FORM OF COORDINATED NATIONAL
ESTIMATES, TRANSCENDS IN SCOPE AND BREADTH THE INTEREST AND COMPETENCE OF ANY SINGLE
INTELLIGENCE AGENCY," BUT THE CIA'S "PRODUCES ESTIMATES...ON THE BASIS OF ITS OWN RESEARCH
AND ANALYSIS AND OFFERS ITS PRODUCT AS COMPETITIVE WITH THE SIMILAR PRODUCT OF OTHER

---

[21] Ibid.

[22] Ibid.

[23] Zegart, *Flawed by Design,* 188.

[24] Mark M. Lowenthal, *U.S. Intelligence Evolution and Anatomy* (Westport, Connecticut: Praeger, 1992*),* 20.

[25] "Summary", *Central Intelligence Organization and National Organization for Intelligence,* (known as the 'Dulles-Jackson-Correa- Report'), 15 January 1949. n.p.

AGENCIES, RATHER THAN AS THE COORDINATED RESULT OF THE BEST INTELLIGENCE PRODUCT WHICH EACH OF THE INTERESTED AGENCIES IS ABLE TO CONTRIBUTE."[26]

ALTHOUGH THE DULLES-JACKSON-CORREA REPORT ACCURATELY IDENTIFIED THE PROBLEM, IT DID NOT RECOMMEND GIVING THE CIA AUTHORITY TO DEMAND COOPERATION OR INCENTIVE TO THE OTHER SERVICES TO PROVIDE IT. THE REPORT RELIED ON INITIATIVE AND GOODWILL MORE THAN LAW OR REGULATIONS TO CORRECT INTELLIGENCE COMMUNITY SHORTCOMINGS, SUGGESTING INSTEAD: "COORDINATION CAN MOST EFFECTIVELY BE ACHIEVED BY MUTUAL AGREEMENT AMONG THE VARIOUS AGENCIES."[27] UNFORTUNATELY, THE REPORT FAILED TO DESCRIBE HOW TO ACHIEVE SUCH MUTUAL AGREEMENT.

CONCURRENT WITH THE PRESIDENT'S STUDY OF THE CIA, CONGRESS, AS PART OF ITS "COMMISSION ON ORGANIZATION OF THE EXECUTIVE BRANCH OF THE GOVERNMENT," EXAMINED THE CIA AND OTHER INTELLIGENCE AGENCIES IN WHAT BECAME THE EBERSTADT REPORT. FERDINAND EBERSTADT DETAILED AN "ADVERSARIAL RELATIONSHIP AND LACK OF COORDINATION BETWEEN THE CIA, THE MILITARY, AND THE STATE DEPARTMENT."[28] THE MILITARY AND STATE DEPARTMENTS WERE FAULTED FOR NOT BEING MORE PROACTIVE IN CONSULTING AND SHARING PERTINENT INFORMATION WITH THE CIA.[29] EBERSTADT CONCLUDED, "A SPIRIT OF TEAMWORK MUST GOVERN INTERAGENCY INTELLIGENCE RELATIONSHIPS. THE CENTRAL INTELLIGENCE AGENCY DESERVES AND MUST HAVE A GREATER DEGREE OF ACCEPTANCE AND SUPPORT FROM OLD-LINE INTELLIGENCE SERVICES."[30]

WALTER BEDELL SMITH, WHO BECAME THE DCI IN 1950, SOUGHT TO INSTITUTE THE RECOMMENDATIONS OF THE EBERSTADT REPORT.[31] SMITH USED FORCE OF PERSONALITY, AND ACCESS TO THE PRESIDENT TO GAIN SOME PARTICIPATION BY OTHER AGENCIES IN THE PRODUCTION OF NATIONAL ESTIMATES, BUT

> WAS UNABLE TO WIN SOME OF HIS BATTLES WITH THE JOINT CHIEFS OF STAFF. SMITH ARGUED PASSIONATELY THAT HE COULD NOT PROPERLY ESTIMATE ENEMY INTENTIONS WITHOUT ADEQUATE INFORMATION ON THE US FORCES THAT THE ENEMY WAS FACING. THE JCS, HOWEVER, STUCK RIGIDLY TO THE ILLOGICAL POSITION THAT SUCH INFORMATION WAS NO CONCERN OF THE DCI. THEY INSTRUCTED THAT JCS PAPERS AND MILITARY OPERATIONAL CABLES WERE NOT TO BE TRANSMITTED TO THE CIA.[32]

EVEN WHERE THE EXISTING AGENCIES DID COMPLY, THEY DID SO IN A WAY THAT FURTHERED THEIR OWN INTERESTS. DESPITE SMITH'S BEST EFFORT TO INCORPORATE THE ENTIRE INTELLIGENCE COMMUNITY, THE CIA CAME TO DOMINATE THE NATIONAL INTELLIGENCE ESTIMATE (NIE) PROCESS.

---

[26] Ibid.

[27] Ibid.

[28] RICHARD A. BEST, JR. *PROPOSALS FOR INTELLIGENCE REORGANIZATION, 1949-2004* (WASHINGTON, DC: CONGRESSIONAL RESEARCH SERVICE, LIBRARY OF CONGRESS, 29 JUL7 2004), 4.

[29] Ibid.

[30] Ferdinand Eberstadt, *National Security Organization,* Appendix G, (U.S. Government Printing Office, Washington D.C., 1949),76-77.

[31] Best, *Proposals for Intelligence Reorganization*, 7.

[32] Andrew, *For the President's Eyes Only*, 192.

Smith found it easier to have the CIA produce its own reports and circulate them to the other agencies for comment than to gather raw data and analysis from all agencies to synthesize into one report.[33] By the end of his tenure as DCI, Smith had reversed the role of the CIA from its intended purpose of evaluating and synthesizing the intelligence of other agencies to an independent producer, subject to the review and evaluation of the older agencies.[34]

In 1954, Congress appointed the Second Hoover Commission to review the organization and efficiency of the executive branch. A sub group of the commission, headed by General Mark Clark, examined the various intelligence agencies, which by then consisted of the "NSC [National Security Council], CIA, NSA [National Security Agency], FBI, Department of State, Army, Navy, Air Force, and the Atomic Energy Commission."[35] This report coined the phrase "intelligence community," although skeptics argued that the "intelligence agencies – jealous of their turf, distrustful of one another, loath to share information, close-chested in their operations – hardly had the stuff of community."[36] The Clark report recommended separating the DCI from the CIA, giving him more time to focus on his community responsibilities, but no concrete action was taken on that recommendation.[37]

The Vietnam Order of Battle (OB) controversy between the CIA and the DoD, in which the CIA assessed the enemy's numerical strength to be much higher than the Pentagon assessment, highlighted the reversal of the role of the CIA from Truman's concept of an overall coordinator and evaluator to another competitor in an interest-laden community. The CIA, true to its charter, approached Vietnam from a detached position that integrated "political, economic, and social developments" as well as military factors into their assessments, resulting in "a pessimistic agenda that highlighted the relative lack of progress in South Vietnam compared to the resources that had been devoted to the conflict."[38] The military, in contrast, had a bureaucratic interest in "a positive agenda, based upon the ideas of progress and impending success."[39] As James

---

[33] Lowenthal, *U.S. Intelligence*, 25.
[34] Ibid.
[35] *Preparing for the 21ST Century: An Appraisal of U.S. Intelligenc: Report of the Commission on the Roles and Capabities of the U.S. Intelligence Community* (Washington, DC: Government Printing Office, 1996), A-12.
[36] Thomas F. Troy, "The Quaintness of the U.S. Intelligence Community" in *Strategic Intelligence,* ed. Loch K. Johnson et al. (Los Angeles, California: Roxbury Publishing Company, 2004), 26.
[37] Best, *Proposals for Intelligence Reorganization*, 7.
[38] James J. Wirtz, "Intelligence to Please?" in *Strategic Intelligence,* ed. Loch K. Johnson, 192.
[39] Ibid.

WIRTZ NOTES: "THE ISSUE DRIVING THE ORDER OF BATTLE CONTROVERSY WAS NOT THE DISAGREEMENT OVER THE SIZE OF THE FORCES ARRAYED AGAINST THE ALLIES IN SOUTH VIETNAM. INSTEAD, IT WAS AN ARGUMENT ABOUT WHICH ORGANIZATION WOULD BE ALLOWED TO SET THE GROUND RULES GOVERNING DISCOURSE ABOUT THE WAR."[40] TO AVOID A SPLIT SPECIAL NATIONAL INTELLIGENCE ESTIMATE (SNIE), DCI HELMS AGREED TO MILITARY ASSISTANCE COMMAND, VIETNAM (MACV)/ DEFENSE INTELLIGENCE AGENCY (DIA) FIGURES IN THE FINAL SPECIAL NATIONAL INTELLIGENCE ESTIMATE DEALING WITH THE STRENGTH OF OPPOSING FORCES IN VIETNAM (SNIE 14.3-67).[41] DESPITE HIS TITLE OF DIRECTOR OF CENTRAL INTELLIGENCE, DULLES ALLOWED THE MILITARY TO DIRECT WHAT INTELLIGENCE WOULD GO FORWARD, NOT ONLY TO MILITARY COMMANDERS, BUT TO CIVILIAN POLICY MAKERS AS WELL.

THE 1970'S BEGAN WITH A NEW DRIVE TO IMPROVE NATIONAL INTELLIGENCE. PRESIDENT NIXON DIRECTED JAMES SCHLESINGER OF THE OFFICE OF MANAGEMENT AND BUDGET (OMB) "TO RECOMMEND HOW THE ORGANIZATIONAL STRUCTURE OF THE INTELLIGENCE COMMUNITY SHOULD BE CHANGED TO BRING ABOUT GREATER EFFICIENCY AND EFFECTIVENESS." IN MARCH OF 1971, THE SCHLESINGER COMPLETED HIS REPORT.[42] IT FAULTED ALL THE PRINCIPAL AGENCIES FOR LARGELY IGNORING OR RESISTING EXTERNAL MANAGEMENT. IT WAS PARTICULARLY CRITICAL OF THE DEPARTMENT OF DEFENSE, WHERE POWERFUL INTERESTS "OPPOSED (AND CONTINUE TO OPPOSE) MORE CENTRALIZED MANAGEMENT OF INTELLIGENCE ACTIVITIES.[43] ALTHOUGH SCHLESINGER RECOMMENDED A SIGNIFICANT REORGANIZATION OF THE IC, THERE WAS LITTLE CONGRESSIONAL INTEREST IN HIS PROPOSALS. IN THE END, NIXON ISSUED A PRESIDENTIAL DIRECTIVE IN NOVEMBER OF 1971, CALLING FOR "AN ENHANCED LEADERSHIP ROLE FOR THE [DCI] IN PLANNING, REVIEWING AND EVALUATING ALL INTELLIGENCE PROGRAMS AND ACTIVITIES, AND IN THE PRODUCTION OF NATIONAL INTELLIGENCE."[44] WITHOUT THE STATUTORY AUTHORITY TO COMPEL COMPLIANCE, HOWEVER, THE DIRECTIVE HAD LITTLE IMPACT ON THE COMMUNITY.

IN THE 1970S, A WAVE OF PUBLIC REVELATIONS OF QUESTIONABLE ACTIVITY BY THE INTELLIGENCE COMMUNITY, RANGING FROM DOMESTIC SPYING ON DISSIDENT GROUPS TO ATTEMPTED ASSASSINATION OF FOREIGN LEADERS, BROUGHT ABOUT NEW CALLS FOR REFORM. ALTHOUGH THE FOCUS WAS NOW HOW TO REIGN IN THE IC RATHER THAN HOW TO IMPROVE ITS EFFICIENCY, THE INVESTIGATIONS REPEATED THE NOW FAMILIAR CALLS TO GIVE THE DCI MORE AUTHORITY TO EXERCISE CENTRALIZED CONTROL. DESPITE THE FANFARE AND CALLS FOR REFORM, WHEN THE FUROR SUBSIDED, THE OLD-LINE INTELLIGENCE ORGANIZATIONS FOUND THEMSELVES WITH NO LESS AUTONOMY THEN THEY ENJOYED BEFORE.

---

[40] Ibid., 186, 191.
[41] Ibid., 188.
[42] *Preparing for the 21st Century,* A-14.
[43] JAMES SCHLESINGER, *A REVIEW OF THE INTELLIGENCE COMMUNITY* (10 MARCH 1971), N.P. ON-LINE INTERNET.
AVAILABLE FROM HTTP://WWW.FAS.ORG/IRP/CIA/PRODUCT/REVIEW1971.PDF. 16.
[44] Best, *Proposals for Intelligence Reorganization,* 16.

WHILE BOTH HOUSES OF CONGRESS CONDUCTED INVESTIGATIONS OF THE INTELLIGENCE COMMUNITY IN THE 1970S, THE SENATE'S EFFORT, LED BY THE POLITICALLY AMBITIOUS SENATOR FRANK CHURCH (WHO HIGHLIGHTED HIS AGGRESSIVE INVESTIGATIONS IN A 1976 PRESIDENTIAL BID), WAS BOTH THE MOST DRAMATIC IN ITS CRITIQUE OF THE STATUS QUO AND AMBITIOUS IN ITS PROPOSALS FOR REFORM. [45] THE CHURCH COMMITTEE FOUND:

> IN ORDER TO PROVIDE FIRM DIRECTION FOR THE INTELLIGENCE AGENCIES, THE COMMITTEE FINDS THAT NEW STATUTORY CHARTERS OF THESE AGENCIES MUST BE WRITTEN THAT TAKE ACCOUNT OF THE EXPERIENCE OF THE PAST THREE AND A HALF DECADES. FURTHERMORE, THE COMMITTEE FINDS THAT THE RELATIONSHIP AMONG THE VARIOUS INTELLIGENCE AGENCIES AND BETWEEN THEM AND THE DIRECTOR OF CENTRAL INTELLIGENCE SHOULD BE RESTRUCTURED IN ORDER TO ACHIEVE BETTER ACCOUNTABILITY, COORDINATION, AND EFFICIENT USE OF RESOURCES. [46]

RATHER THAN RELYING ON THE GOODWILL OF THE COMMUNITY, CHURCH MADE SPECIFIC RECOMMENDATIONS FOR STRENGTHENING THE DCI. THE REPORT RECOMMENDED THAT "NATIONAL INTELLIGENCE FUNDING BE APPROPRIATED TO THE DCI, THEREBY GIVING HIM CONTROL OVER THE ENTIRE IC BUDGET."[47] SIMILAR TO PREVIOUS REPORTS, THE CHURCH COMMITTEE RECOMMENDED SEPARATING THE DCI FROM THE CIA TO ALLOW HIM TO FOCUS ON HIS COMMUNITY ROLE.[48] ADDITIONALLY, THE CHURCH COMMITTEE CALLED FOR REDUCING THE INFLUENCE OF THE DIA AND MAKING THE DIRECTORS OF BOTH THE DIA AND NSA APPOINTEES OF THE PRESIDENT SUBJECT TO SENATE CONFIRMATION, GOING SO FAR AS TO PROPOSE "THAT EITHER THE DIRECTOR OR DEPUTY DIRECTOR OF DIA AND OF NSA SHOULD BE CIVILIANS."[49]

IN 1978, SENATOR WALTER HUDDLESTON AND REPRESENTATIVE EDWARD BOLAND INTRODUCED A 170 PAGE DRAFT NATIONAL INTELLIGENCE REORGANIZATION AND REFORM ACT TO ACCOMPLISH MANY OF THE RECOMMENDATIONS OF THE CHURCH COMMITTEE TO INCLUDE PROVIDING STATUTORY CHARTERS FOR ALL INTELLIGENCE AGENCIES AND CREATING A DIRECTOR OF NATIONAL INTELLIGENCE (DNI). [50] BY THIS TIME HOWEVER, SENATOR CHURCH'S ASPIRATIONS FOR THE PRESIDENCY HAD BEEN DASHED, AND THERE WAS NO ONE TO CHAMPION A CAUSE ALREADY FADING FROM THE PUBLIC'S MIND.[51] AFTER SEVERE CRITICISM IN HEARINGS, THE BILLS DIED WITHOUT EVER BEING REPORTED OUT OF COMMITTEE. [52] CHARTER LEGISLATION FOR THE INTELLIGENCE AGENCIES WOULD NOT

---

[45] Zegart, *Flawed by Design, 197.*
[46] "FOREIGN AND MILITARY INTELLIGENCE" IN BOOK I, *FINAL REPORT OF THE SELECT COMMITTEE TO STUDY*
  GOVERNMENTAL OPERATIONS WITH RESPECT TO INTELLIGENCE ACTIVITIES, COMMONLY REFERRED TO AS THE CHURCH
  REPORT, (WASHINGTON, DC: U.S. GOVERNMENT PRINTING OFFICE. 1976), *426.*
[47] Larry C. Kindsvater, "The Need to Reorganize the Intelligence Community," *Studies in Intelligence: Journal of the American Intelligence Professional* 47, No.1 (2003): n.p. On-line Internet. Available from http://www.cia.gov/csi/studies/vol47no1/index.html.
[48] *Preparing for the 21ˢᵗ Century,* A-16.
[49] Best, *Proposals for Intelligence Reorganization,* 23.
[50] Ibid., 26.
[51] Andrew, *For the President's Eyes Only,* 421.
[52] Best, *Proposals for Intelligence Reorganization,* 26.

STAND A SERIOUS CHANCE UNTIL NEW SCANDALS RAISED THE SALIENCY OF THE TOPIC AGAIN IN THE 1990S.

THE EXECUTIVE BRANCH DID TAKE MORE CONCRETE ACTION TO BOLSTER THE DCI, THOUGH IT STILL FELL SHORT OF CREATING A TRUE DIRECTOR OF NATIONAL INTELLIGENCE, ONE WITH THE FULL LINE AUTHORITY TO EXERCISE THE RESPONSIBILITIES INHERENT IN THAT TITLE. PRESIDENT FORD, IN EO 11905, MADE THE DCI CHAIRMAN OF A NEW COMMITTEE ON FOREIGN INTELLIGENCE (CFI), WITH RESPONSIBILITY FOR CONTROLLING "BUDGET PREPARATION AND RESOURCE ALLOCATION FOR THE NATIONAL FOREIGN INTELLIGENCE PROGRAM" (NFIP)[53] PRESIDENT CARTER WENT FURTHER IN 1977, GIVING THE DCI "FULL AND EXCLUSIVE AUTHORITY FOR APPROVAL" OF THE NFIP BUDGET "PRIOR TO ITS PRESENTATION TO THE PRESIDENT."[54] THIS MEANT APPROVING NOT ONLY THE BUDGET OF THE CIA, BUT ALSO NATIONAL INTELLIGENCE PROGRAMS WITHIN THE DEPARTMENT OF DEFENSE, SUCH AS THE NATIONAL RECONNAISSANCE OFFICE (NRO) AND NSA. THE SECRETARY OF DEFENSE, HOWEVER, RETAINED RESPONSIBILITY FOR SUPERVISING THE DAY-TO-DAY OPERATIONS OF THOSE ORGANIZATIONS. PRESIDENT REAGAN, IN EXECUTIVE ORDER (EO) 12333, GRANTED THE DCI "FULL RESPONSIBILITY FOR [THE] PRODUCTION AND DISSEMINATION OF NATIONAL FOREIGN INTELLIGENCE," INCLUDING THE AUTHORITY TO TASK NON-CIA INTELLIGENCE AGENCIES, AND THE ABILITY TO DECIDE ON COMMUNITY TASKING CONFLICTS. THE ORDER ALSO SOUGHT TO GRANT THE DCI MORE EXPLICIT AUTHORITY OVER THE DEVELOPMENT, IMPLEMENTATION, AND EVALUATION OF NFIP."[55]

WHILE THE POWERS SPECIFIED IN EXECUTIVE ORDERS SOUND IMPRESSIVE, PUTTING THEM INTO PRACTICE WAS PROBLEMATIC. AS THE ASPIN/BROWN COMMISSION WOULD LATER NOTE: "THE DCI APPEARS TO HAVE CONSIDERABLE AUTHORITY VIS-À-VIS OTHER ELEMENTS OF THE INTELLIGENCE COMMUNITY. IN PRACTICE, HOWEVER, THIS AUTHORITY MUST BE EXERCISED CONSISTENT WITH THE AUTHORITY OF THE DEPARTMENT HEADS TO WHOM THESE ELEMENTS ARE SUBORDINATE."[56] SUCH DEPARTMENT HEADS HAVE THEIR OWN STATUTORY AUTHORITY AND DECADES OF BUDGETING AND PERSONNEL MANAGEMENT PRECEDENCE TO COUNTER ATTEMPTS BY DCIS TO FUNDAMENTALLY ALTER THE OPERATION OF THEIR INTELLIGENCE ORGANIZATIONS. WHAT FORMAL AUTHORITY THE DCI HAD ON PAPER WAS RARELY EXERCISED IN PRACTICE.[57]

THE NEXT SIGNIFICANT PUSH TO PASS LEGISLATION REFORMING THE INTELLIGENCE COMMUNITY CAME IN 1992, WHEN SENATOR BOREN AND REPRESENTATIVE MCCURDY EACH PROPOSED OMNIBUS

---

[53] EXECUTIVE ORDER 11905. UNITED STATES FOREIGN INTELLIGENCE ACTIVITIES, 18 FEBRUARY 1976, 5.

[54] JEFFERY T. RICHELSON, ED. "FROM DIRECTOR OF CENTRAL INTELLIGENCE TO DIRECTOR OF NATIONAL INTELLIGENCE." IN
NATIONAL SECURITY ARCHIVE ELECTRONIC BRIEFING BOOK NO. 144, (17 DECEMBER 2004), N.P. ON-LINE INTERNET.
AVAILABLE FROM HTTP://WWW.GWU.EDU/~NSARCHIV/NSAEBB/NSAEBB144/.

[55] Ibid.

[56] Aspin-Brown Commission, *The Evolution of the U.S. Intelligence Community,* 49.

[57] STEPHEN DAGGETT, *THE US INTELLIGENCE BUDGET: A BASIC OVERVIEW* (WASHINGTON, DC: CONGRESSIONAL
RESEARCH SERVICE, LIBRARY OF CONGRESS, 24 SEPTEMBER 2004), 4.

BILLS TO RESTRUCTURE THE INTELLIGENCE COMMUNITY IN RESPONSE TO CALLS TO CUT US DEFENSE RELATED SPENDING IN LIGHT OF THE ENDING OF THE COLD WAR. THE BOREN MCCURDY PROPOSALS WOULD HAVE GIVEN STATUTORY AUTHORITY TO THE OPERATIONAL AUTHORITY ALREADY PROVIDED TO THE DCI BY EXECUTIVE ORDERS, AND WOULD HAVE INCREASED HIS CONTROL OF THE COMMUNITY EVEN FURTHER. BOTH BILLS RECOMMENDED CREATING A SEPARATE DNI WITH "CLEAR STATUTORY AUTHORITY OVER *ALL* INTELLIGENCE AGENCIES AND BUDGETS THROUGHOUT THE COMMUNITY.[58] NATURALLY, THESE BILLS PROVOKED "STRONG OPPOSITION FROM THE DEFENSE DEPARTMENT AND …THE ARMED SERVICES COMMITTEES."[59] IN LIEU OF THESE BILLS, WHICH FAILED TO PASS, CONGRESS INSTEAD PASSED THE WATERED DOWN INTELLIGENCE ORGANIZATION ACT OF 1992, WHICH CLARIFIED, BUT DID NOT ALTER, THE INTELLIGENCE FRAMEWORK CREATED IN 1947. THE ACT REAFFIRMED THE INDEPENDENCE OF THE MILITARY INTELLIGENCE APPARATUS WITH ONLY A NOD TO THE ROLE OF THE DCI, IN THAT IT REQUIRED THE SECRETARY OF DEFENSE TO CONSULT WITH THE DCI PRIOR TO APPOINTING THE DIRECTORS OF THE NSA, NRO, AND DIA.[60] THIS CONSULTATION DID NOT REQUIRE APPROVAL; THE SECRETARY OF DEFENSE COULD FORWARD A NOMINATION AFTER NOTING THE DCI'S NON-CONCURRENCE.[61]

THE NEXT EFFORT TO REFORM INTELLIGENCE CAME THREE YEARS LATER IN RESPONSE TO THE ALDRICH AMES SPY SCANDAL AND THE DISCLOSURE THAT THE NRO HAD LOST ONE BILLION DOLLARS. THE CLINTON ADMINISTRATION ESTABLISHED THE ASPIN/BROWN COMMISSION TO ADDRESS THE ISSUE. THE COMMISSION'S EFFORTS AT REFORM "FACED ENTRENCHED OPPOSITION FROM TWO SIDES: DEFENSE DEPARTMENT OFFICIALS WHO WANTED TO MAINTAIN CONTROL OVER THEIR OWN INTELLIGENCE AGENCIES AND CONGRESSIONAL DEFENSE COMMITTEE MEMBERS WHO WANTED TO KEEP A TIGHT HOLD ON THESE AGENCIES' PURSE STRINGS."[62] RICHARD HASS, WHO LED THE 1996 COUNCIL ON FOREIGN RELATIONS STUDY OF INTELLIGENCE REFORM, SUMMARIZED THE SITUATION: "EVERYONE WHO LOOKED AT [INTELLIGENCE REFORM] CAME OUT WITH THE QUESTION OF HOW TO STRENGTHEN THE DCI, BUT NO ONE WAS WILLING TO DO WHAT IT TAKES TO GIVE HIM REAL CONTROL. THAT WAS TOO MUCH FOR THE SYSTEM TO BEAR AND THEY WILL END UP ONLY TINKERING."[63] DURING THEIR DELIBERATIONS, ONE COMMISSION MEMBER ASKED THE ACTING DCI, ADM. WILLIAM STUDEMAN, "WHAT IF WE PLACED THE ENTIRE INTELLIGENCE BUDGET UNDER THE CONTROL OF THE DCI?" BEFORE STUDEMAN COULD ANSWER THE COMMISSION CHAIRMAN, FORMER SECRETARY OF DEFENSE ASPIN INTERJECTED "MAJOR HEART ATTACK AT THE DOD!"[64] IN THE END, THE COMMISSION CONCLUDED: "THE DCI'S EXISTING LEGAL AUTHORITIES WITH RESPECT TO THE INTELLIGENCE COMMUNITY ARE, ON THE WHOLE, SUFFICIENT."[65]

---

[58] Zegart, *Flawed By Design*, 201.

[59] Best, *Proposals for Intelligence Reorganization*, 30.

[60] Aspin-Brown Commission, *The Evolution of the U.S. Intelligence Community*, 24

[61] US SENATE. SPE*CIAL REPORT OF THE SELECT COMMITTEE ON INTELLIGENCE*, 105TH CONG., 1ST SESS., 1997, S. DOC.
  105-1.

[62] Zegart, *Flawed by Design,* 202.

[63] Ibid., 205.

[64] LOCH K. JOHNSON, "THE ASPIN-BROWN INTELLIGENCE INQUIRY: BEHIND THE CLOSED DOORS OF A BLUE RIBBON

Concurrent with the Aspin/Brown Commission, the House Intelligence Committee conducted its own study of intelligence entitled IC21: The Intelligence Community in the 21st Century.[66] IC21 began as "the boldest, most innovative and most radical of the proposals for IC reform" since its inception.[67] It recommended, among other things, giving the DCI "greater programmatic control of intelligence budgets and intelligence personnel," and "a stronger voice in the appointment of the directors of NFIP defense agencies."[68] These proposals stirred Deputy Secretary of Defense John White to send a letter to the Senate Armed Services Committee raising fears that "greater intelligence centralization would create a Frankenstein 'monolithic' intelligence structure. In particular, he argued against provisions granting the DCI power to transfer funds in and out of Pentagon intelligence agencies and providing for DCI approval of the defense secretary's top appointments to key Defense Department intelligence agencies.[69]

In response to IC21 both the House and Senate proposed bills that would substantially increase the DCI's authority. Early drafts of what eventually became the 1997 Intelligence Authorization Act "pitted DoD and its allies against supporters of a stronger DCI. This, with the important addition of a DCI whose eyes were then on the job of Secretary of Defense...ultimately explains DOD's victory over reform's supporters."[70] The Military was not the only one to oppose the intelligence reforms, FBI Director Louis Freeh "objected strenuously to [a provision in the bill] requiring the DCI to be consulted before the Attorney General appoints the head of the FBI's National Security Division."[71]

In the resulting legislation, "any increase in the DCI's power or that of offices subordinate to his was granted in only a qualified manner."[72] Specifically, it increased the powers of the DCI "in a way that notably avoided subordinating the position of the Secretary of Defense to the DCI."[73] In the spirit of IC21, the bill required the DCI to "improve collection requirements, determine collection priorities, and resolve conflicts in such priorities levied on national collection assets," but then curtailed that responsibility with the phrase "except as otherwise agreed with the Secretary [of

Commission." *Studies in Intelligence* 48, no. 3 (2004), 8.

[65] Zegart, *Flawed by Design*, 203.

[66] US House. *IC21: The Intelligence Community in the 21st Century*. 104th Cong. Staff Study by the
    Permanent Select Committee on Intelligence, 1996. #IC21011

[67] Abraham H. Miller and Brian Alexander, "Structural Quiescence in the Failure of IC21 and Intelligence
    Reform," *International Journal of Intelligence and CounterIntellignece* no 14, (2001), 235.

[68] Best, *Proposals for Intelligence Reorganization, 33.*

[69] Zegart, *Flawed by Design*, 204.

[70] Miller, "Structural Quiescence" 245.

[71] Ibid., 255.

[72] Ibid., 242.

[73] Ibid.

DEFENSE] PURSUANT TO THE DIRECTION OF THE PRESIDENT."[74] WHERE IC21 SOUGHT TO ESTABLISH A CENTRAL MANAGER TO "OVERSEE INTELLIGENCE AS AN END-TO-END PROCESS," THE BILL, WHILE INCREASING THE DCI'S ROLE IN THE PROCESS, ONLY REQUIRED THE SECRETARY OF DEFENSE TO "CONSULT WITH THE DCI BEFORE REPROGRAMMING FUNDS MADE AVAILABLE UNDER JMIP [JOINT MILITARY INTELLIGENCE PROGRAM]."[75]

DUE TO THE INFLUENCE OF PRO-MILITARY FORCES, "[OF] IC21'S THIRTEEN RECOMMENDATIONS TO INCREASE THE DCI'S AUTHORITY OVER THE IC, ONLY FIVE WERE DIRECTLY IMPLEMENTED THROUGH THE IAAFY97 [1997 INTELLIGENCE AUTHORIZATION ACT]… THE EFFECT HAS BEEN TO INCREASE THE DCI'S INPUT OR ABILITY TO MONITOR, WITHOUT ANY ACTUAL INCREASE IN REAL MANAGEMENT AUTHORITY OVER, THE ENTIRE INTELLIGENCE COMMUNITY."[76] IN SEPTEMBER 1966, DENVER'S *ROCKY MOUNTAIN NEWS* OBSERVED, "IN THE FACE OF DOD OPPOSITION TO INTELLIGENCE REFORM PROPOSALS, GAINS BY THE CIA OVER THE PENTAGON IN CONTROL OVER THE INTELLIGENCE COMMUNITY WERE A GOAL THAT APPEARED DOOMED, THE VICTIM OF OPPOSITION FROM PRO-DEFENSE LAWMAKERS."[77] THE SAME ARTICLE NOTED THAT AS "THE DEFENSE DEPARTMENT WOULD ASSUME CONTROL OVER THE NEWLY ESTABLISHED NIMA [NATIONAL IMAGERY AND MAPPING AGENCY], THE DOD HAD ACTUALLY MANAGED TO GAIN SOME ADDITIONAL CONTROL OVER THE IC FROM THE REFORM PROCESS."[78]

ALTHOUGH 50 YEARS OF STUDIES AND INVESTIGATIONS OF THE US NATIONAL INTELLIGENCE ORGANIZATION ALMOST UNIVERSALLY RESULTED IN RECOMMENDATIONS TO STRENGTHEN THE ROLE OF A DCI OR DNI TO COORDINATE AND CONTROL THE COMMUNITY, THE IC ENTERED A NEW MILLENNIUM WITH ESSENTIALLY THE SAME FRAMEWORK CREATED FOR IT IN 1947.[79] NEITHER SCANDALS NOR THE END OF THE COLD WAR PROVED SUFFICIENT IMPETUS FOR CONGRESS TO PASS INTELLIGENCE REFORM OVER THE OPPOSITION OF THE VARIOUS DEPARTMENTAL ORGANIZATIONS. WHAT AUTHORITY EXECUTIVE ORDERS OR WATERED-DOWN LEGISLATION GRANTED THE DCI ON PAPER DID LITTLE TO ALTER HIS RELATIONSHIP WITH THE OTHER DEPARTMENTS IN PRACTICE. WHILE THE DCI REMAINED THE NOMINAL HEAD OF THE INTELLIGENCE COMMUNITY, HE HAD LITTLE POWER TO COMPEL COMPLIANCE FROM ANY INTELLIGENCE ORGANIZATION OTHER THAN THE CIA.

FACTOR 2: ASSOCIATION WITH COVERT OPERATIONS

THE DIFFICULTY IN ENFORCING COMPLIANCE, LET ALONE WILLING PARTICIPATION, FROM A HOSTILE INTELLIGENCE COMMUNITY, LED THE DCI AND CIA TO FOCUS THEIR EFFORTS IN AREAS THAT RECEIVED LESS OPPOSITION. COVERT ACTION PROVED TO BE ONE SUCH AREA, AND DESPITE A

---

[74] Ibid.

[75] Ibid.

[76] Ibid., 243.

[77] Ibid., 255.

[78] Ibid.,

[79] Michael Warner, ed., *Central Intelligence: Origin and Evolution (Washington DC:* Center for the Study of Intelligence, Central Intelligence Agency, 2001), 2.

RELUCTANT START, THE CIA CAME TO EMBRACE IT WHOLEHEARTEDLY. BY 1971, THE CIA'S COVERT OPERATIONS, DEFINED AS "CLANDESTINE OPERATIONS DESIGNED TO INFLUENCE FOREIGN GOVERNMENTS, EVENTS, ORGANIZATIONS, OR PERSONS IN SUPPORT OF UNITED STATES FOREIGN POLICY," ACCOUNTED FOR "OVER HALF OF THE CIA'S ANNUAL TOTAL BUDGET."[80] WHILE ONE CAN DEBATE THE VALUE THESE COVERT OPERATIONS PROVIDE FOREIGN POLICY, THE ASSOCIATION OF THE CIA AND DCI WITH SUCH OPERATIONS HAS BEEN DETRIMENTAL TO THE ACCOMPLISHMENT OF THEIR CENTRAL TASK OF UNIFYING THE COMMUNITY'S INTELLIGENCE EFFORTS AND IMPROVING THE INTELLIGENCE PRODUCTS PROVIDED TO NATIONAL POLICY MAKERS. COVERT OPERATIONS, EVEN WHEN SUCCESSFUL, DIVERT LIMITED TIME, EFFORT, AND RESOURCES AWAY FROM INTELLIGENCE COLLECTION, COORDINATION, AND ANALYSIS. WHEN THEY FAIL OR ARE EXPOSED, THE INTELLIGENCE PRODUCTION SIDE OF THE CIA AND THE DCI SHARE IN THE ENSUING BACKLASH OF NEGATIVE PUBLICITY AND REGULATORY OVERSIGHT.

WHILE COVERT OPERATIONS MAY BE CENTRAL TO THE POPULAR IMAGE OF THE CIA TODAY, SUCH AN ASSOCIATION WAS NEVER THE INTENT OF PRESIDENT TRUMAN, WHO FEARED CREATING AN "AMERICAN GESTAPO."[81] IN HIS MEMOIRS, TRUMAN CLAIMED, "I NEVER HAD ANY THOUGHT WHEN I SET UP THE CIA . . . THAT IT WOULD BE INJECTED INTO PEACETIME CLOAK AND DAGGER OPERATIONS."[82] ORIGINALLY, "THE CIA'S LEGAL MANDATE WAS TO COLLECT, ANALYZE AND DISTRIBUTE FOREIGN INTELLIGENCE TO APPROPRIATE GOVERNMENT OFFICIALS AND TO ADVISE THE NSC ON NATIONAL SECURITY."[83] COVERT ACTION WAS CONSPICUOUSLY MISSING FROM THE DUTIES LISTED IN THE NATIONAL SECURITY ACT OF 1947. WHEN CONVINCED OF A NEED TO SURREPTITIOUSLY SUPPORT THE DEMOCRATIC GOVERNMENT OF ITALY AGAINST A GROWING COMMUNIST MOVEMENT, TRUMAN TRIED TO CONVINCE SECRETARY OF STATE GEORGE C. MARSHALL TO COORDINATE A COVERT PSYCHOLOGICAL CAMPAIGN AGAINST IT. "MARSHALL, HOWEVER, WISELY FEARED THAT HIS 'MARSHALL PLAN' FOR . . . POSTWAR EUROPE WOULD BE GRAVELY COMPROMISED IF THE STATE DEPARTMENT WERE DISCOVERED TO BE INVOLVED IN COVERT ACTION."[84] DCI HILLENKOETTER, WHOSE "WARTIME EXPERIENCE HAD LED HIM TO BELIEVE THAT AN AGENCY CANNOT EFFECTIVELY ENGAGE IN BOTH INFORMATION GATHERING (WHICH WAS THE CIA'S MISSION) AND COVERT ACTIONS," AND WHOSE ATTORNEY ADVISED HIM "THAT COVERT OPERATIONS WERE ILLEGAL," RESISTED. UNDER CONTINUED PRESSURE, HILLENKOETTER

---

[80] *"Controversy Over Covert Operations," Congressional Digest*, 59 Issue 5, (May 1980), 131.; and David Canon, "Intelligence and Ethics: The CIA's Covert Operations" in *The Journal of Libertarian Studies* IV, No. 2 (Spring 1980) 201.

[81] Amy B. Zegart, *Flawed by Design*, 163.

[82] Andrew, *For the President's Eyes Only,* 171.

[83] Mary H. Cooper, "Reforming the CIA," *The CQ Researcher* 6, no 5, (2 February 1996), 106.

[84] Andrew, *For the President's Eye's Only*, 172.

RELUCTANTLY ACCEPTED THE RESPONSIBILITY.[85] THE ENSUING SUCCESS IN ITALY LED TO RAPID EXPANSION OF THIS AUXILIARY ROLE FOR THE CIA.

LESS THAN A YEAR AFTER CREATING THE CIA, TRUMAN SIGNED NSC 10/2 ORDERING THE CIA TO CREATE AN OFFICE TO PLAN AND ENGAGE IN:

> "PROPAGANDA; ECONOMIC WARFARE; PREVENTATIVE DIRECT ACTION, INCLUDING SABOTAGE, ANTI-SABOTAGE, DEMOLITION AND EVACUATION MEASURES; SUBVERSION AGAINST HOSTILE STATES, INCLUDING ASSISTANCE TO UNDERGROUND RESISTANCE MOVEMENTS, GUERILLAS AND REFUGEE LIBERATION GROUPS, AND SUPPORT OF INDIGENOUS ANTI-COMMUNIST ELEMENTS IN THREATENED COUNTRIES OF THE FREE WORLD."[86]

ALTHOUGH UNCOOPERATIVE TOWARD THE CIA'S MANDATE TO DIRECT AND COORDINATE THEIR EFFORTS, THE "INTELLIGENCE ORGANIZATIONS IN THE ARMY, NAVY, AIR FORCE, DEFENSE, STATE, AND JUSTICE DEPARTMENTS . . . ENCOURAGED THE AGENCY TO ACQUIRE COVERT CAPABILITIES."[87] NOT ONLY DID SUCH ACTIVITIES DISTRACT THE CIA FROM ITS COORDINATION ROLE, "NONE OF THE SERVICES WANTED TO BE BOTHERED WITH CLANDESTINE ACTIVITIES THAT COULD SULLY THEIR HANDS AND DETRACT FROM THEIR OWN WORK."[88] WHETHER OR NOT THE CIA WAS THE PROPER AGENCY FOR COVERT ACTIONS, TRUMAN'S DIRECTIVE SET THE PRECEDENT, ALLOWING FUTURE PRESIDENTS AND DCIS WHO DID NOT SHARE TRUMAN'S OR HILLENKOETTER'S APPREHENSIONS TO ENTHUSIASTICALLY EMBRACE THE MISSION.

TRUMAN'S SUCCESSOR, DWIGHT D. EISENHOWER, WAS ONE SUCH PRESIDENT. UPON HIS ELECTION IN 1953, HE CHOSE ALLEN DULLES, AN OSS VETERAN WITH A HISTORY OF COVERT OPERATIONS, TO REPLACE THEN-CURRENT DCI WALTER BEDDELL SMITH—PARTLY BECAUSE SMITH LACKED ENTHUSIASM FOR COVERT OPERATIONS, WHICH HE FEARED WERE "USURPING THE PRIMARY MISSION OF THE CIA TO COLLECT AND INTERPRET INTELLIGENCE."[89] DULLES'S ENTHUSIASM FOR COVERT OPERATIONS BECAME SUCH A PREOCCUPATION THAT IT NOT ONLY LED TO HIS SLIGHTING THE TASK OF INTELLIGENCE COORDINATION, BUT ACTIVELY STONEWALLING IT. THOUGH EISENHOWER WAS GENERALLY HAPPY WITH THE RESULTS OF COVERT OPERATIONS, MOST NOTABLY THE OVERTHROW OF THE IRANIAN AND GUATEMALAN GOVERNMENTS, THE DOMINANCE OF COVERT OPERATIONS OVER INTELLIGENCE COORDINATION LED TO A MAJOR FOREIGN POLICY FAILURE FOR HIS SUCCESSOR, JOHN F. KENNEDY.

THE CIA, WITH EISENHOWER'S APPROVAL, BEGAN PLANNING WHAT ULTIMATELY BECAME THE BAY OF PIGS INVASION WELL BEFORE KENNEDY'S ELECTION. DULLES AND HIS DEPUTY DIRECTOR FOR PLANS (A FORERUNNER TO TODAY'S OPERATIONS), RICHARD BISSELL, BRIEFED THE INCOMING PRESIDENT ON THE OPERATION, WHICH THEY STRONGLY ADVOCATED. ABSENT FROM THE BRIEF WERE THE DISSENTING OPINIONS OF THE STATE DEPARTMENT, THE MILITARY, AND EVEN ANALYSTS WITHIN THE

---

[85] David Fromkin, "Daring Amateurism: The CIA's Social History," *Foreign Affairs,* (January/February 1996), n.p. online at http://www.foreignaffairs.org/19960101fareviewessay4181/david-fromkin/daring-amateurism-the-cia-s-social-history.html.

[86] Andrew, *For the President's Eye's Only,* 172-173.

[87] Zegart, *Flawed By Design,* 212.

[88] Ibid.

[89] Andrew, *For the President's Eyes Only,* 201.

CIA, LEAVING THE PRESIDENT WITH THE IMPRESSION THAT THE MISSION ENJOYED WIDESPREAD BACKING. BOTH ROGER HILSMAN, DIRECTOR OF THE STATE DEPARTMENT'S BUREAU OF INTELLIGENCE, AND SHERMAN KENT, CHAIRMAN OF THE CIA BOARD OF NATIONAL ESTIMATES, OPPOSED THE CONCEPT OF AN INVASION BUT WERE NEVER CONSULTED BY THE CIA, OR EVEN OFFICIALLY INFORMED OF THE PLAN.[90] RATHER THAN SEEKING TO COORDINATE THE EFFORTS OF THE INTELLIGENCE COMMUNITY AND PROVIDE THE PRESIDENT WITH INTELLIGENCE THAT REFLECTED COMMUNITY CONSENSUS, HELMS AND BISSELL ACTIVELY EXCLUDED PARTICIPATION: "THE PLANS DIRECTORATE HAD DONE THEIR BEST TO KEEP THE WHOLE OPERATION SECRET FROM THE INTELLIGENCE DIRECTORATE."[91] ROBERT AMORY, THE CIA'S DEPUTY DIRECTOR FOR INTELLIGENCE AND A VETERAN OF TWENTY-SIX ASSAULT LANDINGS IN THE SOUTH PACIFIC, WAS DELIBERATELY KEPT OUT OF THE OPERATION.[92] AFTER OFFERING HIS ASSISTANCE AND BEING REBUFFED, AMORY "LATER RECALLED THAT ON THE MORNING OF SUNDAY, APRIL 16 [THE DAY OF THE ATTEMPTED INVASION], 'I CAME IN AND OPENED THE CABLES FROM URUGUAY AND NIGERIA AND SO ON AND SO FORTH, AND WENT HOME AND PLAYED FIVE SETS OF TENNIS. I SAID SCREW EM!'"[93] IN RETROSPECT, HAD THE DCI FOCUSED ON HIS COMMUNITY INTELLIGENCE ROLE, RATHER THAN ON THE PLANNING OF COVERT OPERATIONS, IT IS POSSIBLE THE PRESIDENT WOULD HAVE CALLED OFF THE INVASION EARLY IN THE PLANNING PHASE.

IN RESPONSE TO THE BAY OF PIGS, PRESIDENT KENNEDY AUTHORIZED THE TAYLOR COMMISSION TO "ASCERTAIN THE REASONS FOR THE INVASION'S FAILURE."[94] RESTORING THE PRIMACY OF ANALYSIS AND COORDINATION TO THE CIA, HOWEVER, WAS NEVER A FOCUS OF THE INVESTIGATION. RATHER THAN ABOLISHING COVERT ACTIONS, IT SOUGHT TO IMPROVE THEM. "THE TAYLOR COMMITTEE RECOMMENDED THAT THE CIA BE RESPONSIBLE ONLY FOR COVERT POLITICAL ACTION, LEAVING ... PARAMILITARY ACTIVITIES TO THE PENTAGON."[95] ALTHOUGH THE PRESIDENT SOUGHT TO IMPLEMENT THIS RECOMMENDATION, LATER ACTIONS BY THE CIA IN VIETNAM, LAOS, NICARAGUA, AND MOST RECENTLY IN AFGHANISTAN DEMONSTRATE THE TENDENCY OF COVERT OPERATORS TO CREATIVELY, OR EVEN ILLEGALLY, STRETCH THEIR MANDATES.[96]

ANOTHER INDIRECT RESULT OF THE BAY OF PIGS WAS THE CREATION OF THE DEFENSE INTELLIGENCE AGENCY (DIA) BY SECRETARY OF DEFENSE MCNAMARA, TO PROVIDE THE SECRETARY AND THE PRESIDENT WITH "ANOTHER SOURCE FOR EVALUATION OF ANY PROPOSED OPERATION."[97] THE DIA WAS DESIGNED TO ACCOMPLISH WHAT THE CIA HAD FAILED TO DO: COORDINATE THE INTELLIGENCE ACTIVITIES OF THE SERVICES. BUT LIKE THE CIA, IT "QUICKLY SURPASSED THAT RATHER LIMITED ROLE AND BECAME ANOTHER INDEPENDENT PRODUCER OF INTELLIGENCE AND AN OFTEN INTENSE RIVAL OF THE

---

[90] Trumbull Higgins, *The Perfect Failure, Kennedy, Eisenhower, and the CIA at the Bay of Pigs*, (W.W. Norton & Company, New York, 1987), 85.

[91] Andrew, *For the President's Eyes*, 261.

[92] Andrew, *For the President's Eyes*, 261.

[93] Ibid., 264.

[94] CRS, *Proposals for Intelligence Reorganization*, 12.

[95] Higgens, *The Perfect Failure*, 157.

[96] Ibid.

[97] Ibid., 159.

CIA."[98] "THIS PROLIFERATION OF THE INTELLIGENCE JUNGLE HARDLY SERVED TO RESOLVE THE CIA'S FAILURE ADEQUATELY TO SEVER THE EVALUATION OF INTELLIGENCE FROM ITS RESPONSIBILITY FOR EVEN THE SMALL-SCALE COVERT OPERATIONS STILL PERMITTED IT, LET ALONE TO COMPENSATE FOR THE CIA'S FAILURE TO EXERCISE MINIMAL CENTRALIZATION OF THE WHOLE INTELLIGENCE COMMUNITY."[99]

THE COMBINATION OF REGULATIONS, OVERSIGHT, AND COMPETITION DID LITTLE TO DAMPEN THE PREFERENCE OF EITHER THE CIA OR FUTURE DCIS FOR OPERATIONS OVER ANALYSIS OR COMMUNITY MANAGEMENT. AS THE SENATE'S SELECT COMMITTEE TO STUDY GOVERNMENTAL OPERATIONS WITH RESPECT TO INTELLIGENCE ACTIVITIES, BETTER KNOWN AS THE CHURCH COMMITTEE, WAS TO FIND 15 YEARS LATER, "CLANDESTINE OPERATIONS BECAME AND CONTINUED TO BE THE AGENCY'S PREEMINENT ACTIVITY."[100] THE CHURCH REPORT POINTED OUT THAT SUCCESSFUL COVERT ACTIONS WERE THE QUICKEST ROUTE TO CAREER PROGRESSION WITHIN THE AGENCY, AND OF THOSE "DCIS WHO HAVE BEEN AGENCY CAREERISTS, ALL HAVE COME FROM THE CLANDESTINE SERVICE."[101] IRONICALLY, THE FIRST CAREER "ANALYTICAL" INTELLIGENCE OFFICER NOMINATED FOR THE POSITION OF DCI, ROBERT GATES, WOULD FAIL TO RECEIVE SENATE RATIFICATION BECAUSE HIS ASSOCIATION WITH ANOTHER EXAMPLE OF OPERATIONAL EXCESS, THE IRAN CONTRA AFFAIR.[102] THE CHURCH COMMITTEE, IN ITS CONCLUSION, NOTED: "GIVEN THE LIMITATION ON THE DCI'S AUTHORITY, ONLY BY MAKING COMMUNITY ACTIVITIES A FIRST ORDER CONCERN AND BY PURSUING THE PROBLEMS ASSERTIVELY, COULD A DCI BEGIN TO MAKE A DIFFERENCE IN EFFECTING BETTER MANAGEMENT.[103] THE REPORT FAULTED THE THEN-CURRENT DCI, RICHARD HELMS, FOR FOCUSING ON AGENCY OPERATIONS AND NOT PURSUING HIS MANDATE TO COORDINATE THE ENTIRE COMMUNITY WITH ANY VIGOR.[104]

ALTHOUGH THE CHURCH COMMITTEE IDENTIFIED A FUNDAMENTAL CONFLICT THAT PREVENTS THE DCI AND THE CIA FROM EFFECTIVELY COORDINATING THE EFFORTS OF THE INTELLIGENCE COMMUNITY, IT, AS ALONG WITH CONCURRENT INVESTIGATIONS BY THE EXECUTIVE BRANCH AND HOUSE OF REPRESENTATIVES, ACTUALLY DELAYED ACTION ON IMPLEMENTING ANY MEANINGFUL REFORMS. FOLLOWING REVELATIONS OF THE CIA'S ATTEMPTS TO INFILTRATE DOMESTIC ANTI-WAR MOVEMENTS AND ASSASSINATE FOREIGN LEADERS, BOTH BRANCHES OF CONGRESS AND THE ADMINISTRATION WERE EAGER TO PUBLICLY INVESTIGATE THE INTELLIGENCE COMMUNITY. BY FOCUSING ON SENSATIONAL INTELLIGENCE ABUSES, THE INVESTIGATION IGNORED LESS DRAMATIC INTELLIGENCE INEFFICIENCIES. "LEGISLATORS WERE PRINCIPALLY CONCERNED WITH PROTECTING AMERICAN CIVIL LIBERTIES RATHER THAN WITH DEVISING WAYS OF MAKING THE INTELLIGENCE MACHINERY WORK BETTER."[105] THUS, THE AGENDA FOR INTELLIGENCE REFORM SET BY "CHURCH AND HIS COLLEAGUES UNWITTINGLY ENSURED

[98] Lowenthal, *U.S. Intelligence*, 31-32.
[99] Higgens, *The Perfect Failure,* 159.
[100] Church Report, Part Five, Conclusion, 92.
[101] Church Report, Part Five, Conclusion, 92.
[102] Lowenthal, *U.S. Intelligence,* 81.
[103] *Church Report*, Part Five, Conclusion, 91.
[104] *Church Report*, Part Five, Conclusion, 91-92.
[105] Zegart, *Flawed by Design*, 197.

THAT MORE FUNDAMENTAL COORDINATION ISSUES WOULD BE KEPT OFF THE TABLE FOR THE NEXT TWENTY YEARS."[106]

IN THE END, AND DESPITE THE FUROR, CONGRESS PLACED FEW IMPEDIMENTS ON THE CIA'S ABILITY TO CONDUCT COVERT OPERATIONS. WHILE CONGRESS DEBATED EXTENSIVE REFORM LEGISLATION, SOVIET-BACKED SUBVERSIVE ACTIVITIES IN ETHIOPIA, ANGOLA, AND MOZAMBIQUE, ALONG WITH THE OVERTHROW OF THE SHAH IN IRAN AND THE SOVIET INVASION OF AFGHANISTAN, MUTED ANY RESISTANCE TO CIA COVERT OPERATIONS. THE WINDOW FOR SIGNIFICANT CHANGE HAD PASSED. A 263-PAGE NATIONAL INTELLIGENCE REFORM AND REORGANIZATION BILL, SUBMITTED BY SENATOR HUDDLESTON IN 1978, PASSED TWO YEARS LATER AS THE WATERED DOWN FOUR-PAGE INTELLIGENCE OVERSIGHT ACT OF 1980.[107]

THE EXECUTIVE BRANCH WAS ONLY SLIGHTLY MORE SUCCESSFUL IN IMPOSING RESTRAINT THROUGH EXECUTIVE ORDERS. IN EO 11905, PRESIDENT CARTER SPECIFICALLY PROHIBITED ASSASSINATION AND CREATED AN OPERATIONS ADVISORY GROUP TO ADVISE THE PRESIDENT ON "SPECIAL ACTIVITIES."[108] TWO YEARS LATER, PRESIDENT FORD SIGNED EO 12036, CREATING THE NATIONAL SECURITY COUNCIL SPECIAL COORDINATION COMMITTEE TO REVIEW AND APPROVE "PROPOSALS FOR SENSITIVE FOREIGN INTELLIGENCE COLLECTION OPERATIONS."[109] IN 1981, HOWEVER, THE TREND REVERSED WHEN PRESIDENT REAGAN SIGNED EO 12333, WHICH SERVED AS THE PRIMARY MANDATE FOR THE INTELLIGENCE COMMUNITY UNTIL THE PASSAGE OF THE INTELLIGENCE REFORM ACT OF 2004. THIS LATTER LEGISLATION GRANTED "BROADER POWERS TO THE CIA, INCLUDING THE AUTHORITY TO CONDUCT DOMESTIC COVERT OPERATIONS."[110] DURING HIS PRESIDENCY, REAGAN APPROVED "MORE THAN A DOZEN MAJOR COVERT OPERATIONS FROM LATIN AMERICA TO THE MIDDLE EAST TO AFRICA."[111] IN 1988, COVERT ACTIVITIES STILL ACCOUNTED FOR OVER HALF OF THE CIA'S TOTAL BUDGET.

WHILE NEITHER HOUSE OF CONGRESS PLACED EFFECTIVE LEGISLATIVE CONTROLS ON COVERT OPERATIONS, BOTH DID MOVE TO CREATE OVERSIGHT MECHANISMS. IN MAY OF 1976, THE SENATE CREATED THE SELECT COMMITTEE ON INTELLIGENCE, AND A LITTLE MORE THAN A YEAR LATER THE HOUSE CREATED THE PERMANENT SELECT COMMITTEE ON INTELLIGENCE. ALONG WITH RESPONSIBILITY TO "AUTHORIZE EXPENDITURES FOR INTELLIGENCE ACTIVITIES," EACH REQUIRED THAT THEY BE "INFORMED OF INTELLIGENCE ACTIVITIES UNDER THEIR PURVIEW."[112] EVEN THESE REPORTING REQUIREMENTS CONTAINED LOOPHOLES AND CAVEATS, HOWEVER. "DESPITE SOME NEW LEGISLATION,

---

[106] Ibid., 198.
[107] Ibid., 198-199.
[108] EO 11905
[109] EO 12036
[110] Zegart, *Flawed by Design*, 199.
[111] Ibid., 207.
[112] *Preparing for the 21st Century,* A-18.

TODAY'S PRESIDENTS CAN STILL UNDERTAKE CLANDESTINE OPERATIONS WITHOUT LEGISLATIVE APPROVAL OR, IN SOME CASES NOTIFICATION."[113]

THE INTENSE SCRUTINY ENDURED BY THE CIA DURING THE 1970S AND THE RESULTING OVERSIGHT AND REPORTING REQUIREMENTS WERE IN MARKED CONTRAST TO THE AGENCY'S EARLIER EXPERIENCES. FOR THE FIRST COUPLE OF DECADES AFTER ITS FOUNDATION, TRUST CHARACTERIZED THE CIA'S RELATIONSHIP WITH CONGRESS. WHILE THE DCI HAD NO DIRECT MANDATE TO REPORT CLANDESTINE EFFORTS TO THE HOUSE AND SENATE COMMITTEES ON ARMED SERVICES AND APPROPRIATIONS THAT NOMINALLY OVERSAW CIA ACTIVITIES, SOME MADE IRREGULAR ATTEMPTS TO DO SO. "AMONG THE FOUR COMMITTEES, THE CIA WAS SUBJECTED TO ABOUT TWENTY-FOUR HOURS OF LEGISLATIVE HEARINGS PER YEAR FOR MOST OF THE 1950S AND 1960S"[114] TODAY, THE DCI SPENDS A GREAT DEAL OF TIME RESPONDING TO CONGRESSIONAL REQUESTS FOR REPORTS OF VARIOUS TYPES.[115] GIVEN THE PUBLIC EXPOSURE OF UNRESTRAINED COVERT ACTIONS, THE CIA IS UNLIKELY REGAIN THE FREE REIGN IT ONCE ENJOYED. ALTHOUGH THE SENSATIONAL PUBLICITY OF THE INVESTIGATIONS AND THE RESULTING LEVELS OF OVERSIGHT LIKELY CURBED MUCH OF THE EXCESSES OF THE COVERT COMMUNITY, THEY ALSO DID "GENUINE DAMAGE" TO THE ABILITY OF THE COMMUNITY TO PROVIDE TIMELY AND ACCURATE INTELLIGENCE TO NATIONAL POLICY MAKERS AS WELL.[116]

"THE REPORTING REQUIREMENTS IMPOSED ON THE AGENCIES AND THE OVERSIGHT ACTIVITIES PERFORMED BY THE HOUSE AND SENATE HAVE HAD SOME INFLUENCE (HOWEVER SMALL) ON HOW THE INTELLIGENCE INSTITUTIONS DO BUSINESS ON A DAILY BASIS. TIME AND MONEY ARE SPENT ON FULFILLING CONGRESSIONAL REQUIREMENTS," AND SECURITY CONCERNS CURB LEGITIMATE COLLECTION OPERATIONS.[117] THE PROPONENTS OF GREATER INDEPENDENCE FOR THE CIA CLAIM THAT PROVIDING THE REQUIRED INFORMATION ON "SPECIAL ACTIVITIES" TO "SOME EIGHT COMMITTEES AND UP TO 200 MEMBERS AND STAFF" CONSTITUTES "AN UNACCEPTABLY HIGH RISK OF 'LEAKS,' WHICH IN TURN ACTS TO INHIBIT RECRUITMENT AND OPERATIONS."[118]

THE GREATEST DAMAGE AN ASSOCIATION WITH COVERT ACTION HAS DONE TO THE DCI AND CIA'S ABILITY TO COORDINATE THE INTELLIGENCE COMMUNITY, HOWEVER, IS NOT THE COST OF REPORTING REQUIREMENTS, OR THE RESULTING DIFFICULTY IN CONDUCTING CLANDESTINE COLLECTIONS, WHICH, AT MOST, WAS NEVER INTENDED TO BE MORE THAN A PERIPHERAL ROLE. THE GREATEST HARM IS THE RESULTING LOSS OF POLITICAL CAPITAL AND PRESTIGE—WITH CONGRESS, THE OTHER INTELLIGENCE AGENCIES, AND THE EXECUTIVE OFFICE. MOREOVER, AS THE SCANDALS OF THE IRAN CONTRA AFFAIR IN THE 1980S DEMONSTRATED, "REGARDLESS OF THE CHANGES IN OVERSIGHT AND

---

[113] Zegart, *Flawed by Design,* 205.

[114] Cynthia M. Nolan "Seymour Hersh's Impact on the CIA," in *Intelligence and Counterintelligence Journal* 12, no. 1, (1 March, 1999): 23.

[115] *Summary and Analysis, 9/11 Commission Recommendations,* (22 July, 2004), n.p. On-line Internet. Available from http://www.milnet.com/9-11-Commission/analysis1.html.

[116] Lowenthal, *U.S. Intelligence,* 46.

[117] Cynthia M. Nolan "Seymour Hersh's Impact on the CIA," 19.

[118] "Controversy Over Covert Intelligence Operations," 1.

MANAGEMENT," AS LONG AS THE CIA RETAINS A CAPACITY FOR COVERT OPERATIONS, "SUCH OPERATIONAL PROBLEMS AND SUCH SENSATIONAL PUBLIC PROBES" WILL CONTINUE.[119]

"FROM THE BAY OF PIGS TO NICARAGUA AND IRAN-CONTRA, IT IS COVERT OPERATIONS THAT HAVE CAUSED THE C.I.A. AND THE COUNTRY THE MOST EMBARRASSMENT."[120] MELVIN GOODMAN, AN INTELLIGENCE VETERAN OF THE CIA AND STATE DEPARTMENT, AND NOW A PROFESSOR AT THE NATIONAL WAR COLLEGE, ARGUES: "THE DEMISE OF THE SOVIET UNION DEMANDS A REEXAMINATION OF EVERY ASPECT OF ESPIONAGE AND COVERT ACTION."[121] SUCH EXAMINATIONS HAVE OCCURRED, BUT THEY DID NOT BRING GOODMAN'S DESIRED END TO COVERT OPERATIONS IN THE CIA. IN THE 1990S, A PRESIDENTIAL COMMISSION, THE COUNCIL ON FOREIGN RELATIONS (CFR), AND THE HOUSE SELECT INTELLIGENCE COMMITTEE ALL EXAMINED THE CIA'S USE OF COVERT OPERATIONS. ALL THREE REPORTS "GIVE A HIGH PRIORITY TO CONTINUED COVERT ACTION, WITH THE CFR URGING A PERIODIC REVIEW OF CONSTRAINTS ON CLANDESTINE ACTIVITY... TO ENSURE THAT THEY DO NOT UNDULY LIMIT THE EFFECTIVENESS OF THIS TOOL."[122] ENTERING THE NEW MILLENNIUM, COVERT OPERATIONS, WHILE CONTROVERSIAL, REMAINED PROMINENT IN BOTH THE RESPONSIBILITIES AND SELF-IMAGE OF THE CIA AND ITS DIRECTOR.

FACTOR 3: RELATIONAL AUTHORITY VERSUS STATUTORY AUTHORITY

AS DISCUSSED EARLIER, THE PRE-EXISTING INTELLIGENCE ORGANIZATIONS ENSURED THAT THE NATIONAL SECURITY ACT OF 1947 DID NOT PROVIDE THE NEW CIA AND DCI SUFFICIENT STATUTORY AUTHORITY TO COMMAND COMMUNITY WIDE COMPLIANCE. THE ONLY REAL AUTHORITY DCIS HAD WITHIN THE COMMUNITY CAME FROM THEIR TRADITIONALLY PRIVILEGED ACCESS TO THE PRESIDENT; YET NOTHING IN THE NATIONAL SECURITY ACT GUARANTEED SUCH ACCESS. DIFFERENT DCIS EXPERIENCED VARYING DEGREES OF REFLECTED AUTHORITY BASED ON THE DYNAMICS OF THEIR PARTICULAR RELATIONSHIP WITH THE PRESIDENT. RECOGNIZING THE NEED FOR GREATER POWER IN THE POSITION OF DCI, AND UNWILLING TO FIGHT THE BUREAUCRATIC BATTLES NECESSARY TO LEGISLATE SUCH POWERS, PRESIDENTS STARTING WITH FORD ATTEMPTED TO BOLSTER THE RELATIONSHIP OF THE DCI TO THE OFFICE OF PRESIDENT THROUGH EXECUTIVE ORDER. SUCH ORDERS, HOWEVER, ARE NO GUARANTEE THAT FUTURE PRESIDENTS WILL HAVE EITHER THE INTEREST OR INCLINATION TO SUPPORT THE DCI'S ROLE IN THE INTELLIGENCE COMMUNITY. DCIS ARE PUT IN A DELICATE PREDICAMENT, ACCESS TO THE PRESIDENT IS NEEDED TO CARRY OUT THEIR RESPONSIBILITIES, BUT SEEKING SUCH ACCESS RUNS THE RISK OF THE PERCEPTION, IF NOT THE ACTUALITY, OF POLITICIZING INTELLIGENCE. HISTORY SHOWS THAT TYING THE DCI'S AUTHORITY TO HIS PERSONAL RELATIONSHIP WITH THE PRESIDENT IS A POOR METHOD FOR CENTRALIZING CONTROL OF THE INTELLIGENCE COMMUNITY.

---

[119] Lowenthal, *U.S. Intelligence,* 46.
[120] Melvin A. Goodman, "The Road to Intelligence Reform: Paved with Good Intentions," n.p. On-line Internet. Available from http://bss.sfsu.edu/fischer/IR%20360/REadings/Mel%20Goodman htm.
[121] Ibid.
[122] Ibid.

THE WORDING OF THE PORTION OF THE NATIONAL SECURITY ACT THAT DEALT WITH THE CHARTER OF THE CIA AND DCI NEVER ADDRESSED THE RELATIONSHIP OF EITHER TO THE OFFICE OF THE PRESIDENT, OTHER THAN THE PRESIDENT'S ROLE IN NOMINATING THE DCI. SECTION 403 (D) OF THE ACT, WHICH DELINEATES THE DUTIES OF THE CIA, INSTRUCTS THE AGENCY "TO MAKE RECOMMENDATIONS TO THE NATIONAL SECURITY COUNCIL FOR THE COORDINATION OF SUCH INTELLIGENCE ACTIVITIES OF THE DEPARTMENTS AND AGENCIES OF THE GOVERNMENT AS RELATE TO THE NATIONAL SECURITY."[123] ALTHOUGH THE DCI IS A MEMBER OF THE NSC, SO TOO ARE THE SECRETARIES OF STATE AND DEFENSE, TWO OF THE MAJOR PLAYERS IN THE INTELLIGENCE COMMUNITY AND TRADITIONAL DETRACTORS OF CENTRALIZING POWER. FORTUNATELY FOR EARLY DCIS, PRESIDENT TRUMAN ESTABLISHED A PRECEDENT OF READY ACCESS, PARTICULARLY IN HIS ACCEPTANCE OF THE PRESIDENTS DAILY BRIEFING, WHICH ALLOWED THE DCI TO BE ONE OF THE FIRST OFFICIALS TO TALK WITH THE PRESIDENT EACH DAY.

TRUMAN'S FIRST DCI, REAR ADMIRAL SIDNEY SOUERS, SERVED AS THE HEAD OF THE CENTRAL INTELLIGENCE WORKING GROUP BEFORE THE CREATION OF THE CIA. SOUERS BEGAN THE TRADITION OF SENDING REGULAR INTELLIGENCE SUMMARIES TO THE PRESIDENT, "WHO SEEMED TO VALUE THEM MORE THAN WHAT HE HAD BEEN GETTING FROM THE STATE DEPARTMENT, THEREBY CREATING A TRADITION THAT HAS LASTED IN VARIOUS FORMS TO THE PRESENT."[124] HOWEVER, AS ARTHUR S. HULNICK, A 35-YEAR INTELLIGENCE VETERAN AND FORMER EDITOR OF THE PRESIDENT'S DAILY BRIEF, NOTES:

> THE DCI REMAINS THE PRESIDENT'S CHIEF INTELLIGENCE OFFICER, BUT OVER THE YEARS NUMEROUS FACTORS HAVE INTERVENED TO DILUTE THAT ROLE. THERE WAS NO NATIONAL SECURITY COUNCIL IN 1946, NOR WAS THERE A NATIONAL SECURITY ADVISER. THERE WAS NO CONGRESSIONAL OVERSIGHT OF INTELLIGENCE, AND INTELLIGENCE WAS A SUBJECT NOT OFTEN COVERED IN THE PRESS. THERE WAS NO IC, AND NO OTHER INTELLIGENCE AGENCIES VYING FOR THE PRESIDENT'S ATTENTION. IN THAT SIMPLE WORLD, IT WAS RELATIVELY EASY FOR THE DCI TO BE A TRUSTED CONFIDANT OF THE PRESIDENT."[125]

ROSCOE HILLENKOETTER, SOUERS' SUCCESSOR AS DCI AND THE FIRST HEAD OF THE CIA, CONTINUED THE TRADITION OF BEING THE PRESIDENT'S FIRST BRIEFER OF THE DAY, BUT FAILED TO USE THAT ACCESS AS LEVERAGE OVER THE LARGER INTELLIGENCE COMMUNITY. ONE OBSERVER COMMENTED: "IN THE HIERARCHICAL MAZE OF OFFICIAL WASHINGTON, HIS AUTHORITY SCARCELY EXTENDED BEYOND THE FRONT DOOR."[126] HILLENKOETTER'S SUCCESSOR, GEN. WALTER BEDDELL SMITH, USED HIS ACCESS TO THE PRESIDENT TO COMPENSATE FOR STATUTORY AUTHORITY MUCH MORE EFFECTIVELY. ALTHOUGH "INTERDEPARTMENTAL RIVALRIES DID NOT SUDDENLY DISAPPEAR . . . NO ONE

---

[123] Public Law 61-253. *National Security Act (NSA) of 1947*. 26 July 1947, Section 403 (d) (2).
[124] ARTHUR S. HULNICK. "DOES THE U.S. INTELLIGENCE COMMUNITY NEED A DNI?" *INTERNATIONAL Journal of Intelligence and Counterintelligence* 17, no. 4 (Winter 2004-2005): 711.
[125] Ibid., 712.
[126] Andrew, *For the President's Eyes Only*, 170.

WANTED GENERAL SMITH TO HEAR THAT HE OR HIS AGENCY WAS HINDERING THE PRODUCTION OF ESTIMATES."[127]

EVEN THOUGH THE NEXT DCI, JOHN FOSTER DULLES, HAD LITTLE INTEREST IN COMMUNITY MANAGEMENT, HE ENJOYED A CLOSE RELATIONSHIP WITH PRESIDENT EISENHOWER WHO SHARED HIS INTEREST IN COVERT OPERATIONS. WHEN KENNEDY REPLACED EISENHOWER, A PERSONAL RELATIONSHIP WITH THE PRESIDENT WAS EVEN MORE IMPORTANT THAN PREVIOUSLY, AS THE NEW PRESIDENT "DID NOT HOLD REGULARLY SCHEDULED NSC MEETINGS AS EISENHOWER AND TRUMAN HAD DONE."[128] DULLES, HOWEVER, FAILED TO MAKE A STRONG FIRST IMPRESSION ON KENNEDY, AND AFTER THE BAY OF PIGS INCIDENT, THE PRESIDENT LARGELY DENIED HIM ACCESS. DULLES' SUCCESSOR TO THE POSITION, JOHN MCCONE, FARED BETTER INITIALLY, BUT HIS RELATIONSHIP WITH KENNEDY, IRONICALLY, BECAME STRAINED, NOT FROM AN INTELLIGENCE FAILURE, BUT FROM A SUCCESS. ALTHOUGH MCCONE WAS ONE OF THE FEW VOICES WARNING THE PRESIDENT OF THE POSSIBILITY OF SOVIET MISSILES IN CUBA, "THE PRESIDENT DID NOT LIKE MCCONE'S PUBLIC REFERENCES TO THIS FACT, AND THEIR RELATIONSHIP COOLED NOTICEABLY."[129] ALTHOUGH MCCONE INITIALLY BUILT A STRONG RELATIONSHIP WITH PRESIDENT JOHNSON, IT SOURED WHEN THE DCI BEGAN EXPRESSING A PESSIMISTIC OUTLOOK ON THE PRESIDENT'S PREFERRED POLICY FOR VIETNAM. "BY MARCH OF 1964, JOHNSON CLEARLY HAD LOST CONFIDENCE IN MCCONE AND INTEREST IN HIS REGULAR INTELLIGENCE UPDATES."[130] ALTHOUGH BY DESIGN, THE DCI WAS TO HAVE DIRECT ACCESS TO THE PRESIDENT THROUGH THE NSC, LIKE KENNEDY, JOHNSON RARELY CALLED A MEETING OF THE NSC. "JOHNSON'S MAIN DECISION-MAKING GROUP FOR THE VIETNAM WAR BECAME NOT THE NSC BUT THE SO-CALLED TUESDAY LUNCH" WHICH INCLUDED SECRETARY OF DEFENSE MCNAMARA, AND SECRETARY OF STATE RUSK, BUT TO WHICH DCI MCCONE WAS NEVER INVITED.[131] JOHNSON PICKED VICE ADM. WILLIAM RABORN TO SUCCEED MCCONE, NOT BECAUSE HE THOUGHT RABORN WOULD YIELD EFFECTIVE CONTROL OVER THE INTELLIGENCE COMMUNITY, BUT RATHER "HE SAW IN RABORN A RELIABLY COMPLIANT DCI WHOSE ADMINISTRATIVE EFFICIENCY WOULD ENSURE THE AGENCY DID NOT ROCK THE PRESIDENTIAL BOAT."[132] JOHNSON, AND NIXON AFTER HIM, SOUGHT FOREIGN INTELLIGENCE FROM SOURCES OTHER THAN THE DCI; SUBSEQUENTLY, WHATEVER PRIORITIES AND GUIDANCE THEY HAD FOR THE INTELLIGENCE COMMUNITY WERE NOT COMMUNICATED THROUGH THE DCI. NIXON, WHO RELIED ON SECRETARY OF STATE HENRY KISSINGER AS HIS "MAIN INTELLIGENCE ADVISER," EVEN ATTEMPTED TO EXCLUDE DCI HELMS FROM NSC MEETINGS.[133]

---

[127] Andrew, *For the President's Eyes Only*, 189.
[128] John L. Helgerson, *CIA Briefings of Presidential Candidates 1952-1992,* (Washington DC: Center for the Study of Intelligence, Central Intelligence Agency, 1996), n.p. On-line Internet. Available from http://www.cia.gov/csi/books/briefing/.
[129] Ibid.
[130] Ibid., *21.*
[131] Andrew, *For the President's Eyes Only*, 316.
[132] Ibid., 324.
[133] Ibid., 353.

STAKING THE DCI'S AUTHORITY TO HIS ACCESS TO THE PRESIDENT ENJOYED INTERMITTENT SUCCESS AT BEST. EACH PRESIDENT HAD DIFFERENT INTERESTS AND EXPECTATIONS OF THE INTELLIGENCE COMMUNITY AND ITS DIRECTOR, AND EACH DCI HAD DIFFERENT APPROACHES TO DEALING WITH THE PRESIDENT. SOMETIMES THE RELATIONSHIP BECAME AN EFFECTIVE SUBSTITUTE FOR THE DCI'S LACK OF STATUTORY AUTHORITY, BUT OFTEN IT DID NOT. WHEN THE DCI'S INFLUENCE BECAME A PUBLIC ISSUE DURING THE INVESTIGATIONS OF THE 1970S, BUT LEGISLATION FAILED TO ADDRESS THE PROBLEM, PRESIDENT FORD BEGAN AN EFFORT TO BOLSTER THE DCI'S AUTHORITY THROUGH EXECUTIVE ORDER. IN 1976, FORD, FOR THE FIRST TIME, SPECIFIED THAT THE DCI "SHALL BE RESPONSIBLE DIRECTLY TO THE NATIONAL SECURITY COUNCIL AND THE PRESIDENT."[134] IN THE SAME ORDER, HE TASKED THE DCI WITH "PROVIDING LEADERSHIP, GUIDANCE AND TECHNICAL ASSISTANCE TO OTHER GOVERNMENT DEPARTMENTS AND AGENCIES FORMING FOREIGN INTELLIGENCE ACTIVITIES."[135] BY TASKING THE DCI DIRECTLY, FORD ESSENTIALLY CONFERRED HIS AUTHORITY ON THE DCI. IN 1978, PRESIDENT CARTER SUPERSEDED FORD'S ORDER WITH EO 12036, "WHICH REAFFIRMED THE DCI'S COMMUNITY-WIDE AUTHORITY OVER PRIORITIES, TASKINGS, AND THE BUDGET."[136] IN A SUBTLE MOVE, PRESIDENT REAGAN'S EO 12333 LISTED THE DCI'S RELATIONSHIP TO THE PRESIDENT BEFORE THE NSC: "THE DIRECTOR OF CENTRAL INTELLIGENCE SHALL BE RESPONSIBLE DIRECTLY TO THE PRESIDENT AND THE NSC." AND AGAIN REINFORCED THE DCI'S ROLE AS "THE PRIMARY ADVISER TO THE PRESIDENT AND THE NSC ON NATIONAL FOREIGN INTELLIGENCE."[137] REAGAN WENT EVEN FURTHER, GIVING HIS FIRST DCI, WILLIAM CASEY, CABINET RANK. INDEED, THE GREATER INTELLIGENCE COMMUNITY WAS WELL AWARE OF CASEY'S CLOSE RELATIONSHIP WITH THE PRESIDENT. CASEY "COULD NOT RUN THE DoD ELEMENTS, BUT HIS POSITION IN THE ADMINISTRATION MOTIVATED THE OTHER AGENCY LEADERS TO COOPERATE."[138]

CASEY'S PROXIMITY TO THE PRESIDENT, HOWEVER, CAME WITH A PRICE. HAVING SERVED AS REAGAN'S CAMPAIGN MANAGER, IT WAS IMPOSSIBLE FOR CASEY TO MAINTAIN THE DCI'S TRADITIONAL IMAGE OF DETACHED NEUTRALITY TO POLICY. CASEY WAS WIDELY CHARGED WITH INTENTIONALLY SEEKING AND SELECTING ANALYSIS SUPPORTING PRESIDENT REAGAN'S FOREIGN POLICY OBJECTIVES.[139] YEARS LATER WHEN CASEY'S DIRECTOR OF INTELLIGENCE, WILLIAM GATES, SOUGHT SENATE CONFIRMATION AS DCI, ANALYSTS FROM CASEY'S ERA CONTINUED TO CLAIM THEY RECEIVED PRESSURE TO PRODUCE INTELLIGENCE TO SUPPORT THE ADMINISTRATION'S POLICIES. WHEN REAGAN NOMINATED

---

[134] EO 11905
[135] EO 11905
[136] *Preparing for the 21st Century*, A-18.
[137] Executive Order 12333. United States Intelligence Activities, 4 December 1981.
[138] ARTHUR S. HULNICK. "DOES THE U.S. INTELLIGENCE COMMUNITY NEED A DNI?" *INTERNATIONAL Journal of Intelligence and Counterintelligence* 17, no. 4 (Winter 2004-2005): 715.
[139] H. BRADFORD WESTERFIELD, "INSIDE IVORY BUNKERS: CIA ANALYSTS RESIST MANGERS' PANDERING." IN
STRATEGIC INTELLIGENCE, ED. LOCH K. JOHNSON, 199-200.

JUDGE WILLIAM WEBSTER TO REPLACE CASEY AS DCI, WEBSTER MADE A POINT OF DECLINING CABINET STATUS FOR THE EXPRESS PURPOSE OF KEEPING HIS DISTANCE FROM THE PRESIDENT.[140]

PRESIDENT GEORGE H.W. BUSH, HIMSELF A FORMER DCI, "HAD A CLOSER WORKING RELATIONSHIP THAN ANY PREVIOUS PRESIDENT WITH THE CIA."[141] WHEN CLINTON CAME TO OFFICE HOWEVER, HE DID NOT SHARE REAGAN OR BUSH'S INTEREST IN INTELLIGENCE OR RELIANCE ON THE DCI. ALTHOUGH REAGAN'S EXECUTIVE ORDER REMAINED IN EFFECT UNTIL SUPERSEDED BY LEGISLATION IN 2004, CLINTON, WHO INITIALLY FOCUSED ON HIS DOMESTIC AGENDA, LARGELY DID AWAY WITH THE PRESIDENT'S DAILY BRIEF.[142] DCI WOOLSEY, NOMINATED BY CLINTON IN 1993, HAD SUCH LITTLE ACCESS TO THE PRESIDENT THAT HE LATER CLAIMED, "IN THE FALL OF '94, WHEN THAT LITTLE CESSNA AIRPLANE CRASHED INTO THE SOUTH LAWN OF THE WHITE HOUSE, THE WHITE HOUSE STAFF JOKE WAS, THAT MUST BE WOOLSEY STILL TRYING TO GET AN APPOINTMENT WITH [THEN-PRESIDENT BILL] CLINTON."[143] ALTHOUGH PRESIDENT CLINTON RELUCTANTLY SIGNED THE INTELLIGENCE ACT FOR 1997, WHICH HAD SOME PROVISIONS FOR INCREASING COOPERATION THROUGHOUT THE INTELLIGENCE COMMUNITY, THIS DID NOT SIGNAL A STRONG BACKING FOR THE DCI. CLINTON SPECIFICALLY OBJECTED TO "PROVISIONS THAT REQUIRED THE CONSULTATION OF THE DIRECTOR OF CENTRAL INTELLIGENCE (DCI) BEFORE THE APPOINTMENT OF CERTAIN INTELLIGENCE OFFICIALS…AS AN INTRUSION ON PRESIDENTIAL PREROGATIVES"[144]

IN A DECEMBER 1998 MEMO TO THE INTELLIGENCE COMMUNITY, CLINTON'S FOURTH DCI, GEORGE TENET, "DECLARED WAR ON OSAMA BIN LADEN." [145] AS THE 9-11 COMMISSION NOTED, "THERE WAS NO EVIDENT RESPONSE."[146] IF TENET WAS COUNTING ON PRESIDENTIAL BACKING TO SET THE AGENDA FOR THE INTELLIGENCE COMMUNITY, IT FAILED HIM. BOLSTERING THE DCI BY GIVING HIM RELATIONAL POWER, NOT AUTONOMOUS POWER, IS AT BEST A TEMPORARY SOLUTION. THOMAS TROY, A

[140] Ronald Kessler, *Inside the CIA, Revealing the Secrets of the Worlds Most Powerful Spy Agency*, (New York: Pocket Books, 1992), 186.

[141] Christopher Andrew, "Foreword," in *CIA Briefings of Presidential Candidates 1952-1992,"* John L. Helgerson, ed. (Washington DC: Center for the Study of Intelligence, Central Intelligence Agency, 1996), n.p. On-line Internet. Available from http://www.cia.gov/csi/books/briefing/cia-1.htm.

[142] Hulnick, "Does the U.S." 717.

[143] R. JAMES WOOLSEY, IN A FORUM MODERATED BY WALTER H. PINCUS FOR THE COUNCIL ON FOREIGN RELATIONS,
NEW YORK, (12 MAY 2004), N.P. TRANSCRIPT ON-LINE INTERNET. AVAILABLE FROM HTTP://WWW.CFR.ORG/

PUB7022/STANSFIELD_TURNER_R_JAMES_WOOLSEY_WILLIAM_H_WEBSTER_WALTER_H_PINCUS/THE_CENTRAL_
INTELLIGENCE_AGENCY.PHP.

[144] Miller "Structural Quiescence,"235.

[145] JOSEPH LIEBERMAN, "GOVERNMENTAL AFFAIRS COMMITTEE HEARING ON THE PRESIDENT'S PROPOSAL FOR A
TERRORISM THREAT INTEGRATION CENTER." STATEMENT TO THE SENATE GOVERNMENTAL AFFAIRS COMMITTEE, 14
FEBRUARY 2003, ON-LINE INTERNET. AVAILABLE FROM HTTP://WWW.FAS.ORG/IRP/CONGRESS/2003_HR/.

[146] Ibid.

CIA VETERAN, DESCRIBES THE DCI'S PREDICAMENT WELL: "HE HAS NO COMMAND AUTHORITY OVER, FOR INSTANCE THE 80 TO 85 PERCENT OF THE COMMUNITY'S PERSONNEL AND RESOURCES CONTROLLED BY VARIOUS UNITS OF THE DEPARTMENT OF DEFENSE. WHAT PULL HE HAS WITH THEM RESTS UPON PRESIDENTIAL EXHORTATION, WHICH ARE WORDS IN THE WIND, AND UPON EXECUTIVE ORDERS, WHICH ARE AS CHANGEABLE AS THE EXECUTIVES MIND."[147] DESPITE FIFTY YEARS OF EFFORTS TO STRENGTHEN THE DCI, WHEN THE PRESIDENT LACKED THE DESIRE OR INTEREST TO BECOME INVOLVED, THE DCI HAD NO PULL AT ALL.

FACTOR 4: PROLIFERATION OF INTELLIGENCE AGENCIES AND ACTIVITIES

SINCE WOULD-BE REFORMERS OF THE INTELLIGENCE COMMUNITY FOUND INSURMOUNTABLE POLITICAL OBSTACLES TO INVESTING THE DCI AND THE CIA WITH SUFFICIENT AUTHORITY TO EXERT CENTRAL CONTROL, THEY OFTEN CREATED NEW AGENCIES OR ORGANIZATIONS TO CONTROL THE COMMUNITY, OR AT LEAST SOME ASPECT OF IT. LIKE THE CIA, THESE NEW AGENCIES RARELY REPLACED ANY OF THE DUTIES OF THE VARIOUS AGENCIES THEY OSTENSIBLY COORDINATED. INSTEAD, THEY TOO DEVELOPED THEIR OWN NICHES WITHIN THE COMMUNITY, COMPLETE WITH THEIR OWN CUSTOMER BASES, PRIORITIES, AND COMPETING DEMANDS FOR RESOURCES. "VIRTUALLY EVERY PAST 'INTELLIGENCE FAILURE' HAS LED TO REFORMS THAT HAVE RESULTED IN MORE, NOT FEWER, SUB-ORGANIZATIONS TO COORDINATE."[148] THIS PROLIFERATION OF AGENCIES AND SUB-AGENCIES, THOUGH DONE IN THE NAME OF CENTRALIZATION, MAKES THE COMMUNITY EVEN MORE DIVERSE, UNWIELDY AND RESISTANT TO EFFECTIVE COORDINATION.

THE NATIONAL SECURITY ACT OF 1947 ENVISIONED THE DCI USING THE ORGANIZATION OF THE CIA TO SET PRIORITIES, ELIMINATE WASTEFUL REDUNDANCIES, AND SYNTHESIZE INTELLIGENCE PRODUCTS OF THE ENTIRE INTELLIGENCE COMMUNITY. AT ITS CREATION, THE CIA "WAS THE ONLY AGENCY TASKED WITH PRODUCING NATIONAL INTELLIGENCE. OTHERS HANDLED INTELLIGENCE OF NATIONAL IMPORTANCE, BUT ONLY THE CIA HAD DUTY TO PRODUCE IT."[149] WHEN IT WAS SIGNED, THE "EXISTING INTELLIGENCE AGENCIES" CITED IN THE NATIONAL SECURITY ACT CONSISTED OF "THE RELATIVELY SMALL INTELLIGENCE COMPONENTS IN THE ARMED SERVICES, THE DEPARTMENTS OF STATE AND THE TREASURY, [AND] THE FBI."[150] TODAY THE COMMUNITY CONTAINS 15 SEPARATE AGENCIES, MORE THAN MANY PROFESSIONALS IN THE COMMUNITY CAN QUICKLY NAME.[151] SEVERAL OF THESE AGENCIES NOW PRODUCE NATIONAL INTELLIGENCE. ALLOWING THEM TO MAKE END RUNS AROUND THE CIA TO SENIOR POLICY MAKERS. AS A RESULT, THE "CIA TODAY IS NOT THE CENTER OF EVEN THE CIA'S PIE CHART. IT IS ON THE PERIPHERY, ONE OF A DOZEN SPOKES. IT HAS HAD TO YIELD THE CENTER TO

[147] Troy, "The Quaintness of the U.S. Intelligence Community," 27.
[148] Taylor, "Intelligence Reform,"418.
[149] Warner, *Central Intelligence,* 5
[150] Best, *Proposals for Intelligence Reorganization,* 1.
[151] ROBERT F. DORR, "A BIGGER INTELLIGENCE BUREAUCRACY DOESN'T EQUAL BETTER INTELLIGENCE." *ARMY TIMES, (*31
JANUARY 2005): 46.

THE DCI AND HIS COMMUNITY STAFF."[152] BLUNTLY PUT, THE CIA IS NOT A CENTRAL AGENCY. WHILE THE DCI STILL HAS THE NOMINAL RESPONSIBILITY FOR COMMUNITY WIDE AFFAIRS, PREOCCUPATION WITH THE DAY-TO-DAY RUNNING OF THE CIA ALLOWS LITTLE TIME TO EXERCISE WHAT LITTLE AUTHORITY REMAINS TO INFLUENCE A COMMUNITY THAT IS CONTINUALLY GROWING IN SIZE AND COMPLEXITY.

IRONICALLY, IT WAS DCI WALTER BEDELL SMITH WHO INITIATED THE PROCESS LEADING TO THE CREATION OF THE FIRST NEW AGENCY TO JOIN THE INTELLIGENCE COMMUNITY FOLLOWING THE CREATION OF THE CIA: THE NATIONAL SECURITY AGENCY (NSA). THE FAILURE OF NATIONAL SIGNALS INTELLIGENCE ASSETS TO PREDICT THE KOREAN WAR, OR EVEN TO WORK TOGETHER IN THE PROSECUTION OF IT, DISMAYED SMITH. ALTHOUGH WELL AWARE OF THE POTENTIAL VALUE OF SIGINT, SMITH'S "LACK OF AUTHORITY OVER IT, DESPITE HIS RESPONSIBILITY AS DCI FOR COORDINATING THE WORK OF THE INTELLIGENCE COMMUNITY" FRUSTRATED THE DCI.[153] IN DECEMBER OF 1951, HE WROTE A MEMORANDUM TO THE NATIONAL SECURITY COUNCIL THAT STATED, "CONTROL OVER, AND COORDINATION OF, THE COLLECTION AND PROCESSING OF COMMUNICATIONS INTELLIGENCE HAD PROVED INEFFECTIVE."[154] THIS MEMORANDUM LED TO THE NSC COMMISSIONING THE BROWNWELL COMMITTEE REPORT, WHICH RECOMMENDED A STRONGER ORGANIZATION WITHIN THE MILITARY TO COORDINATE THE SIGINT OPERATIONS OF EACH SERVICE. ON OCTOBER 24 OF 1952, TRUMAN SIGNED A NEW NSCID 9, ESTABLISHING THE NSA WITHIN THE DoD. ALTHOUGH THE DIRECTIVE CALLED FOR THE DCI TO ASSIST IN THE ESTABLISHMENT OF POLICIES FOR COMMUNICATIONS INTELLIGENCE (COMINT), IT "DESIGNATED THE DEPARTMENT OF DEFENSE AS EXECUTIVE AGENT OF THE GOVERNMENT, FOR THE PRODUCTION OF COMINT INFORMATION."[155] IN THE END, SMITH HAD LESS PRACTICAL CONTROL THEN HE PREVIOUSLY HAD EVEN NOMINALLY.

JUST AS THE CREATION OF THE CIA DID NOT CONSOLIDATE THE INTELLIGENCE PRODUCTION EFFORTS OF THE EXISTING SERVICES, THE CREATION OF THE NSA DID NOT COMBINE OR REPLACE THE OTHER SIGINT ORGANIZATIONS THROUGHOUT THE GOVERNMENT, OR EVEN WITHIN THE MILITARY. TODAY THE NSA, WHILE THE LARGEST OF ALL US INTELLIGENCE AGENCIES, IS MERELY THE LEAD AGENCY OF THE UNITED STATES SIGINT SYSTEM (USSS), WHICH IS COMPOSED OF THE US ARMY INTELLIGENCE AND SECURITY COMMAND (INSCOM), THE NAVAL SECURITY GROUP COMMAND (NAVSECGRU), THE AIR INTELLIGENCE AGENCY (AIA), AND OTHER MILITARY SIGNALS INTELLIGENCE ELEMENTS. ADDITIONALLY, THE NSA EXERCISES OPERATIONAL CONTROL OVER THE JOINT CIA-NSA SPECIAL COLLECTION SERVICE (SCS), AND HAS SIGNIFICANT INFLUENCE WITH THE CIA'S OFFICE OF

---

[152] Troy, "The Quaintness of the U.S. Intelligence Community," 29.
[153] Andrew, *For the President's Eyes Only,* 196.
[154] JEFFERY T. RICHELSON, ED., "THE NATIONAL SECURITY AGENCY DECLASSIFIED." *NATIONAL SECURITY ARCHIVE*
   ELECTRONIC BRIEFING BOOK NO. 24. (13 JANUARY 2000), ON-LINE INTERNET. AVAILABLE FROM HTTP://WWW.GWU.EDU/~NSARCHIV/NSAEBB/NSAEBB23/INDEX2.HTML.
[155] Ibid.

TECHNICAL COLLECTION (OTC).[156] THIS SAME PATTERN WOULD MANIFEST ITSELF AGAIN WITHIN A FEW SHORT YEARS WITH THE CREATION OF THE DEFENSE INTELLIGENCE AGENCY.

BY 1961, IT WAS CLEAR THAT THE CIA HAD ABDICATED ITS RESPONSIBILITY FOR PROVIDING COMMUNITY WIDE GUIDANCE AND COORDINATION. THE TAYLOR COMMISSION, IN ITS STUDY OF THE BAY OF PIGS FAILURE, STATED: "THERE WAS NO SINGLE AUTHORITY SHORT OF THE PRESIDENT CAPABLE OF COORDINATING THE ACTIONS OF CIA, STATE, DEFENSE AND USIA [U.S. INFORMATION AGENCY]."[157] THE WORDING OF THIS FINDING CLEARLY PUTS THE CIA ON CO-EQUAL STATUS WITH THE OTHER AGENCIES. WITH THE CIA JUST ANOTHER AGENCY IN NEED OF COORDINATION, PRESIDENT KENNEDY REVIVED THE BOARD OF CONSULTANTS CREATED BY EISENHOWER TO ASSIST HIM IN RUNNING THE INTELLIGENCE COMMUNITY, AND RENAMED IT THE PRESIDENT'S FOREIGN INTELLIGENCE ADVISORY BOARD (PFIAB). ONE OF THE PFIAB'S PRIMARY CONCERNS WAS HOW TO ORGANIZE AND COORDINATE "THE DIFFUSE DEFENSE INTELLIGENCE SYSTEM."[158] IN OCTOBER OF 1961, IT APPROVED MCNAMARA'S PROPOSAL TO CREATE A DEFENSE INTELLIGENCE AGENCY (DIA), TO COORDINATE AND EXTEND THE WORK OF THE RIVAL SERVICE INTELLIGENCE DEPARTMENTS."[159]

BY THE DIA'S OWN HISTORY, IT WAS CREATED TO FILL "A CRITICALLY IMPORTANT NEED FOR A CENTRAL INTELLIGENCE MANAGER FOR THE DEPARTMENT OF DEFENSE," BUT DURING THE EARLY YEARS OF THE "DIA'S EXISTENCE, AGENCY ATTEMPTS TO ESTABLISH ITSELF AS DOD'S CENTRAL MILITARY INTELLIGENCE ORGANIZATION MET WITH CONTINUING SERVICE OPPOSITION."[160] ALTHOUGH THE DIA OPENED A NEW PRODUCTION CENTER IN 1963, EACH SERVICE KEPT ITS OWN ANALYTICAL CAPABILITIES.[161] IN THE 1970S, "THE AGENCY SHIFTED ITS FOCUS FROM CONSOLIDATING INTERNAL AND EXTERNAL MANAGEMENT ROLES TO ESTABLISHING ITSELF AS A CREDIBLE PRODUCER OF NATIONAL INTELLIGENCE," PREVIOUSLY A PREROGATIVE OF THE CIA ALONE.[162] AS MARK LOWENTHAL NOTES, ALTHOUGH THE DIA WAS DESIGNED TO COORDINATE THE INTELLIGENCE ACTIVITIES OF THE SERVICES, IT "QUICKLY SURPASSED THAT RATHER LIMITED ROLE AND BECAME ANOTHER INDEPENDENT PRODUCER OF INTELLIGENCE AND AN OFTEN INTENSE RIVAL OF THE CIA."[163] LIKE THE CIA AND NSA BEFORE IT, THE DIA, ALTHOUGH CREATED TO BE A COORDINATING AUTHORITY, BECAME AN ADDITIONAL COMPETING PRODUCER. THAT THE DIA DID NOT SATISFY THE NEED FOR INTELLIGENCE COORDINATION WITHIN THE MILITARY IS EVIDENT BY THE DOD'S CONTINUING EFFORTS AT COORDINATION SUCH AS THE CREATION OF THE POSITION OF ASSISTANT SECRETARY OF DEFENSE FOR INTELLIGENCE (ASD/I) IN 1971 (LATER

---

[156] Matthey M. Aid, "The Time of Troubles: The U.S. National Security Agency in the Twenty-First Century," in *Strategic Intelligence,* ed. Loch K. Johnson, 73.

[157] Best, *Proposals for Intelligence Reorganization,* 13-14.

[158] Andrew, *For the President's Eyes,* 272.

[159] Ibid.

[160] *35 YEARS, A BRIEF HISTORY.* (WASHINGTON DC: DIA HISTORY OFFICE,1996), 1/7.

[161] Preparing *for the 21st Century, ,* A-13.

[162] *35 Years, A Brief History,* 9.

[163] Lowenthal, *U.S. Intelligence,* 31-32.

DESIGNATED AS THE DIRECTOR OF DEFENSE INTELLIGENCE WITH THE CREATION OF THE DEFENSE INTELLIGENCE BOARD).[164]

THE NATIONAL RECONNAISSANCE OFFICE, CREATED IN SEPTEMBER OF 1961 TO COORDINATE SPACE RECONNAISSANCE PROGRAMS, NEVER HAD ILLUSIONS OF WIELDING UNIFIED AUTHORITY OVER SUCH PROGRAMS. INSTEAD, IT WAS TO BE "A FEDERATION OF INTELLIGENCE AND MILITARY ORGANIZATIONS THAT, IN ADDITION TO MAINTAINING THEIR SEPARATE IDENTITIES, WERE PART OF THE NRO."[165] AS THE DoD BASED OFFICE GREW, HOWEVER, IT INCREASINGLY SOUGHT TO CONTROL SPACE PROGRAMS, INCLUDING THOSE IN THE CIA. THIS STRUCTURE RESULTED IN OFTEN "FIERCE BATTLES BETWEEN THE CIA AND THE DIRECTOR NRO OVER THE EXTENT OF THE DIRECTOR'S CONTROL."[166]

THE NEXT MAJOR ORGANIZATION TO JOIN THE INTELLIGENCE COMMUNITY, THE NATIONAL IMAGERY AND MAPPING AGENCY (NIMA), DID REDUCE REDUNDANCY BY "CONSOLIDATING THE DEFENSE MAPPING AGENCY, CENTRAL IMAGERY OFFICE, NATIONAL PHOTOGRAPHIC INTERPRETATION CENTER, THE IMAGERY EXPLOITATION ELEMENT OF THE DEFENSE INTELLIGENCE AGENCY, AND PORTIONS OF THE DEFENSE AIRBORNE RECONNAISSANCE OFFICE AND NATIONAL RECONNAISSANCE OFFICE."[167] HOWEVER, NIMA "LEFT THE ACQUISITION AND OPERATION OF SPACE SYSTEMS AND THEIR GROUND STATIONS TO THE NRO," AND DID NOT INTERFERE WITH THE "IMAGERY EXPLOITATION ACTIVITIES OF THE SERVICE INTELLIGENCE ORGANIZATIONS."[168] THIS PROLIFERATION OF INTELLIGENCE AGENCIES, WHICH ACCOMPANIED THE US'S SHIFT TOWARD ELECTRONIC AND PHOTOGRAPHIC TECHNOLOGIES, MADE "COORDINATING AND INTEGRATING THEIR ACTIVITIES… INCREASINGLY PROBLEMATIC."[169]

CONCURRENT WITH THE PROLIFERATION OF INTELLIGENCE AGENCIES, SUB-AGENCY ORGANIZATIONS UNDERWENT A SIMILAR PATTERN. WOULD-BE CENTRALIZERS CREATED SUCH ORGANIZATIONS TO FOCUS DISPARATE ELEMENTS OF THE COMMUNITY ON SPECIFIC INTELLIGENCE TASKS, BUT IN SHORT ORDER THESE BODIES EVOLVED INTO INDEPENDENT COMPETITORS. FOLLOWING A RASH OF TERRORIST INCIDENTS IN THE EARLY 1980S, "DCI WILLIAM CASEY CREATED A COUNTERTERRORISM CENTER (CTC)" UNDER THE CIA'S DIRECTORATE OF OPERATIONS IN 1986, "TO CORRELATE ALL IC COUNTERTERRORIST ACTIVITIES AND TO 'GO AFTER' TERRORISTS."[170] ALTHOUGH THIS ORGANIZATION INCORPORATED PERSONNEL FROM THE DEPARTMENT OF DEFENSE, THE FBI, AND OTHER AGENCIES, THE

---

[164] *35 Years, A Brief History*, 11-12.

[165] JEFFERY T. RICHELSON, *THE U.S. INTELLIGENCE COMMUNITY* (BOULDER, COLORADO: WESTVIEW PRESS. 1999), 38.

[166] IBID.

[167] Ibid., 43.

[168] Ibid.

[169] JAMES JAY CARAFANO, "THE CASE FOR INTELLIGENCE REFORM: A PRIMER ON STRATEGIC INTELLIGENCE AND
TERRORISM FROM THE 1970S TO TODAY," *THE HERITAGE FOUNDATION.* LECTURE #845, (21 JULY 2004), N.P. ON-
LINE INTERNET. AVAILABLE FROM
HTTP://WWW.HERITAGE.ORG/RESEARCH/NATIONALSECURITY/HL845.CFM.

[170] Taylor, "Intelligence Reform," 418-419.

"FBI CONTINUED TO MAINTAIN ITS COUNTERTERRORISM THREAT ASSESSMENT AND WARNING UNIT AND ITS JOINT TERRORISM TASK FORCE (JTTF), AND OTHER AGENCIES AND SUB-AGENCIES CONTINUED TO CONDUCT COUNTERTERRORISM INTELLIGENCE OF VARYING KINDS WITH MINIMAL CENTRALIZED COORDINATION AND INFORMATION SHARING."[171] THE RESULT WAS FURTHER DILUTION, NOT A CONCENTRATION, OF THE EFFORT TO COLLECT AGAINST TERRORIST TARGETS. RATHER THAN PROMOTING A SHARING OF INFORMATION, THE NEW CTC SET OFF INTENSE TURF BATTLES. ONE SENIOR COUNTERTERRORIST OFFICIAL REPORTEDLY SAID: "VICTORY FOR US [AT THE CTC] MEANT THAT WE STOPPED [THOMAS] TWETTEN [THE CHIEF OF THE CLANDESTINE SERVICE'S NEAR EAST DIVISION] FROM WALKING ALL OVER US."[172] SIMILAR PATTERNS OF EXPANSION EXIST IN COUNTERINTELLIGENCE AND OTHER SPECIALTY FIELDS WITHIN THE INTELLIGENCE COMMUNITY.

THE PROLIFERATION OF AGENCIES AND SUB-AGENCIES IS PARALLEL BY THE GROWTH OF PANELS, BOARDS AND COMMITTEES DESIGNED TO HELP THE DCI MANAGE THE GROWING COMMUNITY. ONE OF THE EARLIEST WAS THE OFFICE OF NATIONAL ESTIMATES (ONE), ESTABLISHED IN 1950 TO IMPROVE THE QUALITY OF NATIONAL INTELLIGENCE APPRAISALS.[173] WHILE SUCH BODIES ARE WELL INTENTIONED, THEIR AGGREGATE RESULT IS NOT AN INCREASE IN THE DCI'S AUTHORITY, BUT RATHER AN INCREASE IN RESPONSIBILITIES. IRONICALLY, ONE WAS CREATED IN RESPONSE TO THE EBERSTADT REPORT, WHICH NOTED: "THE ESTABLISHMENT OF STILL ANOTHER INTELLIGENCE ACTIVITY WOULD RENDER MORE DIFFICULT THE TASK OF THE CENTRAL INTELLIGENCE AGENCY'S AUTHORITY – WHICH NEEDS STRENGTHENING RATHER THAN WEAKENING."[174] FOLLOWING SHORTLY AFTER THE CREATION OF ONE, PRESIDENT EISENHOWER ESTABLISHED THE UNITED STATES INTELLIGENCE BOARD (USIB) "AS THE SINGLE FORUM FOR ALL INTELLIGENCE CHIEFS TO PROVIDE ADVICE TO THE DCI ON INTELLIGENCE ACTIVITIES."[175] THE USIB, A PREDECESSOR OF TODAY'S NATIONAL FOREIGN INTELLIGENCE BOARD (NFIB), SOON DEVELOPED "A SOPHISTICATED SET OF PROCEDURES."[176] MARK LOWENTHAL'S DESCRIPTION OF THE USIB AS "A BODY CREATED IN 1958 TO COORDINATE AND MANAGE INTELLIGENCE ACTIVITIES" SOUNDS REMARKABLY SIMILAR TO THE ORIGINAL CHARTER OF THE CIA, WHICH INCREASINGLY FOUND ITSELF CONDUCTING INDEPENDENT OPERATIONS AND PRODUCING INDEPENDENT PRODUCTS.[177]

BY THE EARLY 1960S, THE GROWTH OF INTELLIGENCE ACTIVITIES WITHIN THE DEPARTMENT OF DEFENSE, WHICH BY THEN INCLUDED THE NSA, NRO, AND DIA AS WELL AS THE INTELLIGENCE ORGANIZATION OF EACH MILITARY SERVICE, "SERVED TO ACCENTUATE THE RELATIVE LACK OF THE DCI'S ROLE OVER THE REST OF THE COMMUNITY."[178] THIS LED THE PFIAB, WHICH HAD ORIGINALLY PUSHED FOR THE CREATION OF THE DIA, TO SUGGEST THE ESTABLISHMENT OF AN "OFFICE OF COORDINATION IN

---

[171] Ibid.

[172] Ibid., 419.

[173] Andrew, *For the President's Eyes Only*, 189.

[174] Eberstadt, *National Security Organization*, 77-78.

[175] *Preparing for the 21st Century*, A-12.

[176] Warner, *Central Intelligence*, 8.

[177] Lowenthal, *U.S. Intelligence*, 26.

[178] *Preparing for the 21st Century*, A-13.

THE WHITE HOUSE," HEADED BY THE DCI.[179] ALTHOUGH KENNEDY DID NOT AGREE TO THE PROPOSAL, HE URGED DCI MCCONE TO STRENGTHEN HIS LEADERSHIP OF THE COMMUNITY. THE RESULT WAS THE NATIONAL INTELLIGENCE PROGRAMS EVALUATION STAFF (NIPES), CHARGED WITH REVIEWING AND EVALUATING IC PROGRAMS AND COST EFFECTIVENESS. DCI HELMS LATER AUGMENTED NIPES WITH THE NATIONAL INTELLIGENCE RESOURCES BOARD (NIRB), CHARTERED TO REVIEW ALL COMMUNITY PROGRAMS AND BUDGETS, AND ALSO TO REFEREE COMMUNITY DISPUTES.

IN MARCH OF 1971, THE SCHLESINGER REPORT PROVIDED A COST-BENEFIT ANALYSIS OF THE INTELLIGENCE COMMUNITY, CONCLUDING THAT "AN IMPRESSIVE RISE IN THEIR SIZE AND COST" HAD NOT LED TO "A COMMENSURATE IMPROVEMENT IN THE SCOPE AND OVERALL QUALITY OF INTELLIGENCE PRODUCTS."[180] YET EVEN THE SCHLESINGER REPORT RESULTED IN INCREASED "SIZE AND COST" AS BOTH THE INTELLIGENCE RESOURCES ADVISORY COMMITTEE (IRAC), AND THE INTELLIGENCE COMMUNITY STAFF (ICS) WERE CREATED IN RESPONSE.[181]

UNLIKE MOST OF THE 1970S INTELLIGENCE INVESTIGATIONS THAT CENTERED ON DRAMATIC FAILURES OF THE COMMUNITY, THE PIKE COMMITTEE WAS UNIQUE IN ITS METHODICAL FOCUS ON "THE BASIC FUNCTIONING OF THE COMMUNITY AND … THE QUALITY OF INTELLIGENCE AND ITS ROLE IN SUPPORTING POLICYMAKERS."[182] THE PIKE COMMITTEE'S REPORT RECOMMENDED EMPOWERING THE DCI TO "ELIMINATE DUPLICATION OF EFFORT," AND SPECIFICALLY "RECOMMENDED THAT THE DIA BE ABOLISHED."[183] THE PIKE REPORT WAS NEVER OFFICIALLY PUBLISHED, HOWEVER. A LEAK OF THE CONTENTS TO CBS-TV AND SUBSEQUENT PUBLICATION OF PORTIONS IN THE *VILLAGE VOICE* MIRED THE ENTIRE COMMITTEE IN CONTROVERSY.[184] THE INTELLIGENCE COMMUNITY CONTINUED ITS PATH OF UNGUIDED AND FRAGMENTED, BUT NONETHELESS STEADY EXPANSION.

BOTH PRESIDENTS FORD AND CARTER CONTRIBUTED TO THIS GROWTH THROUGH EXECUTIVE ORDER. FORD'S EO 11905 CREATED THE COMMITTEE ON FOREIGN INTELLIGENCE TO ASSIST THE DCI IN CREATING COMMUNITY BUDGETS.[185] CARTER'S EO 12036 CREATED THE "SHORT-LIVED NATIONAL INTELLIGENCE TASKING CENTER (NTIC) THAT WAS SUPPOSED TO ASSIST THE DCI IN TRANSLATING INTELLIGENCE REQUIREMENTS AND PRIORITIES INTO COLLECTION OBJECTIVES."[186] CONGRESS MADE OTHER ADDITIONS TO THE INTELLIGENCE STRUCTURE, SOMETIMES AGAINST THE WISHES OF BOTH THE PRESIDENT AND THE DCI. IN SIGNING THE INTELLIGENCE AUTHORIZATION ACT FOR FY1997, PRESIDENT CLINTON SPECIFICALLY OBJECTED TO ITS CREATION OF TWO NEW NSC COMMITTEES, AND "NOTED THE 'STRONG OPPOSITION' BY DCI JOHN DEUTCH TO PROVISIONS ESTABLISHING THREE NEW ASSISTANT

---

[179] Ibid., A-14.
[180] Schlesinger, *A Review of the Intelligence Community,* 1.
[181] Best, *Proposals for Intelligence Reorganization,* 17.
[182] Lowenthal, *U.S. Intelligence,* 46.
[183] Best, *Proposals for Intelligence Reorganization,* 14-25.
[184] Lowenthal, *U.S. Intelligence,* 44.
[185] Warner, *Central Intelligence,* 10.
[186] Best, *Proposals for Intelligence Reorganization,* 27.

DCIS."[187] CLINTON ADDED: "I SHARE HIS CONCERN THAT THESE PROVISIONS WILL ADD ANOTHER LAYER OF POSITIONS REQUIRING SENATE CONFIRMATION WITHOUT A CORRESPONDING GAIN IN THE DCI'S AUTHORITY OR ABILITY TO MANAGE THE INTELLIGENCE COMMUNITY."[188] THE COMMITTEE ON FOREIGN INTELLIGENCE (CFI), ONE OF THE TWO NSC COMMITTEES OBJECTED TO BY PRESIDENT CLINTON, ALTHOUGH DESIGNED TO "PROVIDE MORE FOCUS TO INTELLIGENCE ISSUES AT A HIGH LEVEL … ACHIEVED LITTLE MORE THAN TO CREATE STILL ANOTHER LAYER IN THE NSC'S INCREASINGLY ENCUMBERED BUREAUCRACY."[189]

TODAY, THE DCI CHAIRS, BELONGS TO, OR HAS SUPERVISION OF AN ELABORATE AND DIZZYING SYSTEM OF COMMITTEES.[190] A LIST OF BUT A FEW OF THE MORE PROMINENT INCLUDE THE INTELLIGENCE COMMUNITY STAFF (ITSELF COMPOSED OF FOUR SUB-STAFFS AND EIGHT COMMITTEES), THE NATIONAL FOREIGN INTELLIGENCE BOARD (WHICH CONTAINS 13 COMMITTEES), THE NATIONAL INTELLIGENCE COUNCIL (COMPOSED OF VARIOUS ANALYTICAL GROUPS), AND THE INTELLIGENCE PRODUCERS COUNCIL.[191] THE CREATION OF MORE AGENCIES, SUB AGENCIES, COMMITTEES, SUBCOMMITTEES, BOARDS, PANELS, AND OVERSIGHT BODIES, SEEMS TO HAVE REALIZED, ON A GRANDER SCALE, THE FEARS OF ONE OF THE FIRST DCIS, ALLEN DULLES, WHO OPINED THAT IF "THE AGENCY GOT TO BE A GREAT BIG OCTOPUS, IT WOULD NOT FUNCTION WELL."[192] THAT THE SIZE OF THE COMMUNITY IS HARMING ITS ABILITY TO FUNCTION EFFECTIVELY IS WIDELY RECOGNIZED. THE COST IS EVIDENT BOTH IN DOLLARS SPENT AND IN THE QUALITY OF THE PRODUCTS PRODUCED. IN 1996, THE HOUSE PERMANENT SELECT COMMITTEE ON INTELLIGENCE STATED:

> THE GROWTH OF THE INTELLIGENCE COMMUNITY AND THE PROLIFERATION OF DISTINCT AGENCIES HAVE LED TO UNWARRANTED DUPLICATION IN WHAT ARE, ESSENTIALLY, ADMINISTRATIVE AND LOGISTICAL FUNCTIONS. THIS IS NOT ONLY DUPLICATIVE AND COSTLY, BUT ALSO CAN HARM THE ABILITY OF THE INTELLIGENCE COMMUNITY TO OPERATE AS A CORPORATE WHOLE. NUMEROUS STUDIES AND REVIEWS OF THE COMMUNITY, INCLUDING VICE PRESIDENT GORE'S NATIONAL PERFORMANCE REVIEW, HAVE CONCLUDED THAT THERE ARE EFFICIENCIES AND POTENTIAL COST SAVINGS TO BE HAD BY CONSOLIDATING INFRASTRUCTURE AND ``SERVICES OF COMMON CONCERN.[193]

ALTHOUGH CREATING NEW INTELLIGENCE ORGANIZATIONS TO COORDINATE THE COMMUNITY HAS A DISMAL RECORD OF ACCOMPLISHMENT, IT IS EASY TO SEE WHY POLITICIANS CONTINUE THE PRACTICE. IT IS A HIGHLY VISIBLE POSITIVE ACTION TAKEN IN RESPONSE TO A PERCEIVED PUBLIC CONCERN. CREATING A NEW ORGANIZATION IS EASIER THAN MODIFYING OR FORCING EXISTING ORGANIZATIONS, WITH THEIR ENTRENCHED INTERESTS, TO PRACTICE NEW BEHAVIORS. STAN A. TAYLOR AND DAVID GOLDMAN SUM UP THIS PHENOMENON WELL IN *INTELLIGENCE AND NATIONAL SECURITY*:

---

[187] Ibid., 35.

[188] Ibid.

[189] Loch K. Johnson, *Bombs, Bugs, Drugs, and Thugs* (New York: New York University Press, 2000), 114.

[190] Richelson, *The U.S. Intelligence Community*, 384-397.

[191] Troy, "The Quaintness of the U.S. Intelligence Community," 27.

[192] Melvin A. Goodman, "9/11: The Failure of Strategic Intelligence," *Intelligence and National Security* 18, No.4 (Winter 2003): 66.

[193] US HOUSE. *INTELLIGENCE COMMUNITY ACT.* 104TH CONG., 2ND SESS., 1996. H.R. 104-620

"RESTRUCTURING, PARTICULARLY THE CREATION OF NEW AGENCIES OR SUB-AGENCIES, IS USUALLY THE POLITICAL SIREN SONG. THOSE WHO PURSUE IT CAN SAY, 'LOOK WHAT WE HAVE DONE'. BUT THE ALLURE OF RESTRUCTURING IS ALWAYS GREATER THAN THE REALITY. ALL TOO OFTEN RESTRUCTURING MERELY CREATES ADDITIONAL UNITS THAT MUDDY RATHER THAN CLARIFY WHAT IS REALLY NEEDED – BETTER CORRELATION AND COMMUNICATION ACROSS AGENCIES AND SUB-AGENCIES."[194]

FACTOR 5: THE MILITARIZATION OF INTELLIGENCE

THE CREATION OF THE NATIONAL SECURITY AGENCY IN 1952 NOT ONLY MARKED THE BEGINNING OF THE PROLIFERATION OF THE INTELLIGENCE COMMUNITY, IT ALSO MARKED THE BEGINNING THE DEPARTMENT OF DEFENSE'S GROWING ENCROACHMENT ON THE CIA'S CHARTER FOR THE PRODUCTION OF NATIONAL INTELLIGENCE. THE MILITARY LOST ITS NEAR MONOPOLY OVER INTELLIGENCE COLLECTION AND PRODUCTION WITH THE NATIONAL SECURITY ACT OF 1947, AND IT HAS WAGED A LONG CAMPAIGN TO REGAIN ITS PROMINENCE. ALTHOUGH AT ITS CREATION THE CIA WAS THE ONLY AGENCY TASKED WITH PRODUCING NATIONAL INTELLIGENCE, TODAY THE DoD CONTAINS THREE SUCH AGENCIES (DIA, NRO, AND NGA).[195] ADDITIONALLY, ALTHOUGH NATIONAL INTELLIGENCE BY DEFINITION PERTAINS "TO THE INTERESTS OF MORE THAN ONE DEPARTMENT OR AGENCY OF THE GOVERNMENT," THE DoD IS INCREASINGLY MAKING DEMANDS OF THE CIA TO PRODUCE PRODUCTS TAILORED PARTICULARLY TO SUPPORT THE MILITARY.[196] THIS GROWTH OF THE MILITARY, AS BOTH A PRODUCER AND CONSUMER OF NATIONAL INTELLIGENCE, SERVES TO MARGINALIZE THE ROLE OF THE CIA AND THE DCI.

THE CREATION OF THE CIA AS A CIVILIAN AGENCY RESPONSIBLE TO THE PRESIDENT FOR THE PRODUCTION OF NATIONAL INTELLIGENCE BROKE THE HISTORICAL MODEL OF INTELLIGENCE BEING A MILITARY FUNCTION FOR MILITARY ENDS. EVEN DONOVAN'S OSS EXISTED PRIMARILY TO "SUPPORT MILITARY OPERATIONS IN THE FIELD."[197] ALTHOUGH THE US MILITARY ENJOYED DRAMATIC TACTICAL INTELLIGENCE SUCCESSES IN WORLD WAR II, PEARL HARBOR HIGHLIGHTED THE SHORTCOMINGS OF THE NATION'S STRATEGIC INTELLIGENCE. SOMEHOW, INTELLIGENCE NEEDED TO EXPAND BEYOND THE IMMEDIATE OPERATIONAL AND TACTICAL CONCERNS OF THE MILITARY. BY THE END OF THE WAR THERE WAS A "GROWING CONSENSUS THAT INTELLIGENCE SHOULD NOT BE SOLELY THE PROVINCE OF THE UNIFORMED MILITARY."[198] THE CREATION OF THE CIA IN 1947 BROKE THE MILITARY MONOPOLY IN INTELLIGENCE. ALTHOUGH THE CIA CONTINUED TO COLLECT INTELLIGENCE ON MILITARY TARGETS, THE FOCUS "BECAME LESS TACTICAL AND MORE STRATEGIC, LESS STRICTLY MILITARY AND MORE NATIONAL. . .

---

[194] Taylor, "Intelligence Reform," 421.

[195] Warner, *Central Intelligence,* 5.

[196] US SENATE. *NATIONAL INTELLIGENCE REFORM ACT OF 2004,* 108TH CONG., 2ND SESS., 2004, S.2845,10.

[197] RICHARD L. RUSSELL, "TUG OF WAR: THE CIA'S UNEASY RELATIONSHIP WITH THE MILITARY." *SAIS REVIEW* 22 (SUMMER-FALL 2002): 3.

[198] Gregory F. Treverton, *Reshaping National Intelligence For an Age of Information,* (Cambridge, United Kingdom: Cambridge University Press, 2003), 73.

INTELLIGENCE'S PRIME CONSUMERS WERE CIVILIAN POLICY-MAKERS, NOT JUST MILITARY LEADERS. ITS MISSION WAS STRATEGIC WARNING FIRST AND SUPPORT TO MILITARY OPERATIONS ONLY SECOND."[199]

A STUDY OF HISTORY SHOWS HOW THE MILITARY SERVICES COLLECTIVELY RESISTED THIS NEW INSTITUTION, AND HIGHLIGHTS THEIR SUCCESS IN LIMITING THE CIA OR DCI'S ABILITY TO CONTROL MILITARY INTELLIGENCE FUNCTIONS. THE MILITARY, HOWEVER, HAS NOT MAINTAINED A SOLELY DEFENSIVE STANCE TOWARD CENTRALIZED CIVILIAN AUTHORITY. WHILE KEEPING THE AUTONOMY OF ITS OWN INTELLIGENCE APPARATUS, THE MILITARY HAS CONTINUALLY SOUGHT AND GAINED CONTROL OVER NATIONAL INTELLIGENCE ASSETS. THIS PROCESS, WHICH BEGAN SHORTLY AFTER THE BEGINNING OF THE COLD WAR, ACCELERATED SIGNIFICANTLY UPON ITS CONCLUSION. TODAY, IT IS HARDER THEN EVER TO CENTRALIZE CONTROL OF THE IC IN THE HANDS OF A CIVILIAN, BECAUSE THE COMMUNITY ALREADY HAS A CENTRALIZED LEADER IN THE PENTAGON. THE PROLIFERATION OF INTELLIGENCE AGENCIES ONLY STRENGTHENS THE MILITARY POSITION, AS THE DOD ALONE HAS THE INFRASTRUCTURE TO STAFF, OPERATE, AND FUND SUCH ORGANIZATIONS. DCIS, WITH INTERMITTENT PRESIDENTIAL SUPPORT AT BEST, AND PLAGUED BY SCANDALS, HAVE BEEN UNABLE TO STOP THE CONTINUING MILITARIZATION OF US INTELLIGENCE.

THE KOREAN WAR DEMONSTRATED THE NATION'S COMMITMENT TO CIVILIAN CONTROL OF NATIONAL INTELLIGENCE AT THE BEGINNING OF THE COLD WAR. FEARS OF ANOTHER STRATEGIC SURPRISE ATTACK "ENSURED THAT, DESPITE FIGHTING IN KOREA, OVERHEAD RECONNAISSANCE DURING THE COLD WAR WOULD NOT BE CONTROLLED BY THE UNIFORMED MILITARY."[200] AN INDEPENDENT TASK FORCE SPONSORED BY THE COUNCIL ON FOREIGN RELATIONS DESCRIBED THE ERA:

> DURING THE COLD WAR, WHEN U.S. MILITARY FORCES WERE ENGAGED IN MATTERS OF NATIONAL SURVIVAL, THERE WAS A REASONABLE BALANCE BETWEEN CIVILIAN AND MILITARY PLAYERS BOTH IN THE INTELLIGENCE AND POLICY ARENAS. THREATS FROM THE SOVIET MILITARY ARSENAL WERE ASSESSED BY STRONG SCIENTIFIC AND TECHNICAL CENTERS AT THE NATIONAL LABORATORIES AND AT THE CIA AS WELL AS BY THE MILITARY SERVICES AND DIA. THE NATIONAL RECONNAISSANCE OFFICE WAS UNDER STRONG CIVILIAN INFLUENCE AND MANY OF THE NATIONAL STRATEGIC INTELLIGENCE PROGRAMS WERE DEVELOPED AND OPERATED BY CIVILIANS...THE JCS AND THE OFFICE OF THE SECRETARY OF DEFENSE WERE STRONG BUT NOT DOMINANT PLAYERS. MOST IMPORTANT, THE CIVILIAN SIDE OF U.S. INTELLIGENCE HAD A MAJOR ROLE IN ALLOCATING RESOURCES FOR NATIONAL INTELLIGENCE.[201]

BY THE END OF THE MILLENNIUM, ROLES HAD REVERSED, WITH THE MILITARY AS THE DOMINANT PLAYER IN NATIONAL RECONNAISSANCE AND THE CIA EXERCISING A DIMINISHED INFLUENCE.

ALTHOUGH EARLY INVESTIGATIONS OF THE INTELLIGENCE COMMUNITY, SUCH AS THE SCHLESINGER REPORT, DEEMED THE DUPLICATION IN COLLECTION AND ANALYSIS BETWEEN THE CIA AND

---

[199] Ibid., 70-73.

[200] Treverton, *Reshaping National Intelligence,* 74.

[201] MAURICE R. GREENBERG CHAIRMAN & RICHARD N. HAASS, PROJECT DIRECTOR, *MAKING INTELLIGENCE SMARTER,*
THE FUTURE OF US INTELLIGENCE: REPORT OF AN INDEPENDENT TASK FORCE. THE COUNCIL ON FOREIGN RELATIONS,
N.P. ON-LINE INTERNET. AVAILABLE FROM HTTP://WWW.FAS.ORG/IRP/CFR.HTML.

THE MILITARY AS WASTEFUL, SUCH REDUNDANCY, IN ADDITION TO PACIFYING TURF BATTLES, SHARPENED ANALYSIS AND PROVIDED PRODUCTS BETTER TAILORED TO SPECIFIC CUSTOMERS. NONETHELESS, AS THE NATION BEGAN TO RELY MORE ON ADVANCED TECHNOLOGICAL MEANS TO COLLECT INTELLIGENCE, THE SYSTEMS INVOLVED BECAME TOO EXPENSIVE TO DUPLICATE, AND A FIERCE STRUGGLE EMERGED OVER WHO WOULD CONTROL THEM. THE CONTROL OF OVERHEAD IMAGERY PROVIDED THE CONTEXT FOR THE FIRST SUCH BATTLE.

AFTER THE AIR FORCE PASSED ON LOCKHEED'S BID TO DEVELOP A LONG RANGE HIGH ALTITUDE RECONNAISSANCE JET, THE CIA PROVIDED THE CONTRACTOR $22 MILLION TO DEVELOP IT. THE RESULT, THE U-2 SPY PLANE, FAR EXCEEDED THE AIR FORCE'S RB-47 IN BOTH PERFORMANCE AND AFFORDABILITY. "THE U-2 OPERATION WAS GIVEN TO THE CIA OVER THE OBJECTIONS OF THE AIR FORCE, WHICH DESPERATELY WANTED CONTROL OF THE PLANE AND ITS MISSION."[202] PRESIDENT EISENHOWER WAS "ADAMANT IN NOT WANTING THE AIR FORCE TO CONTROL THE PROGRAM ... OR AERIAL RECONNAISSANCE IN GENERAL."[203] FOR EISENHOWER, "ALLOWING ANY MILITARY SERVICE, BUT PARTICULARLY THE AIR FORCE, TO COMPOSE ITS SHOPPING LIST FOR WEAPONS BASED ON A THREAT ASSESSMENT THAT CAME FROM INTELLIGENCE IT ALONE COLLECTED, PROCESSED, AND INTERPRETED WAS ABSOLUTELY UNTENABLE."[204] BUT THE AIR FORCE WAS NOT WITHOUT INFLUENCE. WHILE THE CIA OWNED THE PLANE AND THE MISSION, THE AIR FORCE OWNED THE FACILITIES AND PILOTS TO MAKE IT OPERATIONAL. THUS BEGAN A COLLABORATIVE PROCESS BETWEEN THE AIR FORCE AND CIA THAT RESULTED IN THE U2 FOLLOW-ON, THE SR-71 SPY PLANE, AND TO THE CORONA SATELLITE SYSTEMS, ALL UNDER THE PRIMARY RESPONSIBILITY OF THE CIA.

AS US SPY SATELLITE CAPABILITIES GREW IN NUMBER AND IMPORTANCE, HOWEVER, "THE AIR FORCE–CIA RIVALRY FOR CONTROL OF THE SPACECRAFT, THEIR TASKING, AND ANALYSIS OF THE PRODUCT ... WAS OFTEN VENOMOUS."[205] DESPITE HIS FEAR OF MILITARY FORCES MAINTAINING RESPONSIBILITY FOR NATIONAL TECHNICAL COLLECTION CAPABILITIES, EISENHOWER'S "EXASPERATIONS WITH THE FEUDING, SELF-INDULGENCE, AND CONCOMITANT WASTE OF TIME AND RESOURCES THAT WENT HAND IN HAND WITH EVERY EFFORT AT SPACE RECONNAISSANCE," ESTABLISHED THE NATIONAL RECONNAISSANCE OFFICE (NRO) IN AUGUST OF 1960.[206] ALTHOUGH DESIGNED TO HAVE CIVILIAN CONTROL (THE DIRECTOR OF THE NRO HAS BEEN AN UNDER SECRETARY OF THE AIR FORCE, AND HIS DEPUTY HAS COME FROM THE CIA), THE CREATION OF THE NRO ADDED ONE MORE AGENCY TO THE DEPARTMENT OF DEFENSE'S GROWING INTELLIGENCE EMPIRE."[207]

"THE ORIGINAL CHARTER OF THE NRO ASSIGNED RESPONSIBILITY FOR MANAGING THE PROGRAMS TO THE SECRETARY OF DEFENSE (HENCE A DIRECTOR FROM DoD) AND THE RESPONSIBILITY

---

[202] Treverton, *Reshaping National Intelligence,* 74.

[203] William E. Burrows, *Deep Black: Space Espionage and National Security* (New York: Berkley Books, 1986), 70.

[204] Ibid.

[205] Ibid., 128.

[206] Ibid., 130.

[207] Ibid., 131.

FOR ESTABLISHING REQUIREMENTS FOR THE PROGRAMS TO THE DCI."[208] AS TECHNOLOGY IMPROVED, THE PENTAGON'S INFRASTRUCTURE BEGAN TO DWARF THE CIA'S ENTREPRENEURIAL WIZARDRY, REFLECTED IN THE U-2 SPY PLANE. IN THE 1970S, THE WHITE HOUSE PROPOSED TO GIVE CONTROL OF THE COLLECTION AGENCIES TO THE DCI. "THEN-SECRETARY OF DEFENSE DONALD RUMSFELD DEFIANTLY REPLIED, IN EFFECT IF NOT IN FACT: 'IF THEY'RE IN MY BUDGET, I'LL RUN THEM."[209] RUMSFELD'S WORDS PROVED PROPHETIC.

ROBERT KOHLER, A CIA VETERAN OF THE NRO, DETAILED HOW OVER TIME THE BUREAUCRATIC MANAGEMENT STYLE OF THE MILITARY, WHICH ELIMINATED COMPETITIVE PROGRAM PROCESSES AND ENCOURAGED RAPID ROTATIONS OF PERSONNEL, INTERFERED WITH THE DCI'S ABILITY TO DRIVE REQUIREMENTS BY SHIFTING POWER FROM PROGRAM MANAGERS TO CONTRACTORS. ACCORDING TO KOHLER, THE DOD AND THE JOINT REQUIREMENTS OVERSIGHT COUNCIL DOMINATE THE NEW REQUIREMENT PROCESS FOR THE NRO; "THE DCI AND THE CIA HAVE LET DOD SIGNIFICANTLY ERODE WHAT SHOULD BE THE DCI'S MAJOR RESPONSIBILITY: THE ARBITRATION, CONSOLIDATION, AND ESTABLISHMENT OF NATIONAL INTELLIGENCE REQUIREMENTS."[210]

IN THE 1990S, AS PART OF THE SO-CALLED PEACE DIVIDEND PROJECTED AS A BENEFIT OF THE END OF THE COLD WAR, A BIG PUSH CAME TO DECREASE THE NUMBER OF EXPENSIVE NRO SATELLITES. OVER TIME, THE DEBATE OVER WHICH SATELLITES TO CUT SHIFTED TO WHAT TYPE OF SATELLITES THE NATION NEEDED. "CIVILIAN ANALYSTS PREOCCUPIED WITH "NATIONAL" PURPOSES WANTED TO LISTEN TO THE CONTENT OF PARTICULAR COMMUNICATIONS, COMINT, AND FOR THAT PURPOSE, HAVING FEWER SATELLITES IN GEOSYNCHRONOUS ORBITS WAS GOOD ENOUGH …. FOR THE WAR-FIGHTERS, BY CONTRAST, WHAT WAS MORE IMPORTANT WAS … ELINT [ELECTRONIC INTELLIGENCE] – NOT THE CONTENT OF CONVERSATIONS BUT SIGNALS IDENTIFYING TECHNICAL CHARACTERISTICS OF UNITS OR WEAPONS *AND* THEIR LOCATION."[211] FOR ELINT COLLECTION, SATELLITES IN HIGH EARTH ORBIT (HEO) WERE PREFERABLE TO GEOSYNCHRONOUS SATELLITES. "IN THE END, THE WAR FIGHTERS TRIUMPHED OVER THE BUDGET CUTTERS, AND THE ARCHITECTURE COMPRISED MORE SATELLITES. INCLUDING HEO ONES."[212]

THE END OF THE COLD WAR AND THE DEMISE OF THE SOVIET UNION LEFT STRATEGIC INTELLIGENCE ORGANIZATIONS WITHOUT A PRIMARY TARGET. THE DOD QUICKLY FILLED THIS VACUUM BY SHIFTING THE SATELLITE INFRASTRUCTURE TO SUPPORT OPERATIONAL AND TACTICAL ENDS. IN A

---

[208] ROBERT J. KOHLER, "ONE OFFICER'S PERSPECTIVE: THE DECLINE OF THE NATIONAL RECONNAISSANCE OFFICE."
STUDIES IN INTELLIGENCE, JOURNAL OF THE AMERICAN INTELLIGENCE PROFESSIONAL 46, NO. 2, (2002), 16.
[209] GREGORY F. TREVERTON, "INTELLIGENCE SINCE COLD WAR'S END." IN *IN FROM THE COLD.* ALLEN E. GOODMAN,
GREGORY F. TREVERTON, AND PHILIP ZELIKOW. (NEW YORK: THE TWENTITH CENTRUY FUND PRESS, 1996), 103.
[210] Kohler, "One Officer's Perspective", 17.
[211] Treverton, *Reshaping National Intelligence,* 79-80.
[212] Ibid.

MODERN DAY EQUIVALENT OF SQUATTER'S RIGHTS, ONCE THE MILITARY GAINED CONTROL OF SATELLITES, IT CLAIMED THEY WERE TOO VITAL TO MILITARY SUCCESS TO GIVE UP. TODAY THE NRO, LIKE THE OTHER MAJOR TECHNICAL COLLECTION AGENCIES, THE NSA AND NATIONAL GEOSPATIAL-INTELLIGENCE AGENCY (NGA, FORMERLY NIMA), IS CLASSIFIED A COMBAT SUPPORT AGENCY, "WITH AN EMPHASIS ON OPERATIONAL AND TACTICAL APPLICATIONS RATHER THAN THE STRATEGIC OR NATIONAL APPLICATIONS."[213]

THE NSA, LIKE THE NRO, BEGAN ITS EXISTENCE AS A NATIONAL ASSET UNDER CIVILIAN CONTROL. PRESIDENT TRUMAN CREATED THE AGENCY THROUGH A SECRET PRESIDENTIAL MEMORANDUM ON NOVEMBER 4, 1952. SINCE THE NEW AGENCY DREW ITS WORKERS, EQUIPMENT, AND EXPERTISE FROM EXISTING MILITARY SERVICE ORGANIZATIONS, IT WAS HOUSED IN THE DOD. THE SAME PRESIDENTIAL MEMORANDUM THAT CREATED IT, HOWEVER, ALSO GAVE THE DCI GREATER POWER TO OVERSEE THE COORDINATION OF SIGINT WITH OTHER INTELLIGENCE ACTIVITIES THROUGH A STRENGTHENED UNITED STATES COMMUNICATIONS INTELLIGENCE BOARD (USCIB).[214] "ALTHOUGH THE NSA REMAINED UNDER THE CONTROL OF THE DEPARTMENT OF DEFENSE, IT WAS A CIVILIAN AGENCY RESPONSIVE TO WIDER NATIONAL CONCERNS AS WELL AS THE NEEDS OF THE ARMED FORCES."[215] IN FACT, "WHEN CONGRESS ENACTED SECTION 193 OF TITLE 10, WHICH SPECIFIED THE COMBAT SUPPORT AGENCIES OF THE DEPARTMENT OF DEFENSE, CONGRESS SPECIFICALLY DECLINED TO LIST THE NATIONAL SECURITY AGENCY AS A COMBAT SUPPORT AGENCY BECAUSE NSA SERVES CUSTOMERS OUTSIDE THE DEPARTMENT OF DEFENSE."[216] WITH THE DEPARTMENT OF DEFENSE CONTROLLING THE AGENCY'S FUNDING AND PERSONNEL, SUCH INDEPENDENCE COULD NOT LAST LONG. "NSA WAS DESIGNATED A COMBAT SUPPORT AGENCY IN 1988 BY THE SECRETARY OF DEFENSE IN RESPONSE TO THE GOLDWATER-NICHOLS DEPARTMENT OF DEFENSE REORGANIZATION"[217]

UNLIKE THE NRO OR NSA, THE NATIONAL IMAGERY AND MAPPING AGENCY WAS CREATED AS A COMBAT SUPPORT AGENCY DESPITE THE FACT THAT IT ABSORBED THE CIA'S NATIONAL PHOTOGRAPHIC INTERPRETATION CENTER AND THE CENTRAL IMAGERY OFFICE AS WELL AS THE MILITARY'S DEFENSE

---

[213] ROBIN MIYOSHI LANDRY, "REFORMING INTELLIGENCE: SELLING CHANGE" (WASHINGTON DC: NATIONAL DEFENSE UNIVERSITY, NATIONAL WAR COLLEGE), 5.

[214] ANDREW, *FOR THE PRESIDENT'S EYES ONLY*, 197.

[215] FINNEGAN, *MILITARY INTELLIGENCE* (WASHINGTON, DC: CENTER OF MILITARY HISTORY, UNITED STATES ARMY,
1998), CHAPTER 7, PARAGRAPH 111.

[216] US SENATE. *AUTHORIZING APPROPRIATIONS FOR FISCAL YEAR 1997 FOR MILITARY ACTIVITIES OF THE DEPARTMENT OF
DEFENSE, FOR MILITARY CONSTRUCTION, AND FOR DEFENSE ACTIVITIES OF THE DEPARTMENT OF ENERGY, TO PRESCRIBE
PERSONNEL STRENGTHS FOR SUCH FISCAL YEAR FOR THE ARMED FORCES, AND FOR OTHER PURPOSE*, 104TH CONG., 2ND
SESS., 1996. S. DOC 104-278.

[217] "PROFILES OF THE U.S. INTELLIGENCE COMMUNITY," TOTSE.COM, N.P. ON-LINE INTERNET. AVAILABLE FROM
HTTP://WWW.TOTSE.COM/EN/POLITICS/CENTRAL_INTELLIGENCE_AGENCY/PROFUSIC.HTML

MAPPING AGENCY.[218] THE SENATE SELECT COMMITTEE ON INTELLIGENCE OBJECTED TO THE COMBAT-SUPPORT DESIGNATION, NOTING THAT, "UNLIKE THE DEFENSE MAPPING AGENCY, NIMA WILL ALSO HAVE IMPORTANT RESPONSIBILITIES TO PROVIDE IMAGERY TO NON-MILITARY CUSTOMERS. ACCORDINGLY, THE COMMITTEE BELIEVES IT WOULD BE A MISTAKE TO ESTABLISH NIMA 'AS A COMBAT SUPPORT AGENCY,' EVEN IF OTHER STATUTORY PROVISIONS SPECIFICALLY STATE THAT NIMA ALSO HAS NATIONAL MISSIONS. THE IMPLICATION WOULD BE LEFT THAT NIMA'S PRIMARY PURPOSE IS TO PROVIDE COMBAT SUPPORT."[219]

NOT ONLY DID THE ARMED SERVICES COMMITTEE PREVAIL OVER THE SELECT COMMITTEE ON INTELLIGENCE IN DESIGNATING NIMA AS A COMBAT SUPPORT AGENCY, IT SUCCEEDED IN LIMITING THE DCI'S AUTHORITY TO ENSURE THE NEW AGENCY MET THE NEEDS OF NATIONAL CONSUMERS OUTSIDE OF THE MILITARY. THE INTELLIGENCE COMMITTEE ATTACHED THE FOLLOWING STATEMENT TO THE FINAL BILL:

> THE COMMITTEES DISAGREED ON THE APPROPRIATE ROLE OF THE DCI IN REPRESENTING THESE NATIONAL CUSTOMERS, INCLUDING THE PRESIDENT AND THE NATIONAL SECURITY COUNCIL...GIVEN THE ADMINISTRATION'S DECISION TO ESTABLISH NIMA AS AN AGENCY WITHIN THE DEPARTMENT OF DEFENSE, WITH ITS BUDGET CONTROLLED BY THE SECRETARY OF DEFENSE, AND TO DESIGNATE IT AS A COMBAT SUPPORT AGENCY SUBJECT TO REVIEW BY THE JOINT CHIEFS OF STAFF, THE DEPARTMENT OF DEFENSE CLEARLY WILL BE ABLE TO ENSURE APPROPRIATE CONSIDERATION OF DOD'S IMAGERY NEEDS, BOTH TACTICAL AND NATIONAL. THE ISSUE DEBATED BY THE COMMITTEES WAS WHETHER THE SECRETARY OF DEFENSE SHOULD BE ABLE TO EFFECTIVELY BLOCK ADJUSTMENTS IN THE PROGRAMS AND POLICIES OF NIMA THAT MIGHT BE NEEDED TO ADDRESS DEFICIENCIES IN THE IMAGERY AGENCY'S ABILITY TO MEET THE NEEDS OF OTHER NATIONAL CUSTOMERS... THE COMMITTEE WAS CONCERNED THAT THE PROPOSALS OF THE ARMED SERVICES COMMITTEE WOULD ALLOW THE SECRETARY OF DEFENSE TO EFFECTIVELY VETO CHANGES NEEDED TO MEET THESE OTHER NATIONAL NEEDS[220]

THE LAW THAT CREATED NIMA OFFICIALLY GAVE THE DCI AUTHORITY TO PRIORITIZE ASSIGNMENTS FOR "NATIONAL IMAGERY COLLECTION ASSETS," BUT AT THE SAME TIME, IT TOOK SUCH ASSETS OUT OF THE CIA AND PUT THEM IN THE DAY-TO-DAY CONTROL OF THE DOD.[221] *THE NATIONAL JOURNAL'S* JAMES KITFIELD TOOK THE CIA'S SIDE, ARGUING: "THE TRANSFER OF ALL IMAGERY ANALYSIS CAPABILITIES IN THE CIA TO A PENTAGON AGENCY HEADED BY A FLAG RANK MILITARY OFFICER... HAS CAUSED CONCERN...THAT THE INTELLIGENCE COMMUNITY HAS ALREADY BEEN UNDULY FOCUSED ON MILITARY NEEDS."[222] NIMA'S CREATION AS A COMBAT SUPPORT AGENCY, FOLLOWING ON THE HEELS OF THE NRO AND NSA, CEMENTED THE SHIFT FROM CIVILIAN TO MILITARY CONTROL OF NATIONAL TECHNOLOGICAL INTELLIGENCE COLLECTION. SUPPORT TO WAR FIGHTERS WAS A SPILLOVER BENEFIT OF TECHNICAL COLLECTION DURING THE COLD WAR. TODAY IT IS THE MAIN PURPOSE OF NATIONAL SYSTEMS WHILE RESIDUAL NATIONAL TARGETS, SUCH AS MONITORING OTHER NATION'S NUCLEAR

---

[218] AID, "THE TIME OF TROUBLES," 74.
[219] US SENATE. AUTHORIZING APPROPRIATIONS FOR FISCAL YEAR 1997.
[220] Ibid.
[221] Warner, *Central Intelligence,* 15.
[222] Miller "Structural Quiescence," 254.

PROGRAMS, ARE THE SPILLOVER EFFECT.[223] FOR GREGORY TREVERTON, 1991'S OPERATION DESERT STORM MARKED A "DEMARCATION POINT IN THE SHIFT FROM KEEPING TABS ON THE SOVIET UNION TO SUPPORTING MILITARY OPERATIONS," BECAUSE FOR THE FIRST TIME, IT BROUGHT "NATIONAL INTELLIGENCE SYSTEMS TO BEAR ON TACTICAL PURPOSES."[224]

WITH THE NRO, NSA, AND NIMA ALL DESIGNATED AS COMBAT SUPPORT AGENCIES WITHIN THE DoD, THE PENTAGON SECURED ITS DOMINANT POSITION REGARDING THE NATION'S TECHNICAL COLLECTION ASSETS. NOT CONTENT TO REST ON ITS GAINS, THE MILITARY INCREASINGLY HAS BEEN CO-OPTING THE ANALYSIS CAPABILITIES OF AGENCIES OUTSIDE THE DoD, PARTICULARLY THE CIA. WHILE THE END OF THE COLD WAR OBSCURED THE NATIONAL STRATEGIC REQUIREMENTS FOR INTELLIGENCE, FREQUENT DEPLOYMENTS AND CONFLICTS ALLOWED THE MILITARY TO DEMAND MORE OPERATIONAL SUPPORT FROM THOSE REMAINING MEMBERS OF THE INTELLIGENCE COMMUNITY NOT UNDER ITS DIRECT CONTROL. WHILE VARIOUS COMMISSIONS THROUGHOUT THE 1990s SOUGHT TO STRENGTHEN THE DCI'S CONTROL OVER THE INTELLIGENCE COMMUNITY, DESERT STORM GAVE THE MILITARY THE LEVERAGE IT NEEDED NOT ONLY TO BLOCK THESE REFORM EFFORTS, BUT ALSO TO REVERSE THEM. "IN THE AFTERMATH OF THE SUCCESSFUL GULF WAR, LAWMAKERS WERE POISED TO GO OUT OF THEIR WAY TO PAY DEFERENTIAL TREATMENT TO THE MILITARY AND TO FUNNEL NATIONAL-LEVEL RESOURCES TOWARD THEM WITH LITTLE REGARD FOR POTENTIAL ADVERSE CONSEQUENCES FOR CIVILIAN POLICYMAKERS WHO ALSO HAD CRITICAL NEEDS FOR INTELLIGENCE."[225]

GENERAL NORMAN SCHWARZKOPF'S "PUBLIC CRITICISM OF THE CIA'S ANALYTICAL PERFORMANCE DURING THE WAR" GALVANIZED CONGRESS AND THE CIA TO LOOK FOR WAYS THE AGENCY COULD BETTER SUPPORT THE MILITARY.[226] IT IS STRANGE THAT FOLLOWING THE UNSUCCESSFUL VIETNAM WAR, THE CIA'S CONTRARY POSITION TO THE MILITARY ANALYSIS OF ENEMY OB RECEIVED GOOD PUBLICITY, EVEN THOUGH FACTS PROVED THAT MILITARY NUMBERS WERE MORE ACCURATE, WHILE FOLLOWING THE SUCCESSFUL OPERATION DESERT STORM, THE CIA'S CONFLICTING ANALYSIS OVER BATTLE DAMAGE ASSESSMENT (BDA) PLAYED POORLY, EVEN THOUGH IN THIS CASE THE CIA NUMBERS PROVED MORE ACCURATE.[227] IT IS DIFFICULT TO ARGUE WITH SUCCESS. RATHER THAN RESISTING THE MILITARY DOMINANCE OF INTELLIGENCE ASSETS, BOTH FOR COLLECTION AND ANALYSIS, THE CIA BENT OVER BACKWARDS TO DEMONSTRATE ITS ABILITY TO SUPPORT THE MILITARY. STUNG BY SCHWARZKOPF'S CRITIQUE OF THE CIA'S CONTRIBUTIONS AND FURTHER HURT BY THE ENSUING FINDINGS OF THE HOUSE COMMITTEE ON ARMED SERVICES, *INTELLIGENCE SUCCESSES AND FAILURES IN OPERATIONS DESERT SHIELD/STORM*, SUPPORT TO MILITARY OPERATIONS (SMO) BECAME A PRIMARY FOCUS OF THE AGENCY.

---

[223] Treverton, *In From the Cold*, 102-103.

[224] Treverton, *Reshaping National Intelligence*, 67.

[225] Russell, "Tug of War," 7.

[226] Ibid.

[227] Wirtz, "Intelligence to Please," 189.; and
Russell, "Tug of War," 8.

THE FACT THAT THE DoD WAS ABLE TO GET CIA'S SUPPORT TO THE MILITARY ON CONGRESS'S AGENDA SHOWS HOW MUCH THE POLITICAL CLIMATE HAD CHANGED SINCE EBERSTADT'S 1949 REPORT CRITICIZED THE DoD FOR ITS LACK OF SUPPORT TO THE CIA.[228] GENERAL WILLIAM ODOM, FORMER DIRECTOR OF THE NSA, CLAIMED THAT DURING THE COLD WAR THE CIA'S INTELLIGENCE WAS "ALMOST NEVER USED BY THE MILITARY SERVICES."[229] YET IN 1992, THE CIA CREATED THE OFFICE OF MILITARY AFFAIRS (OMA) RESPONSIBLE FOR "DEVELOPING PROCEDURES SO THAT THE CIA IS REGULARLY INFORMED OF MILITARY NEEDS FOR INTELLIGENCE SUPPORT; DEVELOPING PLANS FOR CIA SUPPORT IN NATIONAL, THEATER AND JOINT INTELLIGENCE CENTERS DURING CRISES; AND THE AVAILABILITY OF CIA OFFICERS FOR PARTICIPATING WITH THE MILITARY ON SELECTED EXERCISES."[230]

THE MILITARY CO-OPTION OF THE NATIONAL INTELLIGENCE APPARATUS HAS SOMETIMES RECEIVED AID FROM UNLIKELY QUARTERS. "THE BURGEONING MILITARY DEPLOYMENTS DEMANDED EVER MORE TACTICAL INTELLIGENCE SUPPORT, AND PRESIDENT WILLIAM CLINTON ISSUED A 1995 PRESIDENTIAL ORDER (PDD-35) INSTRUCTING THE INTELLIGENCE COMMUNITY TO PROVIDE IT. EXPLAINING HIS DIRECTIVE AT CIA HEADQUARTERS A FEW MONTHS LATER, HE EMPHASIZED THAT THE COMMUNITY'S FIRST PRIORITY WAS TO SUPPORT THE INTELLIGENCE NEEDS OF OUR MILITARY DURING AN OPERATION."[231] WITH THIS ORDER THE PRESIDENT, ORIGINALLY THE FIRST AND HIGHEST PRIORITY OF THE CIA, WILLINGLY CEDED HIS PRIMACY TO THE DoD. "THE RESULT OF THE COMMITMENT IN PDD-35 WAS A DIVERSION OF SHRINKING NATIONAL, STRATEGIC INTELLIGENCE RESOURCES TO GROWING, TACTICAL MISSIONS."[232] "THE EXECUTIVE BRANCH'S INSISTENCE ON USING DECLINING RESOURCES FIRST AND FOREMOST TO SUPPORT MILITARY OPERATIONS EFFECTIVELY BLUNTED THE CONGRESSIONAL EMPHASIS ON CENTRALIZATION BY LIMITING THE WHEREWITHAL THAT DCIs AND AGENCY HEADS COULD DEVOTE TO NATIONAL AND STRATEGIC OBJECTIVES."[233] MORTON ABRAMOWITZ AND RICHARD KERR, MEMBERS OF THE COUNCIL ON FOREIGN RELATIONS' INDEPENDENT COMMISSION ON INTELLIGENCE, DESCRIBED THE PHENOMENON LIKE THIS:

> SINCE THE END OF THE COLD WAR, THE U.S. MILITARY HAS INCREASINGLY DOMINATED THE INTELLIGENCE PROCESS. THE WATCHWORD TODAY IN THE INTELLIGENCE COMMUNITY IS SUPPORT TO MILITARY OPERATIONS. THE EMPHASIS IS ON CURRENT CRISES AND THE SHORT TERM, IN PART BECAUSE MILITARY INTERVENTION HAS BECOME A MORE FREQUENTLY USED TOOL OF FOREIGN POLICY. FOR ALL PRACTICAL PURPOSES, THE CONTROL OF TECHNICAL INTELLIGENCE COLLECTION HAS BEEN PASSED TO THE DEPARTMENT OF DEFENSE. A WEAKENED CIA-THE MAJOR CIVILIAN PLAYER-PLAYS A LESSER ROLE IN THE NATIONAL SECURITY PROCESS AND SPENDS MORE AND MORE OF ITS RESOURCES TO SUPPORT MILITARY OPERATIONS IN A WORLD WHERE POLITICAL, ECONOMIC, AND SOCIAL ISSUES PRESENT AN INCREASINGLY IMPORTANT CHALLENGE BUT GET MUCH LESS ATTENTION. BECAUSE SO MUCH AUTHORITY FOR NATIONAL INTELLIGENCE PROGRAMS IS MOVING TOWARD DEFENSE, THE CONTROL OF RESOURCES AND THE DETERMINATION OF COLLECTION AND ANALYTIC PRIORITIES HAS MOVED IN

---

[228] Eberstadt, *National Security Organization*, 76-77.
[229] Russell, "Tug of War," 4.
[230] Ibid, 9-10.
[231] Warner, *Central Intelligence,* 13.
[232] Ibid.
[233] Ibid., 17.

THAT DIRECTION AS WELL. WHILE MUCH LIP SERVICE IS PAID TO THE NEEDS OF TOP FOREIGN POLICY AND NATIONAL SECURITY OFFICIALS THERE HAS BEEN LESS ATTENTION AND FEWER RESOURCES DEVOTED TO MEETING THEIR NEEDS. THE NATIONAL INTELLIGENCE BUDGET PROCESS HAS BEEN SUBSUMED BY DEFENSE. WE BELIEVE THIS TREND NEEDS TO BE CHECKED AND A BETTER BALANCE STRUCK BETWEEN CIVILIAN AND MILITARY PARTICIPATION AND IN HOW INTELLIGENCE FUNDS ARE SPENT.[234]

SUMMARY

AT THE END OF THE TWENTIETH CENTURY, THE DCI, FAR FROM FILLING THE CENTRAL ROLE OF SETTING PRIORITIES AND COORDINATING INTELLIGENCE EFFORTS AS ENVISIONED BY THE NATIONAL SECURITY ACT OF 1947, INSTEAD FOUND HIMSELF LEADING ONE AGENCY WITHIN AN EXPANDING COMMUNITY INCREASINGLY CALLED ON BY THE DEPARTMENT OF DEFENSE TO SUPPORT ITS OPERATIONS. GIVEN THE ANIMOSITY OF EXISTING INTELLIGENCE ORGANIZATIONS AND THEIR PARENT DEPARTMENTS TOWARD THE DCI, AND THEIR SUCCESS IN LIMITING THE STATUTORY AUTHORITY GRANTED IN THE 1947 LEGISLATION, SUCH A RESULT WAS PERHAPS INEVITABLE. WHILE THE OCCASIONAL SUPPORT OF PRESIDENTS TEMPORARILY GAVE SEVERAL DCI ADDED WEIGHT IN THE COMMUNITY, THE GROWING INVOLVEMENT OF THE CIA WITH COVERT OPERATIONS, AND THE CONCURRENT GROWING CONTROL OF THE DOD OVER NATIONAL INTELLIGENCE ASSETS, HAMPERED THE ATTEMPTS OF DCIS TO ESTABLISH MEANINGFUL CONTROL OVER THE COMMUNITY.

---

[234]Greenberg, *Making Intelligence Smarter*, np.

CHAPTER 2

CONTEMPORY ATTEMPTS TO CENTRALIZE THE INTELLIGENCE COMMUNITY: 9/11 TO PRESENT

WE TEND TO MEET ANY NEW SITUATION IN LIFE BY REORGANIZING. AND WHAT A WONDERFUL METHOD IT CAN BE FORE CREATING THE ILLUSION OF PROGRESS WHILE PRODUCING CONFUSION, INEFFICIENCY AND DEMORALIZATION.
>   PETRONIUS ARBITER, FIRST-CENTURY ROMAN SATIRIST.

DESPITE THE BEST EFFORTS OF REFORMERS, THE US INTELLIGENCE COMMUNITY ENTERED THE NEW MILLENNIUM WITH THE SAME CHALLENGES TO CENTRAL CONTROL IT SOUGHT TO OVERCOME IN THE PRECEDING FIVE DECADES. THE NATIONAL COMMISSION ON TERRORIST ATTACKS UPON THE UNITED STATES (HEREAFTER REFERRED TO AS THE 9/11 COMMISSION) NOTED THAT WHILE DCI "TENET WAS CLEARLY THE LEADER OF THE CIA, THE INTELLIGENCE COMMUNITY'S CONFEDERATED STRUCTURE LEFT OPEN THE QUESTION OF WHO REALLY IS IN CHARGE OF THE ENTIRE U.S. INTELLIGENCE EFFORT."[235] TENET HAD TRIED TO FOCUS COMMUNITY-WIDE COLLECTION AND ANALYSIS CAPABILITIES AGAINST THE THREAT OF TERRORISM BEFORE SEPTEMBER 11, BUT AS THE COMMISSION FURTHER NOTED: "THE DIRECTOR'S POWER, UNDER FEDERAL LAW, OVER THE LOOSE CONFEDERATED 'INTELLIGENCE COMMUNITY' IS LIMITED."[236] WHILE IT IS UNCERTAIN THAT ANY AMOUNT OF FOCUSED INTELLIGENCE EFFORTS COULD HAVE PREVENTED THE TRAGIC EVENTS OF 9/11, THOSE EVENTS CERTAINLY CHANGED THE FOCUS OF NATIONAL INTELLIGENCE.

AS BRUCE BERKOWTIZ, A RESEARCH FELLOW AT THE HOOVER INSTITUTION NOTES, "WE HAVE ACHIEVED A DUBIOUS MILESTONE: WE ARE NOW APPOINTING NEW COMMISSIONS TO INVESTIGATE U.S. INTELLIGENCE FASTER THAN THE EXISTING ONES CAN PUBLISH THEIR FINDINGS."[237] WITHIN WEEKS OF SEPTEMBER 11, 2001, INVESTIGATORS LINKED THE TRAUMATIC ATTACKS OF THAT DAY TO A PERCEIVED INTELLIGENCE FAILURE. THE INABILITY TO FIND PHYSICAL EVIDENCE OF OPERATIONAL OR NEAR-OPERATIONAL WEAPONS OF MASS DESTRUCTION FOLLOWING OPERATION IRAQI FREEDOM (OIF) ADDED TO THE PUBLIC PERCEPTION OF A BROKEN NATIONAL INTELLIGENCE PROCESS. THE PERCEIVED TWIN FAILURES OF 9/11 AND OIF LED TO THE FIRST SUBSTANTIAL REFORM OF THE INTELLIGENCE COMMUNITY IN 57 YEARS, IN MUCH THE SAME WAY A BELIEF THAT THE SURPRISE ATTACK ON PEARL HARBOR WAS A DIRECT RESULT OF INTELLIGENCE FAILURES LED TO THE CREATION OF THE DCI AND CIA.

RICHARD A. POSNER, A NEW YORK TIMES OP-ED CONTRIBUTOR, NOTED THE SPEED WITH WHICH THE INTELLIGENCE REFORM ACT OF 2004 PASSED: "THE PUBLICATION LAST JULY OF THE REPORT OF THE 9/11 COMMISSION STARTED A POLITICAL STAMPEDE. WITHIN DAYS BOTH PRESIDENTIAL CANDIDATES HAD ENDORSED MOST OF THE COMMISSION'S RECOMMENDATIONS; WITHIN WEEKS THERE

---

[235] 9/11 Commission, *The 9/11 Commission Report* (New York: W.W. Norton, 2004), 93.
[236] Ibid., 86.
[237] Bruce Berkowitz, "Intelligence Reform: Less is More," *Hoover Digest*, No.2, (Spring 2004): n.p. On-line
  Internet. Available from http://www.hooverdigest.org/042/berkowitz.html.

WERE BILLS IN CONGRESS; WITHIN MONTHS THE PRESIDENT HAD SIGNED THE INTELLIGENCE REFORM AND TERRORISM PREVENTION ACT OF 2004."[238]

WHILE IT MAY APPEAR THAT A WIDESPREAD BELIEF LINKING A TRAUMATIC NATIONAL EVENT TO INTELLIGENCE FAILURES IS A PREREQUISITE TO SWEEPING REFORM LEGISLATION, IT IS CRITICAL TO NOTE THAT SUCH UNITY OF PERCEPTION DID NOT MITIGATE THE FACTORS WORKING AGAINST UNIFYING CONTROL OF THE IC IN 2004 ANY MORE THAN IT DID IN 1947. INDEED, THE RESISTANCE OF THE EXISTING AGENCIES, PARTICULARLY THOSE IN THE DOD, IS CLEARLY VISIBLE IN THE POLITICAL NEGOTIATIONS THAT LED TO PASSAGE OF THE BILL. THE RESULT IS AN OPTIMISTICALLY-NAMED NATIONAL INTELLIGENCE DIRECTOR (NID), A FIGUREHEAD WHO ONCE AGAIN REQUIRES THE ACTIVE SUPPORT OF THE PRESIDENT TO DISCHARGE HIS DUTIES EFFECTIVELY. COVERT OPERATIONS, WHILE REMOVED FROM THE DIRECT CONTROL OF THE NID, WILL REMAIN A KEY AND CONTROVERSIAL COMPONENT OF THE IC. WHILE SEEKING TO STREAMLINE THE COMMUNITY, THE BILL CREATES MORE, NOT FEWER ORGANIZATIONS AND LEVELS OF BUREAUCRACY. THROUGHOUT THE LATEST REFORM PROCESS, THE DOD ACTIVELY SOUGHT TO STRENGTHEN ITS EXCLUSIVE CONTROL OF THE NATIONAL INTELLIGENCE ASSETS HOUSED WITHIN IT, AND TO PORTRAY ITSELF AS THE PRIMARY CUSTOMER OF ALL NATIONAL INTELLIGENCE.

BEFORE EXAMINING EACH OF THESE FACTORS IN TURN, IT IS USEFUL TO SUMMARIZE THE INVESTIGATIONS AND RECOMMENDATIONS LEADING TO THE 2004 BILL, ALONG WITH THE CONTENT OF THE BILL ITSELF. THE HOUSE PERMANENT SELECT COMMITTEE ON INTELLIGENCE AND THE SENATE SELECT COMMITTEE ON INTELLIGENCE RELEASED THE FIRST MAJOR INVESTIGATION: THE *REPORT OF THE JOINT INQUIRY INTO THE TERRORIST ATTACKS OF SEPTEMBER 11, 2001,* IN DECEMBER 2002. THIS INVESTIGATION OF INTELLIGENCE FAILURES PRECEDING 9/11 MAKES THE DCI'S LACK OF COMMUNITY-WIDE AUTHORITY CLEAR. NOTING THAT THE DOD CONTROLS 85 PERCENT OF THE IC BUDGET, THE JOINT REPORT CLAIMED: "THE INABILITY TO REALIGN INTELLIGENCE COMMUNITY RESOURCES TO COMBAT THE THREAT POSED BY USAMA BIN LADIN IS A RELATIVELY DIRECT CONSEQUENCE OF THE LIMITED AUTHORITY OF THE DCI OVER MAJOR PORTIONS OF THE INTELLIGENCE COMMUNITY … WHILE THE DCI HAS STATUTORY RESPONSIBILITY THAT SPANS THE INTELLIGENCE COMMUNITY, HIS ACTUAL AUTHORITIES ARE LIMITED TO THE BUDGETS AND PERSONNEL OVER WHICH HE EXERCISES DIRECT CONTROL, I.E., THE CIA, THE OFFICE OF THE DCI, AND THE COMMUNITY MANAGEMENT STAFF."[239] FURTHERMORE, THE "DCI'S COMMUNITY MANAGEMENT STAFF HAS LITTLE AUTHORITY TO ENSURE COMPLIANCE WITH THE DCI'S PRIORITIES. IT CANNOT WITHHOLD FUNDING FROM THE INTELLIGENCE COMMUNITY AGENCIES IF THEY DO NOT COMPLY WITH THOSE PRIORITIES."[240]

THE FIRST RECOMMENDATION OF THE JOINT INQUIRY WAS TO "AMEND THE NATIONAL SECURITY ACT OF 1947 TO CREATE AND SUFFICIENTLY STAFF A STATUTORY DIRECTOR OF NATIONAL INTELLIGENCE

---

[238] Richard A. Posner, "Important Job, Impossible Position," *New York Times*, (9 February 2005). n.p. On-line Internet. Available from www.nytimes.com/2005/02/09/opinion/09posner.html?th.

[239] US HOUSE. *JOINT INQUIRY INTO INTELLIGENCE COMMUNITY ACTIVITIES BEFORE AND AFTER THE TERRORIST ATTACKS OF SEPTEMBER 11, 2001.* 107TH CONG., 2ND SESS., 2002. H.R. 107-792. 43.

[240] Ibid., 30.

WHO SHALL BE THE PRESIDENT'S PRINCIPAL ADVISOR ON INTELLIGENCE AND SHALL HAVE THE FULL RANGE OR MANAGEMENT, BUDGET AND PERSONNEL RESPONSIBILITIES NEEDED TO MAKE THE ENTIRE U.S. INTELLIGENCE COMMUNITY OPERATE AS A COHERENT WHOLE."[241] AS NOTED IN THE PRECEDING CHAPTER, THIS RECOMMENDATION WAS MERELY ANOTHER ADDITION TO "AN IC STRUCTURAL REFORM DEBATE THAT DATES AT LEAST TO 1955, WHEN ARGUMENTS FOR STRONGER IC AUTHORITY BEGAN TO SURFACE."[242]

WHILE THE JOINT INQUIRY ISSUED ITS REPORT FIRST, IT WAS THE 9/11 COMMISSION—AN INDEPENDENT, BIPARTISAN COMMISSION CREATED BY CONGRESSIONAL LEGISLATION AND THE SIGNATURE OF PRESIDENT GEORGE W. BUSH IN LATE 2002—WHOSE REPORT LAID THE BLUEPRINT FOR CHANGE. RELEASED IN JULY OF 2004, THE REPORT FOCUSED LARGELY ON THE BACKGROUND LEADING TO THE TERRORIST ATTACKS IN NYC, BUT ALSO FULFILLED ITS MANDATE "TO PROVIDE RECOMMENDATIONS DESIGNED TO GUARD AGAINST FUTURE ATTACKS."[243] IN DOING SO, IT SOUGHT TO LOOK BEYOND THE IMMEDIATE THREAT OF TERRORISM TO DETERMINE THE BEST ORGANIZATION OF THE INTELLIGENCE COMMUNITY FOR THE "BROADER RANGE OF NATIONAL SECURITY CHALLENGES IN THE DECADES AHEAD." [244]

THE MOST HERALDED RECOMMENDATION OF THE 9/11 COMMISSION WAS THE CREATION OF A NATIONAL INTELLIGENCE DIRECTOR (NID), SEPARATE FROM THE CIA AND WITH GREATER POWER "TO MANAGE THE NATIONAL INTELLIGENCE PROGRAM AND OVERSEE THE AGENCIES THAT CONTRIBUTE TO IT."[245] THE COMMISSION'S GOALS FOR THE COMMUNITY, HOWEVER, ARE FAR MORE COMPREHENSIVE THAN THE CREATION OF A NEW LEADER. LIKE THE JOINT INQUIRY BEFORE IT, THE 9/11 COMMISSION ENCOURAGED CONGRESS TO CHANGE THE ENTIRE CULTURE OF THE INTELLIGENCE COMMUNITY BY PASSING AN INTELLIGENCE EQUIVALENT TO THE MILITARY GOLDWATER-NICHOLS ACT, WHICH IN 1986 FORCED THE MILITARY SERVICES TO "GIVE UP SOME OF THEIR TURF, AUTHORITIES, AND PREROGATIVES," AND INSTILL A SPIRIT OF "JOINTNESS."[246]

FOLLOWING THE "ABORTED ATTEMPT TO RESCUE AMERICAN HOSTAGES IN TEHRAN, WHICH FAILED, IN PART BECAUSE THE AIR FORCE AND THE NAVY DIDN'T COOPERATE," POLICY MAKERS REALIZED THAT "SOMEONE HAD TO BE GIVEN THE POWER TO MAKE THE SERVICES WORK TOGETHER. THEY WERE NOT GOING TO DO IT ON THEIR OWN."[247] IN RESPONSE, THE GOLDWATERS-NICHOLS ACT "WAS MEANT TO PUSH THE NOTION OF JOINT MILITARY OPERATIONS, TO EMPOWER ONE PERSON TO ORDER THE SERVICES

---

[241] *Joint Inquiry into the terrorist attacks,* Recommendations, 1.

[242] Alfred Cumming. "The Position of Director of National Intelligence: Issues for Congress." CRS Report for Congress, Order Code RL32506. (Washington DC: Congressional Research Service, 2004), Summary.

[243] "NATIONAL COMMISSION ON TERRORIST ATTACKS UPON THE UNITED STATES." N.P. ON-LINE INTERNET. AVIALABLE FROM WWW.9-11COMMISSION.GOV.

[244] *The 9/11 Commission Report*, 407.

[245] Ibid., 411.

[246] Ibid., 403.

[247] Dana Priest, "The Changing Roles of the Regional Commanders In Chief," remarks at the Secretary of State's open forum, (23 March 2001), n.p. On-line Internet. Available from http://www.state.gov/s/p/of/proc/tr/3719.htm.

TO WORK TOGETHER."[248] THE ACT CUT POWER FROM THE MILITARY SERVICE CHIEFS, ALLOWING COMMAND TO FLOW DIRECTLY FROM THE PRESIDENT, THROUGH THE SECRETARY OF DEFENSE, AND THEN TO UNIFIED COMBATANT COMMANDS. THE COMBATANT COMMANDS HAVE A BROAD, CONTINUING MISSION UNDER A SINGLE COMMANDER, AND ARE COMPOSED OF FORCES FROM TWO OR MORE MILITARY DEPARTMENTS. THE SERVICES ENDED UP WITH THE LESSER ROLE OF TRAINING AND EQUIPPING FORCES TO MEET THE COMBATANT COMMAND'S PERSONNEL AND MATERIAL NEEDS.[249] ALONG WITH THE STRUCTURAL CHANGE, GOLDWATER-NICHOLS CONTAINED A NUMBER OF PROVISIONS TO INCREASE JOINT INTEROPERABILITY ("JOINTNESS"), SUCH AS REQUIRING DUTY IN AN ORGANIZATION OUTSIDE OF ONE'S PARENT SERVICE FOR PROMOTION.

IN THE 9/11 COMMISSION'S MODEL, THE NID PLAYS A SIMILAR ROLE IN THE IC AS THAT OF THE SECRETARY OF DEFENSE IN THE DOD. FOR THE ROLE OF THE UNIFIED COMBATANT COMMANDS, THE COMMISSION RECOMMENDED THE CREATION OF NATIONAL INTELLIGENCE CENTERS (NICS) "TO PROVIDE ALL-SOURCE ANALYSIS AND PLAN INTELLIGENCE OPERATIONS FOR THE WHOLE GOVERNMENT ON MAJOR PROBLEMS."[250] THE COMMISSION SPECIFICALLY RECOMMENDED THE CREATION OF A NATIONAL INTELLIGENCE CENTER (NIC) FOCUSING ON COUNTERTERRORISM HOUSED IN THE NATIONAL COUNTER TERRORISM CENTER (A NEW ORGANIZATION RECOMMENDED IN THE COMMISSION'S REPORT). "OTHER NATIONAL INTELLIGENCE CENTERS – FOR INSTANCE, ON COUNTERPROLIFERATION, CRIME AND NARCOTICS, AND CHINA – WOULD BE HOUSED IN WHATEVER DEPARTMENT OR AGENCY IS BEST SUITED FOR THEM."[251] IN THE COMMISSION'S PLAN, THE ESTABLISHED AGENCIES WOULD CONTINUE TO EXIST, ORGANIZED PRIMARILY AROUND THEIR COLLECTION METHOD (I.E. HUMINT FOR THE CIA, SIGINT FOR THE NSA, OR IMINT FOR THE NGA). THEY WOULD SHIFT THE BULK OF THEIR ANALYSIS EFFORTS TO THE NICS, ALTHOUGH THEY WOULD CONTINUE TO RECRUIT, TRAIN, AND EQUIP PEOPLE TO STAFF THE NEW CENTERS. THE NICS, BY COMBINING MEMBERS FROM MULTIPLE AGENCIES INTO ONE FUSION CENTER FOCUSED ON A COMMON PROBLEM, SHOULD—IN THEORY—SHARE INFORMATION AND COORDINATE THEIR EFFORTS BETTER THAN BEFORE. THE NID WOULD HAVE THE POWER TO ELIMINATE WHATEVER STRUCTURAL, TECHNICAL, OR CULTURAL BARRIERS TO COOPERATION REMAINED.

IN CREATING THE NATIONAL INTELLIGENCE REFORM ACT OF 2004, CONGRESS LARGELY FOLLOWED THE 9/11 COMMISSION'S RECOMMENDATIONS. IT CREATED THE POSITION OF NATIONAL INTELLIGENCE DIRECTOR AND PROVIDED THE NEW OFFICE WITH EXPANDED AUTHORITIES TO MANAGE AND OVERSEE THE COMMUNITY. IT ALSO ESTABLISHED A NATIONAL COUNTER TERRORISM CENTER (NCTC) THAT ABSORBED THE EXISTING TERRORIST THREAT INTEGRATION CENTER (TTIC) INTO ITS DIRECTORATE OF INTELLIGENCE. THE NCTC IS INTENDED TO SERVE AS A COUNTERTERRORISM NIC, PROVIDING THE EXAMPLE AND GUIDELINES FOR THE CREATION OF MORE NICS. LIKE THE 9/11

---

[248] Ibid.
[249] David S. C. Chu and Nurith Berstein, "Decision Making For Defense" in *New Challenges, New Tools for Defense Decision Making,* Stuart Johnson, Martin Libicki, and Gregory F. Treverton, eds., (Santa Monica, California: Rand Corporation, 2003), 16.
[250] *The 9/11 Commission Report*, 411.
[251] Ibid., 411.

COMMISSION, CONGRESS DREW HEAVILY ON THE EXAMPLE OF THE DEPARTMENT OF DEFENSE'S REORGANIZATION. IN DISCUSSING HOW TO BREAK DOWN THE BARRIERS TO INFORMATION SHARING, THE BILL STATES: "IT IS THE SENSE OF CONGRESS THAT THE MECHANISMS PRESCRIBED UNDER THIS SUBSECTION SHOULD, TO THE EXTENT PRACTICAL, SEEK TO DUPLICATE WITHIN THE INTELLIGENCE COMMUNITY THE JOINT OFFICER MANAGEMENT POLICIES ESTABLISHED BY THE GOLDWATER-NICHOLS DEPARTMENT OF DEFENSE REORGANIZATION ACT."[252]

LIKE THE NATIONAL SECURITY ACT OF 1947, HOWEVER, THE PROVISIONS FOR STRENGTHENING CENTRAL CONTROL IN THE 2004 BILL SUFFERED FROM THE OPPOSITION OF ESTABLISHED AGENCIES AND THEIR CONGRESSIONAL PATRONS. SENATOR PAT ROBERTS, CHAIR OF THE SENATE INTELLIGENCE COMMITTEE, REFERRING TO "THE LONG AND BITTER REARGUARD FOUGHT AGAINST THE IDEA OF A POWERFUL NEW INTELLIGENCE DIRECTOR BY THE PENTAGON AND ITS CONGRESSIONAL ALLIES," NOTED: "THIS WASN'T THE BEST POSSIBLE BILL, BUT IT WAS THE BEST BILL POSSIBLE."[253] ULTIMATELY, THE SUCCESS OF THE BILL DEPENDS ON WHETHER THE IC PROVIDES MORE TIMELY AND USABLE INTELLIGENCE TO NATIONAL POLICY MAKERS AND MILITARY COMMANDERS THAN ITS PREDECESSORS. ONLY TIME WILL TELL. A SECONDARY, ALTHOUGH RELATED ISSUE, IS WHETHER THE NEW ORGANIZATION WILL BE MORE SUCCESSFUL IN EXERTING CENTRALIZED CONTROL OVER THE ENTIRE COMMUNITY. EXAMINING THE BILL AND CURRENT EVENTS IN LIGHT OF THE FACTORS DEVELOPED IN THE PREVIOUS CHAPTER ENABLES SOME JUDGMENTS ON THE LATTER ISSUE. IT APPEARS THAT MANY, IF NOT ALL OF THE FACTORS THAT HAVE WORKED AGAINST CENTRALIZED CONTROL IN THE PAST, WILL CONTINUE TO AFFECT THE COMMUNITY IN THE FUTURE, AND IN FACT ARE ALREADY DOING SO.

FACTOR 1: THE MOTIVE AND ABILITY OF EXISTING INTELLIGENCE ORGANIZATIONS TO RESIST CENTRALIZED CONTROL

THAT THE INTELLIGENCE REFORM ACT OF 2004 DID NOT MAKE THE NID AS POWERFUL IN FACT AS ON PAPER IS UNDOUBTEDLY DUE TO THE SAME REASON POWER DID NOT ACCUMULATE IN THE OFFICE OF DCI IN 1947; THE EXISTING AGENCIES AND THE DEPARTMENTS THAT HOUSE THEM HAVE THE MOTIVE AND POWER TO RESIST EXTERNAL CONTROL OF THEIR INTELLIGENCE ASSETS. WITH THE INCREASED SIZE OF THE INTELLIGENCE COMMUNITY TODAY, THERE ARE MORE AGENCIES TO LOBBY AGAINST GIVING A CENTRAL COORDINATOR INCREASED AUTHORITY THAN PROPONENTS OF CENTRALIZING INTELLIGENCE FACED IN 1947. THE CIA, WHICH PREVIOUSLY TRIED TO ASSERT ITS COMMUNITY-WIDE MANDATE, NOW JOINS THE RANKS OF AGENCIES DEALING WITH THE PROBLEM OF HOW MUCH POWER IT WILL CEDE TO A CENTRAL ORGANIZATION. THE COMBINED INTERESTS OF THE EXISTING AGENCIES AFFECTED HOW THE

---

[252] US SENATE. *NATIONAL INTELLIGENCE REFORM ACT OF 2004*, 108TH CONG., 2ND SESS., 2004, S.2845, 45.

[253] Shaun Waterman, "Congress already tweaking new intel post," *Washington Times*, (21 March 2005): n.p.
  On-line Internet. Available from www.washtimes.com/upi-breaking/20050320-033228-9327r htm.

VARIOUS COMMISSIONS AND PANELS EXAMINED THE ISSUE, STRONGLY IMPACTED WHAT LEGISLATION ULTIMATELY PASSED, AND ARE ALREADY AFFECTING HOW SUCH LEGISLATION IS BEING IMPLEMENTED.

THE MILITARY CONTINUES TO PROVIDE THE GREATEST RESISTANCE TO STRENGTHENING THE NID'S AUTHORITIES. WITH EIGHT OF THE 15 INTELLIGENCE COMMUNITY AGENCIES HOUSED IN THE DEPARTMENT OF DEFENSE, THE MILITARY HAS THE MOST TO LOSE FROM A STRONG CENTRAL POWER, AND THE STRONGEST BASE WITH WHICH TO RESIST IT. THE JOINT INQUIRY, AMONG ITS NUMEROUS RECOMMENDATIONS, SUGGESTED THAT THE NID AND SECRETARY OF DEFENSE MAKE THE "NSA A FULL COLLABORATING PARTNER WITH THE CENTRAL INTELLIGENCE AGENCY AND THE FEDERAL BUREAU OF INVESTIGATION IN THE WAR ON TERRORISM, INCLUDING FULLY INTEGRATING THE COLLECTION AND ANALYTIC CAPABILITIES OF NSA, CIA, AND THE FBI."[254] MAKING RECOMMENDATIONS IS RELATIVELY EASY, BUT ENACTING THEM INTO LAW IS MUCH MORE DIFFICULT. AS ONE OBSERVER NOTED: "TRYING TO WREST THE NATIONAL SECURITY AGENCY AND LIKE AGENCIES FROM THE DEFENSE DEPARTMENT, HOWEVER, WOULD LEAVE CAPITOL HILL AND PENNSYLVANIA AVENUE AWASH IN BLOOD... THE MILITARY SERVICES WILL NEVER ACCEPT DEPENDENCE ON OTHER DEPARTMENTS FOR PERFORMANCE OF THEIR CORE FUNCTIONS, WHICH INCLUDE TACTICAL INTELLIGENCE COLLECTION, AND POLITICIANS WILL NOT OVERRIDE MILITARY PROTESTS THAT THEIR COMBAT EFFECTIVENESS IS BEING PUT AT RISK."[255] LEAVING FULL CONTROL OF THE NATION'S TECHNICAL COLLECTION ASSETS IN THE DEPARTMENT OF DEFENSE, HOWEVER, LEAVES THE NATIONAL INTELLIGENCE AUTHORITY DEPENDENT ON ANOTHER DEPARTMENT FOR PERFORMANCE OF MANY OF ITS CORE FUNCTIONS.

THE 9/11 COMMISSION HAD THE UNENVIABLE JOB OF PROVIDING A BLUEPRINT FOR LEGISLATION THAT WOULD EMPOWER A NID, WHILE PLACATING PENTAGON CONCERNS THAT THE MILITARY WOULD LOSE CONTROL OF INTELLIGENCE ASSETS CRITICAL TO MODERN WARFIGHTING.
THE COMMISSION BEGAN WITH A KEEN AWARENESS OF THE CHALLENGE. NOTING THAT THAT THE STRUCTURE OF THE CIA AS DESIGNED IN 1947 "BUILT IN TENSIONS BETWEEN THE CIA AND THE DEFENSE DEPARTMENT'S INTELLIGENCE AGENCIES," THE COMMISSIONERS SOUGHT TO DEFUSE SUCH TENSIONS.[256] THE CONGRESSIONAL RESEARCH SERVICE PRODUCED A PAPER ENTITLED "INTELLIGENCE COMMUNITY REORGANIZATION: POTENTIAL EFFECTS ON DOD INTELLIGENCE AGENCIES" THAT CONCLUDED: "PROPOSALS TO ESTABLISH A DNI/NID WOULD AFFECT THE CONTROL OF THE SECRETARY OF DEFENSE OVER AGENCIES THAT ARE CLOSELY INTEGRATED INTO THE OPERATIONAL CAPABILITIES OF THE MILITARY SERVICES. FEW OBSERVERS DOUBT THAT SENIOR DOD OFFICIAL AND SOME MEMBERS OF CONGRESS WOULD RAISE CONCERNS ABOUT PROVISIONS TO TRANSFER MANAGEMENT AUTHORITY FOR DOD INTELLIGENCE AGENCIES TO THE NEWLY CREATED DNI/NID."[257] THE REPORT QUOTED FORMER DCI

---

[254] Joint Inquiry, *Recommendations*, 10.
[255] RICHARD K. BETTS "THE NEW POLITICS OF INTELLIGENCE: WILL REFORMS WORK THIS TIME?" *FOREIGN AFFAIRS* 83, NO. 3 (MAY-JUN. 2004): 6.
[256] *The 9/11 Commission Report*, 89.
[257] "RICHARD A. BEST, *INTELLIGENCE COMMUNITY REORGANIZATION: POTENTIAL EFFECTS ON DOD INTELLIGENCE AGENCIES.*(WASHINGTON DC: CONGRESSIONAL RESEARCH SERVICE, 2004), 8-9.

ROBERT GATES: "IN THE REAL WORLD OF WASHINGTON BUREAUCRATIC AND CONGRESSIONAL POLITICS, THERE IS NO WAY THE SECRETARY OF DEFENSE OR THE ARMED SERVICES COMMITTEES OF CONGRESS ARE SIMPLY GOING TO HAND THOSE AGENCIES OVER TO AN INTELLIGENCE CZAR SITTING IN THE WHITE HOUSE. INDEED, FOR THE LAST DECADE, INTELLIGENCE AUTHORITY HAS BEEN QUIETLY LEACHING FROM THE C.I.A. AND TO THE PENTAGON, NOT THE OTHER WAY AROUND." IN AN UNDERSTATEMENT THE REPORT CLAIMED THAT THE ISSUE OF WHETHER OR NOT TO GIVE A NEW DNI/NID "THE AUTHORITY TO APPOINT AND DISMISS HEADS OF INTELLIGENCE AGENCIES OF THE DEFENSE DEPARTMENT, TO EXECUTE ALL FUNDS APPROPRIATED FOR THE NATIONAL FOREIGN INTELLIGENCE PROGRAM, OR TO TRANSFER FUNDS AND PERSONNEL AMONG DIFFERENT INTELLIGENCE ACTIVITIES OVER THE OBJECTIONS OF RELEVANT DEPARTMENT HEADS" IS "LIKELY TO BE CONTROVERSIAL." [258]

IN THE END, PROVIDING THE NEW NID WITH FULL AUTHORITY TO RUN THE IC PROVED NOT ONLY CONTROVERSIAL, BUT ALSO IMPOSSIBLE. "CONCERNED ABOUT LOSING ITS CLOUT OVER SPY SATELLITES AND ELECTRONIC EAVESDROPPING, THE PENTAGON AND ITS ALLIES ON CAPITAL HILL, WITH QUIET SUPPORT FROM THE WHITE HOUSE, FOUGHT AGAINST GIVING THE DNI MUCH POWER. AFTER A SERIES OF COMPROMISES, THE DNI ENDED UP WITH ONLY SLIGHTLY STRONGER FORMAL AUTHORITY THAN TODAY'S DIRECTOR OF CENTRAL INTELLIGENCE TO RUN THE COMMUNITY."[259] MICHAEL O'HANLON, A DEFENSE-BUDGET EXPERT AT THE BROOKINGS INSTITUTION, NOTES: "THE ORIGINAL SENATE LEGISLATION WOULD HAVE GIVEN THE INTELLIGENCE DIRECTOR THE AUTHORITY TO SHIFT UNLIMITED FUNDS AND UNLIMITED PERSONNEL FROM ONE INTELLIGENCE FUNCTION TO ANOTHER. UNDER PRESSURE FROM HOUSE REPUBLICANS SYMPATHETIC TO THE PENTAGON, THE FINAL BILL GRANTS THE DIRECTOR THE POWER TO SET OVERALL INTELLIGENCE-AGENCY BUDGET PARAMETERS, SUBJECT TO CONSULTATION WITH THE AGENCY HEADS AND FINAL ARBITRATION BY THE PRESIDENT AND HIS OFFICE OF MANAGEMENT AND BUDGET."[260] PUT SOME SORT OF CONNECTOR HERE, ONE QUOTE AFTER ANOTHER IS POOR FORM: "THE BILL DOES GRANT THE DNI LIMITED NEW POWER TO MOVE MONEY AND PERSONNEL. BUT THE DNI CAN INDEPENDENTLY MOVE FUNDS ONLY AS LONG AS THEY ARE LESS THAN $150 MILLION AND 5 PERCENT OF AN AGENCY'S BUDGET – WHAT ONE CRITIC CALLS 'DECIMAL DUST' IN MULTIBILLION-DOLLAR AGENCIES"[261]

A KEY PENTAGON ALLY ON CAPITOL HILL, HOUSE ARMED SERVICES COMMITTEE CHAIR DUNCAN HUNTER, OPPOSED EARLY DRAFTS OF THE BILL. A CONTEMPORARY NEWS ARTICLE NOTED: "CRUCIAL TO WINNING HUNTER'S SUPPORT IS ENSURING THAT THE DEFENSE DEPARTMENT WOULD RETAIN DIRECT CONTROL OVER THE AGENCIES THAT OPERATE THE NATION'S SPY SATELLITES AND

---

[258] Ibid., 10.

[259] David E. Kaplan and Kevin Whitelaw, "Intelligence reform--at last", *USNews.com*, (20 December 2004),

  n.p. On-line Internet. Available from http://www.usnews.com/usnews/news/articles/041220/20intell htm.

[260] *NATIONAL INTELLIGENCE REFORM ACT OF 2004*, 247.

[261] Kaplan, "Intelligence reform--at last," n.p.

ANALYZE THE INFORMATION THEY PICK UP."[262] IN ASKING FOR COMPROMISE LANGUAGE TO ENSURE THAT THE PENTAGON WOULD MAINTAIN CONTROL OVER INTELLIGENCE SATELLITES, HUNTER STATED: "WE NEED TO HAVE HERE A STRONG CHAIN OF COMMAND BETWEEN THE COMBAT SUPPORT AGENCIES – THOSE ARE THE SATELLITE AGENCIES AND THOSE WHO DO THE SIGNAL INTELLIGENCE AND THE PICTURES – AND THE WARFIGHTERS ON THE GROUND IN THE DEPARTMENT OF DEFENSE."[263] THE POWER OF THE PENTAGON TO OPPOSE LEGISLATION PROMPTED JOHN DIAMOND TO WRITE IN *USA TODAY*: "THE IRRESISTIBLE FORCE OF POST-SEPT. 11 LEGISLATION TO RESTRUCTURE THE NATION'S INTELLIGENCE SYSTEM HAS RUN INTO THE IMMOVABLE OBJECT OF OPPOSITION FROM THE PENTAGON... THE IMPASSE TESTIFIES TO THE POLITICAL INFLUENCE OF THE MILITARY, PARTICULARLY IN WARTIME, AND THE DIFFICULTY OF PASSING LEGISLATION THAT REQUIRES POWERFUL COMMITTEE LEADERS TO GIVE UP POWER."[264] THE ARTICLE FURTHER NOTED: "IF THE SENATE'S MORE POWERFUL INTELLIGENCE DIRECTORSHIP IS CREATED, HUNTER'S COMMITTEE WOULD LOOSE CONTROL OVER BILLIONS OF DOLLARS IN SPENDING ON SPY SATELLITES, MUCH OF WHICH GOES TO CONTRACTORS IN HIS HOME STATE OF CALIFORNIA."[265]

PENTAGON ADVOCATES ONLY SUPPORTED THE LEGISLATION AFTER "NEGOTIATORS ADDED LANGUAGE TO THE BILL EXPLICITLY PREVENTING INTELLIGENCE OFFICIALS FROM INTERFERING IN THE MILITARY CHAIN OF COMMAND."[266] GENERAL MYERS, CHAIR OF THE JOINT CHIEFS OF STAFF, WHO PREVIOUSLY "WROTE A LETTER TO CONGRESS IN OCTOBER ARGUING THAT CONTROL OVER THREE INTELLIGENCE AGENCIES THAT PROVIDE COMBAT SUPPORT – THE NATIONAL SECURITY AGENCY (NSA), THE NGA, AND THE NRO – SHOULD STAY WITH THE PENTAGON," DECLARED N DECEMBER 2, 2004, THAT "MEASURES IN THE COMPROMISE BILL HAD ADDRESSED HIS CONCERNS."[267]

IN THE FINAL BILL, "BUDGETARY PROVISIONS GIVE THE NID THE RESPONSIBILITY FOR DEVELOPING A 'CONSOLIDATED BUDGET FOR THE NATIONAL INTELLIGENCE PROGRAM,' AND PERMIT THE NID'S 'PARTICIPATION' IN FORMULATING BUDGETS FOR TACTICAL AND OTHER MILITARY INTELLIGENCE. BUT THE POWER TO DEVELOP AND PARTICIPATE IS HARDLY THE POWER TO HELM AND CONTROL."[268]

---

[262] "TWO ISSUES STALLING INTEL OVERHAUL BILL," *NEWSMAX WIRES*. (2 DECEMBER 2004): N.P. ON-LINE INTERNET.
  AVAILABLE FROM HTTP://WWW.NEWSMAX.COM/ARCHIVES/ARTICLES/2004/12/2/155222.SHTML.
[263] Ibid.
[264] John Diamond, "Pentagon's objections block overhaul of U.S. intelligence," *USA Today*, (2 November 2004): 12A.
[265] Ibid.
[266] ESTHER, PAN, "INTELLIGENCE LEGISLATIVE REFORM," (NEW YORK: COUNCIL ON FOREIGN RELATIONS, 31MARCH
  2005), N.P. ON-LINE INTERNET. AVAILABLE FROM
WWW.CFR.ORG/BACKGROUND/BACKGROUND_INTELLIGENCE_
  REFORM.PHP?PRINT=1.

[267] Ibid,
[268] Bob Barr, "Is it Time to Reform Intelligence Reform?," *FindLaw's Legal Commentary*, (21 January 2005), n.p. On-line Internet. Available from
  http://writ news findlaw.com/commentary/20050121_barr html.

ADDITIONALLY, THE BILL "ONLY MANAGED TO GARNER ENOUGH VOTES FOR PASSAGE AFTER SPONSORS AGREED TO INCLUDE A PROVISION SPECIFYING THAT NOTHING IN IT WOULD 'ABROGATE' THE STATUTORY AUTHORITY OF OTHER HEADS OF DEPARTMENTS. BUT THAT'S A BIG PROBLEM: THE DEFENSE SECRETARY, FOR INSTANCE, HAS VAST STATUTORY AUTHORITY OVER INTELLIGENCE GATHERING, AUTHORITY THAT IS SEEMINGLY PRESERVED UNDER THIS LITTLE-NOTICED SECTION."[269] DOD INFLUENCE IN THE CREATION OF THE BILL IS SEEN AGAIN IN THE NID'S POWER TO OVERSEE THE ACQUISITION OF MAJOR SYSTEMS FOR THE IC. IN DEVELOPING AN ACQUISITION PROGRAM, THE NID SERVES "AS EXCLUSIVE MILESTONE DECISION AUTHORITY" FOR ALL AGENCIES, "EXCEPT WITH RESPECT TO DEPARTMENT OF DEFENSE PROGRAMS THE DIRECTOR SHALL SERVE AS MILESTONE DECISION AUTHORITY JOINTLY WITH THE SECRETARY OF DEFENSE OR THE DESIGNEE OF THE SECRETARY."[270]

AFTER THE BILL'S PASSAGE IN DECEMBER OF 2004, RESISTANCE TO THE NEW POSITION DID NOT STOP WITHIN THE GREATER COMMUNITY. REP ELLEN TAUSCHER, A MEMBER OF THE HOUSE ARMED SERVICES COMMITTEE, ATTRIBUTED THE DELAY BETWEEN PASSAGE OF THE BILL AND THE WHITE HOUSE'S APPOINTMENT OF A CANDIDATE FOR THE POSITION TO "MURKINESS AND AMBIGUITIES…DIRECTLY RELATED TO COMPROMISES THAT HAD TO BE MADE IN BOTH HOUSES TO GET THE INTELLIGENCE REORGANIZATION BILL PASSED."[271] DURING THAT TIME, THE OTHER AGENCIES HAVE NOT BEEN IDLE. SENATOR HAMILTON, BEFORE THE APPOINTMENT OF NEGROPONTE, "PREDICTED THAT RUMSFELD WOULD TRY TO TEST THE AUTHORITY OF THE NEW CHIEF SAYING 'LAWYERS FROM THE DEPARTMENT OF DEFENSE – AS WELL AS THE FBI AND THE CIA – WERE DOUBTLESSLY ALREADY POURING OVER THE SMALL PRINT LOOKING FOR LOOPHOLES…CONFIRMATION OF THEIR AGENCY'S RIGHT TO RESIST THE (NEW DIRECTORS) ORDERS."[272]

IN MARCH OF 2005, SENATORS SAXBY CHAMBLISS AND BEN NELSON, BOTH MEMBERS OF THE ARMED SERVICES COMMITTEE, INTRODUCED THE MILITARY REORGANIZATION ACT OF 2005 TO CREATE A UNIFIED COMBATANT COMMAND FOR MILITARY INTELLIGENCE (INTCOM).[273] SENATOR CHAMBLISS SUGGESTED SUCH AN ACT WOULD BE AN AID TO THE DNI: "INTCOM CREATES ONE POINT OF CONTACT FOR MILITARY INTELLIGENCE FOR THE NEW DNI AND CREATES A MORE EFFICIENT, RESPONSIVE, AND SIMPLER MILITARY INTELLIGENCE STRUCTURE…TO BE SUCCESSFUL THE NEW DNI WILL NEED A STRUCTURE IN PLACE THAT IS MANAGEABLE AND OUR COMBATANT COMMANDERS NEED A MILITARY

---

[269] Ibid.

[270] *National Intelligence Reform Act of 2004*, 142.

[271] Walter Pincus, "National Intelligence Director Proves to Be Difficult Post to Fill," *Washingtonpost.com*, (31 January 2005): A04.

[272] Waterman, "Congress already tweaking new intel post," n.p.

[273] US SENATE. *A BILL, TO AMEND TITLE 10, UNITED STATES CODE, TO PROVIDE FOR THE ESTABLISHMENT OF A UNIFIED COMBATANT COMMAND FOR MILITARY INTELLIGENCE, AND FOR OTHER PURPOSES.* 109TH CONG. 1ST SESS. 2005, S. DOC. 2778.

OFFICER TO ARTICULATE THEIR INTELLIGENCE REQUIREMENTS TO THE DNI."[274] IT IS NOT HARD TO SEE THIS PROPOSAL AS MORE THAN JUST AN ATTEMPT TO BE HELPFUL TO THE NEW DNI. A RECENT ARTICLE CLAIMED THE PENTAGON IS "LOOKING AT THE CHAMBLISS PROPOSAL AS A WAY TO ENSURE IT HAS AN INTELLIGENCE OFFICER OF SUFFICIENT STATURE AND RANK TO HANDLE DISPUTES THAT MAY ARISE WITH THE NEW INTELLIGENCE CZAR."[275]

DESPITE THE BEST EFFORTS OF THE PENTAGON AND ITS ALLIES, THE INTELLIGENCE REFORM BILL OF 2004 DOES PROVIDE THE NID MORE AUTHORITY THAN THE DCI EVER HAD. AT THE SAME TIME, THE DOD WILL CONTINUE TO BE A POWERFUL COUNTERFORCE WITHIN THE IC. TIME WILL TELL HOW EFFECTIVE JOHN NEGROPONTE, THE FIRST NID, WILL BE IN SETTING PRECEDENTS FOR THE RESTRUCTURED COMMUNITY. EUGENE OREGON'S *REGISTER-GUARD* DESCRIBED THE SITUATION WELL: "DESPITE NEGROPONTE'S IMPRESSIVE JOB DESCRIPTION, IT REMAINS TO BE SEEN IF THE POSITION IS AS POWERFUL AS THE SEPT. 11 COMMISSION ENVISIONED IT. AN EPIC TURF BATTLE LOOMS WITH DEFENSE SECRETARY DONALD RUMSFELD, WHO DIDN'T WANT A NATIONAL INTELLIGENCE CZAR AND IS INTENT ON EXPANDING THE PENTAGON'S INTELLIGENCE CAPACITIES. IT ALSO REMAINS TO BE SEE IF NEWLY APPOINTED CIA DIRECTOR PORTER GOSS WILL COOPERATE WITH NEGROPONTE, OR WHETHER GOSS WILL TRY TO RE-ESTABLISH THE CIA CHIEF'S TRADITIONAL ROLE AS PRE-EMINENT INTELLIGENCE AUTHORITY."[276] MUCH OF NEGROPONTE'S SUCCESS OR LACK THERE OF, WILL DEPEND ON HOW WELL PRESIDENT BUSH SUPPORTS HIM.

FACTOR 2: RELATIONAL AUTHORITY VERSUS STATUTORY AUTHORITY

JUST AS DCIS RELIED ON RELATIONAL AUTHORITY TO INFLUENCE THE INTELLIGENCE COMMUNITY SINCE 1947, NIDS, GIVEN THE SUCCESSFUL INSERTION OF COMPROMISE LANGUAGE IN THE REFORM ACT, WILL BE LARGELY DEPENDENT ON HOW MUCH SUPPORT THEY RECEIVE FROM THE PRESIDENT. BOTH THE INVESTIGATIONS INTO THE IC, AND THE BILL THAT TRANSFORMED IT, RECOGNIZED THE CENTRAL ROLE THE PRESIDENT MUST PLAY FOR REFORM TO SUCCEED. NEITHER, HOWEVER, ENSURES THAT PRESIDENTIAL SUPPORT WILL BE FORTHCOMING.

THE JOINT INQUIRY BY CONGRESS'S INTELLIGENCE COMMITTEES, WHICH SOUGHT TO GIVE THE NID SWEEPING STATUTORY AUTHORITY, RECOGNIZED THAT EVEN WITH SUCH AUTHORITY, THE PRESIDENT WOULD STILL PLAY THE KEY ROLE IN THE COMMUNITY. RIGHT AFTER RECOMMENDING THAT A

---

[274] "Chambliss Helps Introduce Intelligence Reform Bill," *Chattanoogan.com* (16 March 2005): n.p. On-line
   Internet. Available from http://www.chattanoogan.com/articles/article_64105.asp.
[275] John Diamond, "Pentagon mulls military command for intelligence," *USA Today, (*10 January 2005): n.p.
   On-line Internet. Available from http://www.usatoday.com/news/washington/2005-01-10-intel-post_x.htm.
[276] "The spymaster's mission: Negroponte faces huge challenges in new job," *Register-Guard,* Eugene,
   Oregon. (22 February, 2005): n.p. On-line Internet. Available from www registerguard.com/news/
   2005/02/22/ed.edit negroponte.phn.0222.html.

DNI BE ESTABLISHED AND GRANTED "STATUTORY AUTHORITY TO INSURE THAT INTELLIGENCE COMMUNITY AGENCIES AND COMPONENTS FULLY COMPLY WITH COMMUNITY-WIDE POLICY, MANAGEMENT, SPENDING, AND ADMINISTRATIVE GUIDANCE AND PRIORITIES," THE REPORT WENT ON TO SAY: "CONGRESS AND THE PRESIDENT SHOULD ALSO WORK TO ENSURE THAT THE DIRECTOR OF NATIONAL INTELLIGENCE EFFECTIVELY EXERCISES THESE AUTHORITIES… THE PRESIDENT SHOULD TAKE ACTION TO ENSURE THAT CLEAR, CONSISTENT, AND CURRENT PRIORITIES ARE ESTABLISHED AND ENFORCED THROUGHOUT THE INTELLIGENCE COMMUNITY."[277]

LIKEWISE, THE 9/11 COMMISSION, WHICH ACKNOWLEDGES THE "DCI'S REAL AUTHORITY HAS BEEN DIRECTLY PROPORTIONAL TO HIS PERSONAL CLOSENESS TO THE PRESIDENT, WHICH HAS WAXED AND WANED OVER THE YEARS," FAILS TO RECOMMEND GIVING THE NID SUFFICIENT AUTHORITY TO ARBITRATE DISPUTES WITHIN THE COMMUNITY UNILATERALLY.[278] INSTEAD, IT RECOMMENDS THAT THE "NATIONAL INTELLIGENCE DIRECTOR SHOULD PARTICIPATE IN AN NSC EXECUTIVE COMMITTEE THAT CAN RESOLVE DIFFERENCES IN PRIORITIES AMONG THE AGENCIES AND BRING MAJOR DISPUTES TO THE PRESIDENT FOR DECISION."[279] THE IMPLICATION IS THAT THE NID WILL ONLY HAVE THE POWER TO RESOLVE MINOR DISPUTES AND THE OTHER AGENCIES CAN ALWAYS APPEAL SUCH DECISIONS.

THE NATIONAL INTELLIGENCE REFORM ACT OF 2004 EVEN LEGISLATES THE SECRETARY OF DEFENSE'S RIGHT TO APPEAL TO THE PRESIDENT WHEN IN DISAGREEMENT WITH THE NID. AFTER GIVING THE SECRETARY THE RESPONSIBILITY FOR JOINTLY OVERSEEING THE ACQUISITION OF MAJOR SYSTEMS FOR AGENCIES IN THE DOD, THE BILL STATES WHEN THE TWO "ARE UNABLE TO REACH AGREEMENT ON A MILESTONE DECISION… THE DIRECTOR SHALL ASSUME MILESTONE DECISION AUTHORITY SUBJECT TO REVIEW BY THE PRESIDENT AT THE REQUEST OF THE SECRETARY."[280] ALTHOUGH THE BILL GIVES THE NID RESPONSIBILITY FOR ESTABLISHING THE REQUIREMENTS AND PROCEDURES FOR THE CLASSIFICATION, DISSEMINATION, AND REPORTING OF INTELLIGENCE, LATER IT STATES, "NO SINGLE AGENCY CAN CREATE A MEANINGFUL INFORMATION SHARING SYSTEM ON ITS OWN. ALONE, EACH AGENCY CAN ONLY MODERNIZE STOVEPIPES, NOT REPLACE THEM. PRESIDENTIAL LEADERSHIP IS REQUIRED TO BRING ABOUT GOVERNMENTAL CHANGE."[281]

THE 9/11 COMMISSION DID TRY TO BOOST THE NID'S RELATIONAL AUTHORITY BY SUGGESTING THE POSITION BE "LOCATED IN THE EXECUTIVE OFFICE OF THE PRESIDENT," ENABLING THE NID TO, IN EFFECT, SPEAK ON BEHALF OF THE CHIEF EXECUTIVE.[282] THIS RECOMMENDATION, HOWEVER, DID NOT MAKE IT INTO THE FINAL LAW. SECTION 221 OF THE BILL SPECIFICALLY STATES: "THE NATIONAL INTELLIGENCE DIRECTOR SHALL NOT BE LOCATED WITHIN THE EXECUTIVE OFFICE OF THE PRESIDENT."[283] BOTH THE 9/11 COMMISSION RECOMMENDATIONS AND THE REFORM BILL RETAINED THE

---

[277] *Joint Inquiry into the terrorist attacks,* 2-3.
[278] *The 9/11 Commission Report,* 86.
[279] Ibid., 414.
[280] *National Intelligence Act of 2004,* 143.
[281] Ibid., 23, 165.
[282] *The 9/11 Commission Report,* 414.
[283] *National Intelligence Act of 2004,* 209.

NID's access to the President, however, by making her or him the President's principal advisor for intelligence. Unlike the DCI, however, who as head of the CIA owned a powerful all source analysis center, the NID will not have an independent source of intelligence with which to brief the President. The 9/11 Commission even states: "We hope the president will come to look directly to the directors of the national intelligence centers to provide all-source analysis in their areas of responsibility, balancing the advice of these intelligence chiefs against the contrasting viewpoints that may be offered by department heads at State, Homeland Security, Justice, and other agencies."[284] Since many of these NICs will be housed in separate departments, the department heads in effect receive two lines of communication to the President, while the NID is little more than an intermediary relaying second hand information.

Some critics of the 2004 bill suggest that removing the NID from the CIA leaves him or her with less community-wide power than the DCI enjoyed. "Agency officers object that taking the CIA away from the director would be like leaving a general with no troops. Absent any direct means for action, the DNI would be dependent on a set of agencies with their own bureaucracies, roles, and missions. If a director had the kind of real control implied by the term 'intelligence czar,' and could fire at will those who defy him, this objection would lose much of its strength."[285] The 9/11 Commission recommended giving the NID such real control. In the Commission's vision, the NID would have the ability to hire and fire agency heads; grant, move, or withhold funds; and, as a member of the executive office, in effect speak on behalf of the president. The final legislation, however, strips the general of his troops, gives him limited power over funds and personnel, and prohibits him from being in the executive office.

Former DCI Gates concurred: "An intelligence czar with no independent base would have to have authority over the entire intelligence budget to be effective ... When you consider that 85 percent of that budget is under the Defense Department, there's no way any secretary of Defense is going to give up that kind of control over organizations for which he has ultimate responsibility. So you automatically have a situation in which the new intelligence czar sitting over in the Old Executive Office Building has no significantly greater budgetary or management authority than the current director of central intelligence. At the same time, because he does not head the CIA he is stripped of all of his organizational base and independence. That kind of position is guaranteed to fail."[286]

---

[284] *The 9/11 Commission Report*, 414.

[285] John Prados, "Intelligence: No easy fix," *Bulletin of the Atomic Scientists* 60, no. 5 (September/October 2004): 19.

[286] Mary H. Cooper, "Overview: After the Aldrich Ames Spy Scandel," *The CQ Researcher* 6, no. 5 (February, 1996): 4.

While the bill clearly anticipates that the NID will need the support of the President to be effective, it cannot legislate such support. One of the bill's architects, Sept 11 Commission Vice Chairman Lee Hamilton, acknowledged: "The law provides 'sufficiently clear and strong authorities (for the new post) … provided he has the support of the president.'"[287] Following Bush's nomination of Negroponte to the position, Hamilton expressed the same sentiment even more bluntly: "If the president backs him, he'll succeed. If he doesn't, he won't."[288]

"Some reformers worry that Bush, given his lukewarm support for the 9/11 commission and intelligence reform, may not truly empower a DNI."[289] For example: "Former CIA Director Stansfield Turner, who served as U.S. spymaster under former President Jimmy Carter, said it was not clear that Bush would back Negroponte against Rumsfeld given the Pentagon chief's long-standing influence over Bush."[290] Walter Pincus of *The Washington Post* notes, "Negroponte would be the man who gives him [Bush] his daily intelligence briefing… So this NID will have direct and daily access to the president, which is no mean measure of influence and potentially power."[291] Yet the President is capable of withdrawing his support. The PFIAB, led by Brent Scowcroft, a once powerful voice in the administration, saw its influence with the President drop significantly "since Scowcroft became a relatively open critic of the Iraq war."[292] Given Bush's close relationship with the Secretary of Defense, it is hard to predict who he would back if the NID and Rumsfeld ever disagreed on the use of national intelligence assets. Even if Bush does support Negroponte, there is no guarantee that future Presidents will have either the interest or the inclination to empower future NIDs.

Factor 3: Association with Covert Operations

While removing the NID from the CIA may strip away a large power base, it does provide a layer of insulation from the potentially politically hazardous area of covert operations. When these operations—that by definition seek to influence foreign governments undetected—are revealed and subjected to public scrutiny, the result has been embarrassment to the US, which publicly promotes democracy and self-determination abroad. While the NID may not be as closely associated with such operations as DCIs

[287] Waterman, "Congress already tweaking new intel post," n.p.

[288] Ibid.

[289] Kaplan, "Intelligence Reform at – Last," n.p.

[290] David Morgan, "Negroponte takes intelligence reins," *Arizona Daily Star, (*18 February 2005): n.p. On-line Internet. Available from http://www.azstarnet.com/dailystar/relatedarticles/61981.php.

[291] Fred Kaplan, "What NID Needs, Bush's bold choice for national intelligence director?," *Slate,* (17 February 2005): n.p. On-line Internet. Available from http://slate.msn.com/id/2113705.

[292] Walter Pincus, "President Gets to Fill Ranks of New Intelligence Superstructure," *Washingtonpost.com,* (16 December 2004): A35.

DURING THE COLD WAR, AS HEAD OF THE IC, THE DIRECTOR IS STILL LIKELY TO BE TAINTED BY FAILURES ANYWHERE WITHIN THE COMMUNITY. GIVEN THE APPARENT READINESS OF THE NATION TO CONTINUE SUCH OPERATIONS, IT IS LIKELY THAT EVENTUALLY ONE OR MORE WILL FAIL TO REMAIN SECRET, THUS BRINGING SCRUTINY ON THE IC AND THE NID, HURTING THE LATTER'S STATURE AND THEREBY THE ABILITY TO LEAD.

DURING THE 1990S, AFTER THE FALL OF THE SOVIET UNION, MELVIN GOODMAN MADE A STRONG CASE THAT THE US GOVERNMENT SHOULD REDUCE OR ELIMINATE COVERT OPERATIONS, AS THEY WERE BOTH INEFFECTIVE AND IMMORAL: "COVERT ACTION RARELY HAVE BEEN BENEFICIAL AND EVEN SHORT-TERM SUCCESSES – SUCH AS IRAN AND GUATEMALA IN THE 1950S AND AFGHANISTAN IN THE 1980S – HAVE BECOME LONG-TERM FAILURES… THE USE OF COVERT ACTION IS PARTICULARLY QUESTIONABLE, BOTH MORALLY AND POLITICALLY… MOST OF THESE ACTIONS RAISE MORAL AND HUMANITARIAN QUESTIONS THAT TARNISH THE QUEST FOR INTERNATIONAL STABILITY."[293] WHILE HIS ARGUMENTS REMAIN VALID, IT DOES NOT FIND AS ACCEPTING AN AUDIENCE SINCE THE THREAT OF INTERNATIONAL TERRORISM CAME TO THE FORE. THE WINDOW FOR REDUCING USE OF COVERT ACTIONS CLOSED ON 9/11, AND IF ANYTHING, THE US WILL SEE BOTH INCREASED ACCEPTANCE AND USE OF SUCH MEASURES IN THE FUTURE.

THE 9/11 JOINT INQUIRY RECOMMENDED THE DNI DEVELOP A STRATEGY FOR DEALING WITH TERRORISM, WHICH AMONG OTHER THINGS WOULD "MAXIMIZE THE EFFECTIVE USE OF COVERT ACTION IN COUNTERTERRORIST EFFORTS" AND "FACILITATE THE ABILITY OF CIA PARAMILITARY UNITS AND MILITARY SPECIAL OPERATIONS FORCES TO CONDUCT JOINT OPERATIONS AGAINST TERRORIST TARGETS."[294] THE 9/11 COMMISSION SEEMED TO RECOGNIZED THE INHERENT DANGERS OF SUCH OPERATIONS, NOTING THAT "ALTHOUGH COVERT ACTIONS REPRESENT A VERY SMALL FRACTION OF THE AGENCY'S ENTIRE BUDGET, THESE OPERATIONS HAVE AT TIMES BEEN CONTROVERSIAL AND OVER TIME HAVE DOMINATED THE PUBLIC'S PERCEPTION OF THE CIA."[295] YET THE COMMISSION LAMENTED THE DECLINE OF CIA COVERT OPERATIONS, IMPLYING THAT CIA LEADERS WERE OVERLY CAUTIOUS DURING THE 1990S WHEN THEY EXERCISED MORE PRUDENCE AND CONCERN FOR LEGALITY THAN POLICYMAKERS WHO URGED A MORE AGGRESSIVE COVERT AGENDA.[296] THE COMMISSION EVEN CLAIMED THAT PART OF THE CIA'S DIFFICULTY IN TACKLING TERRORISM TODAY COMES FROM HAVING ALLOWED ITS CAPACITY FOR COVERT ACTION TO ATROPHY.[297]

THE NATIONAL INTELLIGENCE REFORM BILL OF 2004, IN DESCRIBING THE RESPONSIBILITIES OF THE CIA, RETAINED THE AMBIGUOUS PHRASE "PERFORM SUCH OTHER FUNCTIONS AND DUTIES RELATED TO INTELLIGENCE AFFECTING THE NATIONAL SECURITY AS THE PRESIDENT OR THE NATIONAL

---

[293] MELVIN A. GOODMAN "THE ROAD TO INTELLIGENCE REFORM: PAVED WITH GOOD INTENTIONS," (1996), N.P. ON-
LINE INTERNET. AVAILABLE FROM HTTP://WWW.US.NET/CIP/DIGEST.HTM.
[294] *Joint Inquiry into the terrorist attacks,* 5.
[295] *The 9/11 Commission Report,* 86.
[296] Ibid., 90.
[297] Ibid., 93.

INTELLIGENCE DIRECTOR MAY DIRECT," THAT WAS USED TO AUTHORIZE COVERT OPERATIONS DURING THE COLD WAR.[298] ELSEWHERE, THE BILL IS MUCH MORE DIRECT, STATING: "LONG-TERM SUCCESS IN THE WAR ON TERRORISM DEMANDS THE USE OF ALL ELEMENTS OF NATIONAL POWER, INCLUDING DIPLOMACY, MILITARY ACTION, INTELLIGENCE, COVERT ACTION, LAW ENFORCEMENT, ECONOMIC POLICY, FOREIGN AID, PUBLIC DIPLOMACY, AND HOMELAND DEFENSE."[299] JEFFERY H. SMITH, A FORMER CIA GENERAL COUNSEL, AND JOHN DEUTCH, FORMER DCI, SEE A POWERFUL ROLE FOR COVERT OPERATIONS IN THE CURRENT WAR ON TERROR. THEY RECOMMEND STREAMLINING THE CIA'S AUTHORIZATION PROCESS, WHICH CURRENTLY REQUIRES A PRESIDENTIAL FINDING AND A REPORT TO CONGRESS, MAKING IT EASIER FOR THE CIA TO PARTICIPATE IN JOINT OPERATIONS WITH THE MILITARY, WHICH HAS NO APPROVAL AND REPORTING REQUIREMENTS.[300]

WHILE THE 9/11 COMMISSION ENCOURAGED A RENEWED EMPHASIS IN COVERT ACTIONS WITHIN THE IC, THE NID WILL NOT DIRECTLY HEAD WHATEVER AGENCY IS RESPONSIBLE FOR CONDUCTING THEM. NEITHER, HOWEVER, WILL THE NID BE A PASSIVE OBSERVER WITH PLAUSIBLE DENIABILITY. THE COMMISSION NOTES: "COVERT OPERATIONS TEND TO BE HIGHLY TACTICAL, REQUIRING CLOSE ATTENTION. THE NATIONAL INTELLIGENCE DIRECTOR SHOULD RELY ON THE RELEVANT JOINT MISSION CENTER TO OVERSEE THESE DETAILS, HELPING TO COORDINATE CLOSELY WITH THE WHITE HOUSE."[301] WITH RESPONSIBILITY FOR THE ENTIRE INTELLIGENCE COMMUNITY, COMES ACCOUNTABILITY FOR ANY FAILURE OR POLITICAL EMBARRASSMENT CAUSED BY ANY MEMBER OF THE COMMUNITY. WHILE SUCCESSES ARE NOT LIKELY TO RECEIVE WIDE COVERAGE, FAILURES FREQUENTLY RECEIVE A GREAT DEAL OF MEDIA ATTENTION. WHILE COVERT OPERATIONS HAVE THE POTENTIAL TO BE VITAL IN THE WAR ON TERROR, THEY ALSO HAVE THE POTENTIAL TO CREATE SPECTACULARLY PUBLIC FAILURES. SUCH FAILURES GIVE OPPONENTS OF THE IC, OR THE CURRENT ADMINISTRATION'S POLICIES, AN OPPORTUNITY TO PAINT THE IC IN GENERAL AND THE NID IN PARTICULAR AS A ROGUE ELEPHANT, AS WELL AS AMMUNITION FOR THOSE WHO WOULD LESSEN THE NID'S POWERS.

FACTOR 4: PROLIFERATION OF INTELLIGENCE AGENCIES AND ACTIVITIES

ALONG WITH COVERT OPERATIONS, ANOTHER INTELLIGENCE TRADITION PROMISES TO CONTINUE IN THE NEW MILLENNIUM: THE TENDENCY OF AGENCIES AND ORGANIZATIONS TO PROLIFERATE, MAKING THE IC INCREASINGLY COMPLEX AND DIFFICULT TO CONTROL. IN ADDITION TO ALL OF THE BUREAUCRATIC STAFFING THAT COMES WITH THE CREATION OF A NEW NATIONAL INTELLIGENCE AUTHORITY AND NATIONAL INTELLIGENCE DIRECTOR, THE 2004 LAW INVITES THE UNLIMITED CREATION OF NATIONAL INTELLIGENCE CENTERS THAT POTENTIALLY ANSWER TO BOTH A DEPARTMENT AND THE NID, BUT RETAIN A SPECIFIC INDIVIDUAL MISSION. THE MILITARY IS ALREADY CREATING NEW INTELLIGENCE

---

[298] *National Intelligence Reform Act of 2004*, 229.
[299] Ibid., 316.
[300] Jeffrey H. Smith and John Deutch, "Smarter Intelligence," *Foreign Policy,* (January/February 2002): 64-69.
[301] *The 9/11 Commission Report*, 415.

ORGANIZATIONS AND POSITIONS THAT PROMISE TO COMPLICATE THE NID'S AUTHORITY OVER NATIONAL INTELLIGENCE ASSETS WITHIN THE DOD. THE AUTHORS OF THE 9/11 COMMISSION AND THE 2004 INTELLIGENCE REFORM ACT HOPED TO MITIGATE THE CONFUSION CAUSED BY THE INCREASINGLY COMPLEX COMMUNITY BY PROMOTING AN ENVIRONMENT OF JOINTNESS AND FREE INFORMATION FLOW. SUCH AN APPROACH ATTEMPTS TO ADDRESS THE SYMPTOM, BUT DOES NOT ATTEND TO THE UNDERLYING PROBLEM: THE COMMUNITY IS TOO LARGE AND DIVERSE, AND IT IS GROWING.

NOT EVERYONE BELIEVES THAT CREATING A NID IS A STEP IN THE RIGHT DIRECTION FOR STREAMLINING THE IC. FORMER DCI STANSFIELD TURNER APPROVES OF SEPARATING A CENTRAL DIRECTOR OF THE COMMUNITY FROM THE CIA, BUT IS CRITICAL OF THE CURRENT BILL'S FORMULA: "THE RECOMMENDED POSITION OF NATIONAL INTELLIGENCE DIRECTOR (NDI) [SIC] ALREADY EXISTS. IT IS THE DIRECTOR OF CENTRAL INTELLIGENCE (DCI) CREATED BY THE NATIONAL SECURITY ACT OF 1947, WITH RESPONSIBILITY FOR COORDINATING THE NATION'S 15 INTELLIGENCE AGENCIES. THE DCI TODAY HAS A STAFF JUST FOR THIS COORDINATING FUNCTION. WE DON'T NEED A NEW LAYER OF BUREAUCRACY. WHAT WE DO NEED IS A REVIEW OF WHAT AUTHORITY A COORDINATOR OF INTELLIGENCE SHOULD HAVE, WHETHER WE CALL HIM OR HER AN NID OR A DCI."[302] JUDGE RICHARD POSNER, A NEW YORK TIMES OP-ED CONTRIBUTOR, ECHOES TURNER'S SENTIMENTS. CLAIMING THAT "SLOTTING IN A NEW BUREAUCRACY (THE DIRECTOR IS AUTHORIZED A STAFF OF 500) ABOVE THE EXISTING AGENCIES WILL NOT INCREASE INFORMATION SHARING. INSTEAD, BY ADDING A LAYER TO THE INTELLIGENCE HIERARCHY, IT WILL DELAY AND DIMINISH THE FLOW OF INFORMATION TO THE PRESIDENT."[303]

NOT ONLY DID THE BILL CREATE A NEW NID, RATHER THAN PLACING THE POSITION IN THE EXECUTIVE OFFICE, AS THE 9/11 COMMISSION RECOMMENDED, THE BILL ESTABLISHED THE NATIONAL INTELLIGENCE AUTHORITY (NIA)—AN "INDEPENDENT ESTABLISHMENT IN THE EXECUTIVE BRANCH OF THE GOVERNMENT," TO HOUSE THE NID.[304] THE NIA SERVES MUCH THE SAME OVERSIGHT FUNCTION AS THE NSC, WHICH CONTINUES TO EXIST AND UNDOUBTEDLY RETAINS AN INTEREST IN INTELLIGENCE FUNCTIONS. JUST AS THE DCI HAD MANY COMMITTEES ESTABLISHED TO ASSIST IN COMMUNITY DUTIES, THE LAW THAT ESTABLISHED THE NID ALSO CREATED A JOINT INTELLIGENCE COMMUNITY COUNCIL (JICC, CONSISTING OF THE NID AND THE SECRETARIES OF STATE, TREASURY, DEFENSE, ENERGY, HOMELAND DEFENSE, THE ATTORNEY GENERAL, AND, OTHERS AS THE PRESIDENT MAY DESIGNATE). THUS, ALL OF THE DCI'S TRADITIONAL RIVALS WILL HAVE A SPECIFIED FORUM IN WHICH TO "ASSIST THE NATIONAL INTELLIGENCE DIRECTOR TO IN [SIC] DEVELOPING AND IMPLEMENTING A JOINT, UNIFIED NATIONAL INTELLIGENCE EFFORT TO PROTECT NATIONAL SECURITY."[305] IF OVER FIFTY YEARS OF EFFORT HAVE FAILED TO MAKE THE NSC, DCI, AND INTELLIGENCE COMMUNITY STAFF PRODUCE SATISFACTORY RESULTS, IT IS UNLIKELY THAT ADDING AN NIA, NID, AND JICC WILL IMPROVE THE RESULT. IN ALL LIKELIHOOD, THESE NEW ADDITIONS WILL FURTHER COMPLICATE ANDENTANGLE THE CHAIN OF COMMAND.

---

[302] Stansfield Turner, "Restructuring," *Washington Post*, (1 August 2004): B01.
[303] Posner, "Important Job, Impossible Position," n.p.
[304] *National Intelligence Reform Act of 2004*, 12.
[305] Ibid., 151.

Although the 9/11 Commission recognized that, "[o]ver the decades, the agencies and the rules surrounding the intelligence community have accumulated to a depth that practically defies public comprehension," rather than eliminating some of the depth, the Commission proposed a "new institution: a civilian led unified joint command for counterterrorism."[306] The 9/11 Commission established this institution as the National Counterterrorism Center (NCTC), directly under the control of the NIA.[307] The NCTC consists of two parts, the Directorate of Planning and the Directorate of Intelligence, the latter of which absorbs the TTIC, but none of the other intelligence community counter-terrorism organizations.[308] Once again, the bill, which states the Intelligence "Directorate shall have primary responsibility within the United States Government for analysis of terrorism and terrorist organizations from all sources of intelligence," seeks to establish unified control over a narrow portion of the IC by creating a new body directly responsible for it. [309]

The NCTC is just the latest in a string a fusion centers designed to address terrorism. The Terrorist Threat Integration Center (TTIC) itself was established in 2003 within the Department of Homeland Security to serve as "an all-source terrorism information fusion center that will dramatically improve the focus and quality of counter terrorism analysis and facilitate the timely dissemination of relevant intelligence information."[310] While this sounds like a laudable goal, it is nearly identical to the mission of the CIA's Counter Terrorism Center (CTC), created in 1986 and still in existence. By the fall of 2004, one observer concluded, "that, in spite of the efforts to centralize counterterrorist intelligence activities, approximately 45 separate governmental units and subunits are [still] responsible for handling the different dimensions of the terrorist threat."[311] So far, creation of such organizations has failed to bring about the desired results, instead serving to dilute the government's emphasis on counterterrorism. A recent investigation of the TTIC by a White House commission studying intelligence found:

> Though they sat side by side, agents and analysts from the different
> agencies were still playing by the old rules: trust our own, and be wary of

[306] *The 9/11 Commission Report*, 403, 410.
[307] Ibid.
[308] *National Intelligence Reform Act of 2004*, 95.
[309] Ibid., 96.
[310] Joseph Lieberman, Lieberman, Joseph, "Governmental Affairs Committee Hearing on the President's
    Proposal for a Terrorism Threat Integration Center." Statement to the Senate Governmental Affairs
    Committee, 14 February 2003, On-line Internet. Available from
    http://www.fas.org/irp/congress/2003_hr/.
[311] Taylor Stan A. and David Goldman, "Intelligence Reform: Will More Agencies, Money, and Personnel
    Help?" *Intelligence and National Security.* 19, No.3 (Autumn 2004): 419.

THE OTHER GUY. THE COMMISSIONERS FOUND THAT THERE WERE NO LESS THAN NINE LEVELS OF CLASSIFIED INFORMATION STORED IN THE CENTER'S COMPUTERS. ANALYSTS FROM DIFFERENT AGENCIES HAD DIFFERENT SECURITY CLEARANCES, MAKING IT DIFFICULT FOR THEM TO TALK TO ONE ANOTHER. THE AGENT FROM HOMELAND SECURITY WAS ESPECIALLY IRRITATED BY THE ARRANGEMENT. WHEN SENSITIVE INFORMATION CAME IN TO THE OFFICE, HE COMPLAINED TO THE COMMISSIONERS, THE CIA AND FBI AGENTS SITTING NEXT TO HIM WOULD GO OFF INTO A PRIVATE, SECURE ROOM AND LOOK AT THE MATERIAL ON SEPARATE COMPUTERS.[312]

THE CREATION OF THE NCTC IS NO MORE LIKELY TO FIX THIS PROBLEM THAN THE CREATION OF THE CTC AND TTIC WERE. SUCH CENTERS WILL ONLY BE EFFECTIVE WHEN THEY LEARN TO COLLABORATE EFFICIENTLY AND SHARE INFORMATION. BREAKING DOWN STRUCTURAL AND CULTURAL BARRIERS TO INTELLIGENCE SHARING IS A CENTRAL THEME OF 2004'S INTELLIGENCE REFORM BILL; BUT SUBDIVIDING THE COMMUNITY INTO SMALLER FIEFDOMS, WITH MORE LAYERS OF MANAGEMENT, ONLY COMPLICATES THAT PROCESS.

THE NTCT, ALTHOUGH GIVEN RESPONSIBILITY TO BE THE NATION'S FOCAL POINT FOR ANALYSIS OF TERRORISM AND TERRORIST ORGANIZATIONS FROM ALL SOURCES OF INTELLIGENCE, DOES NOT HAVE THE AUTHORITY IT NEEDS TO CARRY OUT THIS TASK. IT CAN ONLY "PROPOSE INTELLIGENCE COLLECTION AND ANALYTIC REQUIREMENTS FOR ACTION BY ELEMENTS OF THE INTELLIGENCE COMMUNITY" AND "IMPLEMENT POLICIES AND PROCEDURES TO ENCOURAGE COORDINATION BY ALL ELEMENTS OF THE INTELLIGENCE COMMUNITY."[313] ESSENTIALLY, IT IS RELYING ON THE GOODWILL AND COOPERATIVE SPIRIT OF OTHER AGENCIES—THE DIRECTORATE OF PLANNING, HOWEVER, "ASSIGNS RESPONSIBILITIES FOR COUNTERTERRORISM OPERATIONS TO THE DEPARTMENTS AND AGENCIES OF THE UNITED STATES GOVERNMENT INCLUDING THE DOD, CIA, FBI, AND DHS."[314]

THE NCTC IS JUST THE FIRST OF MANY NARROWLY FOCUSED NATIONAL INTELLIGENCE CENTERS (NICS) ENVISIONED BY THE LAW. ANOTHER IS MANDATED IN THE BILL: "WITHIN ONE YEAR OF ENACTMENT OF THIS ACT THERE SHALL BE ESTABLISHED WITHIN THE NATIONAL INTELLIGENCE AUTHORITY A NATIONAL COUNTERPROLIFERATION CENTER."[315] SIMILAR TO THE UNIFIED COMBATANT COMMANDS OF THE MILITARY, NICS WILL "BE ASSIGNED AN AREA OF INTELLIGENCE RESPONSIBILITY, WHETHER EXPRESSED IN TERMS OF GEOGRAPHIC REGION, IN TERMS OF FUNCTION, OR IN OTHER TERMS."[316] POTENTIAL FOR THE PROLIFERATION OF NICS IS VERY HIGH, AS THE BILL FURTHER PROPOSES CENTERS FOCUSED ON NUCLEAR TERRORISM, CHEMICAL TERRORISM, AND BIOLOGICAL TERRORISM, ALL MORE NARROW AND FOCUSED SUBDIVISIONS OF THE NCTC.[317] IN ADDITION, THE AUTHORS OF THE 9/11 COMMISSION ENVISIONED NICS DEALING WITH CRIME AND NARCOTICS OR

---

[312] MICHAEL ISIKOFF AND DANIEL KLAIDMAN, "LOOK WHO'S NOT TALKING – STILL," *NEWSWEEK*, (4 APRIL, 2005):

N.P. ON-LINE INTERNET. AVAILABLE FROM HTTP://MSNBC.MSN.COM/ID/7306163/SITE/NEWSWEEK.

[313] *National Intelligence Reform Act of 2004*, 96-97.

[314] Ibid., 97.

[315] Ibid., 104.

[316] Ibid., 120.

[317] Ibid.

CHINA.[318] DEPENDING ON WHAT THREAT CAPTURES THE PUBLIC'S ATTENTION IN FUTURE YEARS, NICS COULD EMERGE WITH RESPONSIBILITY FOR EVERYTHING FROM ENVIRONMENTAL TO ECONOMIC INTELLIGENCE. WHEREAS THE CIA USED TO HOUSE ANALYTIC TEAMS IN ONE AGENCY WHERE THEY COULD EASILY INTERACT WITH EACH OTHER, THE CURRENT SYSTEM ALLOWS THE NICS TO BE SCATTERED THROUGHOUT THE COMMUNITY WITHIN VARIOUS DEPARTMENTS, ISOLATING THEM FROM OTHER NICS DEALING IN RELATED SUBJECTS.[319]

ONCE CREATED, THESE CENTERS WILL BE DIFFICULT TO DISBAND. ALTHOUGH THE PERSONNEL STAFFING THE NICS ARE PROVIDED BY THE VARIOUS AGENCIES, JUST AS THE MILITARY SERVICES PROVIDE BODIES TO THE COMBATANT COMMAND, IT WILL BE MUCH HARDER TO RECALL AND REASSIGN A MEMBER OF A NIC THAN IT PREVIOUSLY WAS FOR A MANAGER IN THE CIA, DIA, OR THE STATE DEPARTMENT'S BUREAU OF INTELLIGENCE AND RESEARCH (INR) TO MOVE ANALYSTS BETWEEN TEAMS. AS THE NICS DEVELOP A PERMANENT STAFF OF EXPERTS AND THEIR OWN CUSTOMER BASES, THEY ARE LIKELY TO DEVELOP AN INSTITUTIONAL WILL TO SURVIVE.[320] ALTHOUGH THE INTELLIGENCE REFORM ACT DOES PROVIDE FOR TERMINATING A NIC IF IT IS NO LONGER MEETING ESTABLISHED INTELLIGENCE PRIORITIES, IT ALSO ALLOWS THE NID THE MUCH MORE PALATABLE OPTION OF RECOMMENDING "TO THE PRESIDENT A MODIFICATION OF THE AREA OF INTELLIGENCE RESPONSIBILITY ASSIGNED TO A NATIONAL INTELLIGENCE CENTER."[321] THUS, IT SEEMS THAT LIKE MOST BUREAUCRATIC ENTITIES, THESE NICS, ONCE CREATED, ARE LIKELY TO CONTINUE INDEFINITELY, ASSUMING NEW MISSIONS TO ENSURE THEIR SURVIVAL.[322]

A FINAL AREA WHERE PROLIFERATION OF THE INTELLIGENCE COMMUNITY IS CURRENTLY VISIBLE IS THE DOD'S PROPOSED INTCOM (INTELLIGENCE COMMAND) FUNCTIONAL UNIFIED COMMAND. A RECENT ARTICLE IN THE ARMY TIMES NOTES THAT SUCH A NEW ORGANIZATION "WON'T PUT A SINGLE SATELLITE IN ORBIT. IT WON'T PUT A SINGLE SPY ON THE GROUND. WORST OF ALL IT WON'T PRODUCE ANY NEW INTELLIGENCE[323] WHAT IT WILL DO, THE ARTICLE CONTENDS, IS "ADD A GENERAL OFFICER TO THE PENTAGON'S ALREADY SWOLLEN BEVY OF BRASS AND CREATE YET ANOTHER BUREAUCRACY."[324] SENATOR CHAMBLISS, IN AN ADDRESS TO THE HERITAGE FOUNDATION IN WHICH HE DISCUSSED HIS INTENTION TO REINTRODUCE LEGISLATION TO CREATE A MILITARY INTELLIGENCE COMMAND, STATED: "THE DNI'S TASK WILL BE FAR EASIER TO ACCOMPLISH IF THERE IS AN INTCOM COMMANDER TO COORDINATE THE DISPARATE EIGHT DEPARTMENT OF DEFENSE MEMBERS INTO ONE, THUS REDUCING

---

[318] *The 9/11 Commission Report,* 411.
[319] *National Intelligence Reform Act of 2004*, 120-121.
[320] Gareth Morgan, *Images of Organization* (Thousand Oaks, California: Sage Publications, 1997), 67.
[321] *National Intelligence Reform Act of 2004*, 128.
[322] Morgan, *Images of Organization, 67.*
[323] ROBERT F. DORR, "A BIGGER INTELLIGENCE BUREAUCRACY DOESN'T EQUAL BETTER INTELLIGENCE." *ARMY TIMES,* (31
   JANUARY 2005): 46.
[324] Ibid.

THE TOTAL NUMBER OF INTELLIGENCE COMMUNITY MEMBERS FORM FIFTEEN TO EIGHT."[325] GIVEN THE HISTORY OF SUCH ORGANIZATIONS, HOWEVER, THE EFFECT IS MORE LIKELY TO BE AN INCREASE IN THE NUMBER OF AGENCIES FROM 15 TO 16. CREATION OF A FOUR STAR INTCOM WILL NOT ELIMINATE ANY OF THE EXISTING AGENCIES IN THE DoD, BUT THE NEW ORGANIZATION, JUST AS THE DIA BEFORE IT, WILL FIND A MISSION AND CUSTOMER BASE FOR ITSELF.

THE NATIONAL INTELLIGENCE REFORM ACT OF 2004 HAS AN AGGRESSIVE AGENDA TO BUILD A CULTURE OF JOINTNESS IN THE INTELLIGENCE COMMUNITY, AND TO STANDARDIZE OR STREAMLINE CLASSIFICATION SYSTEMS, SECURITY CLEARANCES, COMMUNICATION NETWORKS, AND OTHER STRUCTURAL OR TECHNICAL BARRIERS TO SHARING INFORMATION. IF IT IS SUCCESSFUL, THEN A DIFFUSE COMMUNITY OF NICs ACTIVELY NETWORKING MAY IMPROVE THE PRODUCT OF THE COMMUNITY. ESTABLISHING SUCH A CULTURE AND COMMON STANDARDS, HOWEVER, REQUIRES STRONG CENTRAL LEADERSHIP. THE LIMITED AUTHORITY GRANTED THE NID, ALONG WITH THE NEW LAYERS OF BUREAUCRACY CREATED BY THE LAW, MAKES THE CAPACITY TO ESTABLISH THESE STANDARDS QUESTIONABLE. THE CONTINUED DIVISION OF THE COMMUNITY INTO MORE AND MORE ENTITIES BEFORE ESTABLISHING SUCH STANDARDS ONLY COMPLICATES THE NID'S JOB. HENCE THE PARADOX OF THE INTELLIGENCE COMMUNITY: A DECENTRALIZED NON-HIERARCHICAL NETWORKING COMMUNITY MAY BE THE LONG-TERM GOAL, BUT A STRONG CENTRAL POWER IS REQUIRED TO ACHIEVE IT. BY SEEKING TO ESTABLISH THE GOAL BEFORE ESTABLISHING THE PREREQUISITE MEANS, THE US RISKS MAKING THE GOAL UNATTAINABLE.

FACTOR 5: THE MILITARIZATION OF INTELLIGENCE

ANOTHER CONTINUING TREND THAT LIMITS THE NID'S ABILITY TO EXERCISE CONTROL OVER THE INTELLIGENCE COMMUNITY IS THE GROWING DEGREE OF CONTROL THE MILITARY WIELDS. HAVING SECURED OWNERSHIP OF THE THREE NATIONAL TECHNICAL COLLECTION AGENCIES DURING THE 1990s, THE DoD CONTINUES TO ASSERT ITS PRIORITY FOR THEIR SERVICES. WITH ONGOING MILITARY OPERATIONS IN THE MIDDLE EAST, THE MILITARY IN ADDITION CONTINUES TO DEMAND ANALYTICAL SUPPORT FROM NON-MILITARY AGENCIES. IN A RECENT MOVE, THE PENTAGON APPEARS TO BE SEEKING A LARGER SHARE OF A COLLECTION MISSION PREVIOUSLY THE DOMAIN OF THE CIA—HUMAN INTELLIGENCE. WITH THE MILITARY OWNING SO MUCH OF THE IC AND DEMANDING EVEN MORE, NEGROPONTE WILL HAVE A DIFFICULT JOB COORDINATING ALL ELEMENTS OF THE IC TO MEET HIS PRIMARY RESPONSIBILITY OF

---

[325] CHAMBLISS, SAXBY. "INTELLIGENCE REFORM AND THE SAFETY OF AMERICA: HAVE WE SUCCEEDED?" *THE HERITAGE FOUNDATION*, WEBMEMO#633, 7 JANUARY 2005. N.P. ON-LINE INTERNET, AVAILABLE FROM WWW.HERITAGE.ORG/RESEARCH/HOMELANDDEFENSE/WM633.CFM.

PROVIDING THE BEST POSSIBLE "NATIONAL INTELLIGENCE TO THE PRESIDENT [AND] TO THE HEADS OF OTHER DEPARTMENTS AND AGENCIES OF THE EXECUTIVE BRANCH."[326]

FORMER DCI JOHN DEUTCH DECLARED: "POST-SEPT. 11 THERE IS AN URGENCY TO HARMONIZE INTELLIGENCE PRIORITIES, PARTICULARLY AS EFFORTS THAT SUPPORT HOMELAND SECURITY AND LAW ENFORCEMENT COMPETE WITH MILITARY USERS FOR SCARCE INTELLIGENCE ASSETS."[327] YET THE MILITARY IS UNRELENTING IN ITS DEMANDS ON THE FIRST PRODUCTS OF THE COMMUNITY. IN RESISTING THE PASSAGE OF THE INTELLIGENCE REFORM ACT OF 2004, THE PENTAGON ARGUED THAT GIVING UP SOME OF ITS BUDGET CONTROL TO A CENTRAL DIRECTOR OF INTELLIGENCE WOULD ALLOW THE NID TO "AFFECT WHICH TECHNOLOGIES GET DEVELOPED OVER THE COMING YEARS, POSSIBLY AT THE EXPENSE OF COMBAT TROOPS, WHO NEED THE FASTEST AND MOST TECHNOLOGICALLY ADVANCED SATELLITE RECONNAISSANCE HELP THEY CAN GET."[328] WHILE IT IS PROPER FOR A SECRETARY OF DEFENSE TO ADVOCATE GETTING THE BEST POSSIBLE EQUIPMENT AND SUPPORT FOR TROOPS, RECOGNIZING AND SUBMITTING TO CIVILIAN AUTHORITY IS A HALLMARK OF THE US MILITARY SYSTEM. YET IN THE INTELLIGENCE ARENA, THE MILITARY SEEMS WILLING TO DEFY EXTERNAL CONTROL.

IF THE MILITARY HAD ITS WAY, THE NSA, NGA, AND NRO WOULD ALL HAVE THE "NATIONAL" IN THEIR TITLE REPLACED WITH "MILITARY," TO CEMENT ITS OWNERSHIP OF THESE VALUABLE ASSETS. IN 2002, A PANEL LED BY NATIONAL SECURITY ADVISER BRENT SCOWCROFT RELEASED A STUDY ON INTELLIGENCE REFORM. THE REPORT RECOMMENDED THAT THE NSA, NIMA (NOW NGA), AND NRO BE PUT UNDER THE CONTROL OF THE DCI. WHEN RUMORS OF THE COMMISSIONS FINDINGS LEAKED IN DECEMBER OF 2001, RUMSFELD LET IT BE KNOWN "THAT HE WAS NOT ABOUT TO LET THE DCI TAKE AWAY THE PENTAGON'S INTELLIGENCE COLLECTION AGENCIES."[329] TO BETTER SECURE THE AGENCIES TO THE MILITARY, RUMSFELD, WITH THE SUPPORT OF CONGRESS, CREATED THE POSITION OF UNDERSECRETARY OF DEFENSE FOR INTELLIGENCE, WHICH DR STEPHEN CAMBONE FILLED IN MARCH OF 2003.[330] "THE OFFICE'S MANDATE WAS DRAWN BROADLY, GIVING CAMBONE DIRECT CONTROL OVER THE DEFENSE INTELLIGENCE AGENCY AND NATIONAL SECURITY AGENCY AS WELL AS THE NATIONAL RECONNAISSANCE OFFICE AND THE NATIONAL IMAGERY AND MAPPING AGENCY."[331] SINCE THESE

---

[326] *National Intelligence Reform Act of 2004*, 16.

[327] John Deutch, "The Smart Approach to Intelligence," *Washington Post,* (9 September 2002): pA17.

[328] John Diamond, "Intelligence Impasse mainly a question of control," *USA Today,* (29 November 2004): 6A.

[329] ARTHUR S. HULNICK. "DOES THE U.S. INTELLIGENCE COMMUNITY NEED A DNI?" *INTERNATIONAL Journal of Intelligence and Counterintelligence* 17, no. 4 (Winter 2004-2005): 718.

[330] GLEN W. GOODMAN, "INTELLIGENCE ON DEMAND: AN INTERVIEW WITH STEPHEN CAMBONE, UNDERSECRETARY OF DEFENSE FOR INTELLIGENCE," *THE ISR JOURNAL,* (3 DEC 2003): N.P. ON-LINE INTERNET. AVAILABLE FROM HTTP://WWW.DEFENSELINK.MIL/USDI/CAMBONEINTERVIEW.HTML.

[331] ROBERT SCHLESINGER, "EXPANDING ROLE OF DEFENSE DEPARTMENT SPURS CONCERNS," *VETERANS FOR PEACE,* (6 AUGUST 2003): N.P. ON-LINE INTERNET. AVAILABLE FROM WWW.VETERANSFORPEACE.ORG/EXPANDING_ROLE_060803.HTM.

AGENCIES ANSWER TO BOTH THE SECRETARY OF DEFENSE AND TO THE DCI, IT IS NOT CLEAR IF THE EXPLICIT AUTHORITY GIVEN CAMBONE WAS TRULY RUMSFELD'S TO GIVE. "JAY FARRAR, A FORMER EMPLOYEE IN THE DEFENSE DEPARTMENT AND NATIONAL SECURITY COUNCIL ... SAID CAMBONE'S BROAD AUTHORITY IS NOT A COINCIDENCE. 'IT'S ONE MORE STEP IN THE DEFENSE DEPARTMENT SEEKING TO CONSOLIDATE MAJOR CONTROL OVER THE INTELLIGENCE APPARATUS OF THE UNITED STATES." [332]

FORMER DCI DEUTCH, WROTE IN THE WASHINGTON POST "RUMSFELD'S PROPOSED CREATION OF A NEW UNDERSECRETARY OF DEFENSE FOR INTELLIGENCE WOULD ALSO FURTHER DISTORT THE ALREADY UNEQUAL BALANCE OF AUTHORITY BETWEEN THE DCI AND THE DEFENSE SECRETARY OVER THESE NATIONAL INTELLIGENCE AGENCIES."[333] TO DEUTCH, THE PROPOSED UNDERSECRETARY "WOULD BE IN AN IDEAL POSITION TO SET BUDGET PRIORITIES AND SAY NO TO ANY PROPOSAL PUT FORWARD BY THE DCI."[334] OTHERS SEE THE CURRENT MOVE BY THE PENTAGON TO CREATE A FOUR STAR INTELLIGENCE COMMAND AS ANOTHER MOVE TO CONSOLIDATE ITS POWER. A RECENT ARTICLE IN *ARMYTIMES* CLAIMS, "BY CREATING A FOUR-STAR INTELLIGENCE CHIEF UNDER THE NID, THE PENTAGON HOPES TO DILUTE THE POWER OF THE NID AND RETAIN CONTROL OVER ITS ASSETS."[335]

WHILE CEMENTING ITS DOMINANCE OF SUPPOSEDLY NATIONAL INTELLIGENCE ASSETS HOUSED WITHIN THE DOD, THE MILITARY CONTINUES ITS CAMPAIGN TO BE THE DOMINANT CUSTOMER FOR NATIONAL INTELLIGENCE ORGANIZATIONS OUTSIDE OF THE DEPARTMENT. ALTHOUGH "CLINTON ADMINISTRATION OFFICIALS DURING THE TRANSITION" TO BUSH'S ADMINISTRATION, NOTED THAT THE INTELLIGENCE "PRIORITY–SETTING PROCESS [PDD-35]... WAS NOT EFFECTIVE FOR COMMUNICATING CHANGING PRIORITIES OVER TIME," IT REMAINED THE GUIDING DOCUMENT OF THE COMMUNITY ON 9/11.[336] PDD-35 LISTED COUNTERTERRORISM AS ONE OF SEVERAL *DE JURE* TOP PRIORITIES FOR THE COMMUNITY, BUT THE STRESS ON SUPPORT TO MILITARY OPERATIONS AS THE *DE FACTO* HIGHEST PRIORITY EFFECTIVELY MOVED ALL OTHERS TO A DISTANT SECOND FOR THE THINLY STRETCHED ANALYSIS CENTERS. IN DISCUSSING HIS DIFFICULTIES IN ALLOCATING RESOURCES TO SUPPORT HIS OWN DECLARED INTELLIGENCE WAR AGAINST USAMA BIN LADIN, DCI TENET TESTIFIED: "AS I 'DECLARED WAR' AGAINST AL-QA'IDA IN 1998 – IN THE AFTERMATH OF THE EAST AFRICA EMBASSY BOMBINGS – WE WERE IN OUR FIFTH YEAR OF ROUND-THE-CLOCK SUPPORT TO OPERATION SOUTHERN WATCH IN IRAQ... IN EARLY 1999, WE SURGED MORE THAN 800 ANALYSTS AND REDIRECTED COLLECTION ASSETS FROM ACROSS THE INTELLIGENCE COMMUNITY TO SUPPORT THE NATO BOMBING CAMPAIGN AGAINST THE FEDERAL REPUBLIC OF YUGOSLAVIA."[337] WHAT INTELLIGENCE WAS GATHERED AND ANALYZED ON TERRORISM TENDED TO HAVE A MILITARY SLANT. THE JOINT INQUIRY FOUND, "THE INTELLIGENCE COMMUNITY'S FOCUS WAS ALSO FAR MORE ORIENTED TOWARD TACTICAL ANALYSIS OF AL-QA'IDA IN SUPPORT OF

---

[332] Ibid.
[333] Deutch, "The Smart Approach to Intelligence," A17.
[334] Ibid.
[335] Dorr, "A bigger intelligence bureaucracy," 46.
[336] *Joint Inquiry into the terrorist attacks,* 49.
[337] Ibid., 47.

OPERATIONS THAN ON THE STRATEGIC ANALYSIS NEEDED TO DEVELOP A BROADER UNDERSTANDING OF THE THREAT AND THE ORGANIZATION."[338]

ONE RECENT ARTICLE IN STUDIES IN INTELLIGENCE SUGGESTED THAT RECENT EVENTS MAY BE WORKING TO WEAKEN MILITARY CONTROL OF NATIONAL ASSETS: "THE RECOGNITION THAT THERE IS A GENUINE THREAT TO THE HOMELAND FROM OTHER THAN FOREIGN MILITARY FORCES MEANS THAT THERE IS A NEW, POWERFUL DYNAMIC NOW IN PLAY. BEFORE SEPTEMBER 11TH, THE PRIORITY OF SUPPORT TO US FORCES OPERATING IN AFGHANISTAN WOULD HAVE BEEN UNQUESTIONED; AFTERWARD, SECURITY FOR THE OLYMPICS IN SALT LAKE CITY HAD A HIGHER PRIORITY."[339] WHILE HOMELAND SECURITY MAY GIVE AGENCIES OUTSIDE THE DoD A CHANCE TO USE NATIONAL ASSETS, THE PENTAGON IS USING THE WAR ON TERROR AS AN EXCUSE TO TAKE ON A COLLECTION ROLE PREVIOUSLY IN THE DOMAIN OF THE CIA, THE ROLE OF HUMAN INTELLIGENCE.

INDEED, WITH ITS COMMUNITY FUNCTIONS NOW FALLING UNDER THE NIA AND THE OFFICE OF THE NID, AND ITS ANALYSIS RESPONSIBILITIES FARMED OUT TO VARIOUS NICS, THE CIA IS LITTLE MORE THAN A HUMINT COLLECTION AGENCY. UNDER THE 2004 REFORM BILL, THE FIRST RESPONSIBILITY LISTED FOR THE CIA IS TO "COLLECT INTELLIGENCE THROUGH HUMAN SOURCES AND BY OTHER APPROPRIATE MEANS."[340] THE BILL FURTHER STATES THAT THE "CIA WILL SERVE AS THE PRIMARY AGENCY FOR COLLECTING NATIONAL INTELLIGENCE OUTSIDE THE US THROUGH HUMAN SOURCES WITH A RESPONSIBILITY TO PROVIDE OVERALL DIRECTION AND COORDINATION TO ALL OTHER DEPARTMENTS, AGENCIES, OR ELEMENTS WHO ARE AUTHORIZED TO UNDERTAKE SUCH COLLECTION."[341] YET DESPITE THE CIA'S NOMINAL PREEMINENCE IN HUMIT, AN ARTICLE IN THE NATIONAL JOURNAL NOTES THAT WITH THE CIA "REELING FROM THREE AND A HALF YEARS OF REVELATIONS ABOUT ITS FAILURES, THE PENTAGON AND THE FBI HAVE MOVED QUICKLY TO TRY TO SEIZE SOME CIA TURF BY BEEFING UP THEIR OWN SPYING ACTIVITIES."[342]

SHORTLY AFTER THE REFORM BILL PASSED, THE PENTAGON CREATED ITS OWN SPY DIVISION, THE STRATEGIC SUPPORT BRANCH.[343] IN AN ARTICLE IN THE 24-31 JANUARY 2005 ISSUE OF THE NEW YORKER ENTITLED "THE COMING WARS: WHAT THE PENTAGON CAN NOW DO IN SECRET," SEYMOUR HERSH MAKES THE POINT THAT "THE PENTAGON IS INCREASINGLY TAKING OVER SOME OF THE CIA'S FORMER ROLES AND BECOMING THE FACILITATOR OF WHITE HOUSE POLICY AT THE EXPENSE OF THE

---

[338] Ibid., 60.

[339] PAPPAS, ARIS A., AND JAMES M. SIMON, JR. "THE INTELLIGENCE COMMUNITY: 2001-2015," STUDIES IN INTELLIGENCE 46, NO. 1 (2002): 41.

[340] *National Intelligence Reform Bill,* 228.

[341] Ibid., 228-229.

[342] SIOBAHN GORMAN, "FEWER, BETTER SPIES KEY TO INTELLIGENCE REFORM, FORMER OFFICIAL SAYS," GOVEXEC, (18 MARCH 2005): N.P. ON-LINE INTERNET. AVAILABLE FROM HTTP://WWW.GOVEXEC.COM/STORY_PAGE.CFM?ARTICLEID= 30798&PRINTERFRIENDLYVERS=1&.

[343] Ibid.

INTELLIGENCE AGENCY."[344] A RECENT ARTICLE IN *INTERNATIONAL RELATIONS AND SECURITY NETWORK* AGREES, STATING: "THE CIA HAS INDEED HAD ITS WINGS CLIPPED, AND THE PENTAGON'S ROLE IN INTELLIGENCE GATHERING AND OPERATIONS HAS BEEN ENHANCED AT ITS EXPENSE."[345]

ALTHOUGH DoD ENCROACHMENT OF THIS CIA ROLE MAY NOT BE A DIRECT CHALLENGE TO THE NID'S CENTRAL AUTHORITY, ANY GROWTH OF THE MILITARY'S INTELLIGENCE CAPABILITY ONLY HIGHLIGHTS THE IMBALANCE BETWEEN IT AND THE NID WHO CONTROLS NO FORCES OF HIS OWN. GIVEN THE PENTAGON'S SUCCESS WITH SIGINT AND IMINT, IT IS REASONABLE TO PREDICT THAT SOMETIME IN THE NEXT SEVERAL DECADES THE CIA WILL MERGE WITH THE MILITARY'S STRATEGIC SUPPORT BRANCH, BE HOUSED IN THE DoD, AND BE DESIGNATED AS A COMBAT SUPPORT AGENCY.

THE MILITARY'S DOMINANT POSITION IN THE IC, BOTH AS A PRODUCER AND A CONSUMER, SIGNIFICANTLY INFLUENCES THE NID'S ABILITY TO EXERT LEADERSHIP OVER THE COMMUNITY. BY NOT DIRECTLY CHALLENGING THE DoD'S CONTROL OF THE NATIONAL INTELLIGENCE AGENCIES HOUSED IN THE DoD, THE 2004 ACT ESSENTIALLY VALIDATES THE MILITARY'S CLAIM TO NEAR EXCLUSIVE PRIORITY FOR THEIR USE. THE UNWILLINGNESS OF CONGRESS TO INSIST THAT OTHER CUSTOMERS HAVE A LEGITIMATE NEED OF THE NATION'S INTELLIGENCE ASSETS DURING WARTIME ALLOWS THE MILITARY TO CONTINUE TO DRIVE THE PRIORITY FOR COLLECTION AND ANALYSIS OF ALL INTELLIGENCE CENTERS REGARDLESS OF WHERE THEY ARE LOCATED. GROWING INTELLIGENCE ORGANIZATIONS AND FUNCTIONS WITHIN THE DoD EXACERBATE THE IMBALANCE. WITHOUT SOLID STATUTORY AUTHORITY, THE NID IS UNLIKELY TO SUCCESSFULLY CHALLENGE THE MILITARY'S CONTROL OVER THE IC ANY MORE THAN 50 YEARS OF DCIs WERE ABLE TO.

SUMMARY

WHILE TIME IS STILL REQUIRED TO DETERMINE THE EFFECTIVENESS OF THE NATIONAL INTELLIGENCE REFORM ACT OF 2004, RECENT EVENTS INDICATE THE FACTORS THAT HISTORICALLY HINDERED THE DCI'S ABILITY TO EXERCISE CENTRAL CONTROL OVER THE IC HAVE NOT BEEN ADEQUATELY ADDRESSED, AND WILL CONTINUE TO PLAGUE THE CURRENT NID AND HIS SUCCESSORS. THE DEPARTMENT OF DEFENSE, ALONG WITH ITS ALLIES IN CONGRESS, SUCCESSFULLY PROTECTED ITS INTERESTS BY LIMITING THE STATUTORY AUTHORITY GIVEN THE NID IN THE BILL. A DIRECTOR MAY STILL BE EFFECTIVE, IF GIVEN STRONG BACKING BY THE PRESIDENT, BUT SUCH BACKING IS NEITHER ASSURED NOR LIKELY TO PROVE PERMANENT EVEN IF IT DOES EXIST INITIALLY. COVERT OPERATIONS REMAIN A KEY ELEMENT OF THE IC, AND WHILE THE NID HAS A GREATER ORGANIZATIONAL DISTANCE FROM SUCH OPERATIONS THAN DCIs EXPERIENCED, ANY FAILURE OR PUBLIC EXPOSURE OF SUCH AN OPERATION WILL COMPLICATE THE NID'S AUTHORITY. WHILE AN IMPROVEMENT IN THE QUALITY OF INTELLIGENCE IS UNCERTAIN, A GROWTH IN BUREAUCRACY AND INTELLIGENCE CENTERS SEEMS ASSURED. FINALLY, THE MILITARY TOOK ADVANTAGE OF THE TURMOIL SURROUNDING THE TRANSFORMATION OF THE IC, COMING

---

[344] Ustina Markus, "CIA in decline, Pentagon on the rise," *ISN Security Watch*, (24 January, 2005): n.p. On-line Internet. Available from http://www.isn.ch/news/sw/details.cfm?ID=10626.
[345] Ibid.

AT THE SAME TIME AS THE WAR ON TERROR, TO CONTINUE ITS GROWING DOMINANCE OF NATIONAL INTELLIGENCE BY DIRECTLY CHALLENGING THE NID'S ABILITY TO "SERVE AS THE HEAD OF THE INTELLIGENCE COMMUNITY."[346]

---

[346] *National Intelligence Reform Act of 2004*, 15.

CHAPTER 3

RECCOMENDATIONS AND CONCLUSIONS

WHILE IT REMAINS TO BE SEEN JUST HOW EFFECTIVELY JOHN NEGROPONTE AND FUTURE NATIONAL INTELLIGENCE DIRECTORS (NIDS) WILL BE, GIVEN THE POWERS GRANTED BY THE INTELLIGENCE REFORM ACT OF 2004, LESSONS LEARNED FROM THE HISTORY OF SIMILAR REFORM EFFORTS ARE NOT PROMISING. THE GROWTH OF THE IC AND ITS DOMINANCE BY THE DEPARTMENT OF DEFENSE (DOD) MAKE STRONG CENTRALIZED CIVILIAN CONTROL MORE DIFFICULT THAN EVER TO IMPLEMENT. WITH ONLY A WEAK CENTRAL AUTHORITY TO BALANCE ITS INTERESTS, THE MILITARY IS DRIVING THE NATION'S INTELLIGENCE APPARATUS TO THE DETRIMENT OF WIDER POLICY-MAKING. TO COUNTER THIS TREND, CONGRESS AND THE PRESIDENT MUST REINFORCE THE POWERS OF THE NID, REVITALIZE THE CENTRAL INTELLIGENCE AGENCY (CIA) TO MAKE IT A TRULY CENTRAL AGENCY, AND TAKE ACTIVE MEASURES TO GUARD AGAINST THE FACTORS WHICH HISTORICALLY ERODE CENTRAL CONTROL OF THE INTELLIGENCE COMMUNITY (IC).

THE FAILURE OF REFORM EFFORTS TO ESTABLISH STRONG CENTRAL CONTROL OVER THE IC HAS RESULTED IN A COMMUNITY IN WHICH ONE GOVERNMENTAL DEPARTMENT HAS OVERWHELMING CONTROL OVER A MAJORITY OF NATIONAL INTELLIGENCE ASSETS. NATIONAL INTELLIGENCE, BY DEFINITION, PERTAINS TO MORE THAN ONE GOVERNMENTAL DEPARTMENT. YET MUCH OF THE US'S NATIONAL INTELLIGENCE APPARATUS IS CONTAINED IN, AND WORKS NEARLY EXCLUSIVELY FOR, THE DEPARTMENT OF DEFENSE, WHICH HAS PRACTICALLY MADE ITS DOMINATION OF THE NATIONAL INTELLIGENCE AGENCIES A *FAIT ACCOMPLI*. NOT ONLY DOES IT OWN THE NATIONAL RECCONAISANCE OFFICE (NRO), NATIONAL GEOSPATIAL-INTELLIGENCE AGENCY (NGA), AND NATIONAL SECURITY AGENCY (NSA), THE DOD HAS SUCCESSFULLY PROPAGATED THE NOTION THAT SUPPORT TO MILITARY OPERATIONS IS THE HIGHEST PRIORITY FOR THE CIA, IN EFFECT MAKING THE CIA A COMBAT SUPPORT AGENCY. THE INTELLIGENCE REFORM ACT OF 2004, BY FAILING TO FULLY EMPOWER THE NID TO STAND UP AGAINST ENTRENCHED INTERESTS BOTH IN THE INTELLIGENCE COMMUNITY AND IN CONGRESS, IS UNLIKELY TO REVERSE THIS TREND.

THE MILITARY'S SUCCESS IN ESTABLISHING AN INTELLIGENCE APPARATUS TO SUPPORT ITS NEEDS IS DUE TO AN APPRECIATION OF THE VALUE AND NATURE OF INTELLIGENCE THAT MANY CIVILIAN POLICY MAKERS LACK. WHILE INTELLIGENCE, LIKE WEALTH, IS THEORETICALLY LIMITLESS, IT REQUIRES A SUBSTANTIAL INVESTMENT IN PERSONNEL, ENERGY, AND TIME TO PRODUCE. RECOGNIZING THIS, THE MILITARY, AFTER A CONTENTIOUS START, APPLIED ITS CULTURALLY METHODICAL APPROACH TO CONTINUOUSLY DETERMINE ITS INTELLIGENCE NEEDS, DEVELOP AND ANALYZE COURSES OF ACTION FOR ACHIEVING THOSE NEEDS, AND EXECUTE A WELL-PLANNED CAMPAIGN TO ACHIEVE ITS DESIRED OBJECTIVES. CIVILIAN LEADERS, ON THE OTHER HAND, OFTEN LACK INTEREST IN INTELLIGENCE—AND EVEN WHEN INTERESTED GENERALLY FAIL TO PROVIDE THE DETAILED GUIDANCE REQUIRED TO OPTIMIZE ITS PRODUCTION AND USE. ALTHOUGH THE DIRECTOR OF CENTRAL INTELLIGENCE (DCI) WAS CREATED

TO OVERSEE THE NATIONAL INTELLIGENCE EFFORT, HE WAS NEVER GIVEN THE AUTHORITY TO MEET HIS RESPONSIBILITIES, OR EVEN A CLEAR PICTURE OF WHAT HE WAS EXPECTED TO ACCOMPLISH.

AS A RESULT, THE IC GREW IN AN UNGUIDED AND HAPHAZARD MANNER. THE CIA STRAYED FAR FROM ITS ORIGINAL PURPOSE OF COORDINATING AND EVALUATING THE EFFORTS OF THE OTHER AGENCIES TO BECOME AN INDEPENDENT COLLECTOR AND OPERATOR. TECHNICAL AGENCIES DEALING WITH SIGNALS INTELLIGENCE (SIGINT) AND IMAGERY INTELLIGENCE (IMINT) EVOLVED INTO COMBAT SUPPORT AGENCIES, DESPITE THE INTENTIONS OF PRESIDENTS WHO INITIATED THEIR DEVELOPMENT AS CIVILIAN ORGANIZATIONS. PERCEIVED FAILURES BY THE IC HAVE BEEN ADDRESSED BY THE CREATION OF NEW ORGANIZATIONS. THESE SUPERFICIAL SOLUTIONS CONCENTRATE ON CORRECTING SPECIFIC PROBLEMS RATHER THAN FINDING AND FIXING THE STRUCTURAL FLAW THAT PROMPTED THE FAILURE, RESULTING IN MORE GROWTH UNGUIDED BY A MASTER PLAN.

TODAY, ALTHOUGH OPTIMIZED TO SUPPORT THE DEPARTMENT OF DEFENSE TO THE POINT THAT MILITARY DOCTRINE NOW USES TERMS SUCH AS INFORMATION DOMINANCE AND TOTAL SITUATIONAL AWARENESS, INTELLIGENCE FAILS TO PROVIDE OPTIMAL SUPPORT TO THE REST OF THE GOVERNMENT. THIS SHORTCOMING DIRECTLY AFFECTS THE POLICIES THE US ADOPTS AND THE WAY IT SEEKS TO ACHIEVE THEM. WITH MUCH OF ITS NATIONAL INTELLIGENCE ASSETS CONTROLLED BY THE MILITARY, THE US TENDS TO PERCEIVE ALL CHALLENGES AS MILITARY ONES, THEREFORE, CORRECTIBLE WITH MILITARY SOLUTIONS. WHILE THE MILITARY SEEKS TO MAINTAIN A LONG-TERM OUTLOOK, THE REQUIREMENTS OF COMBAT FOCUS ITS ATTENTION ON SHORTER-TERM OPERATIONAL AND TACTICAL CONCERNS TO THE DETRIMENT OF STRATEGIC CONSIDERATIONS.

MANY OBSERVERS HAVE NOTED THE EFFECTS OF THIS IMBALANCE. GREG TREVERTON, HEAD OF THE INTELLIGENCE POLICY CENTER AT THE RAND CORPORATION, COMMENTED:

> "WHEN YOU ASK, 'WHY DO WE HAVE SO LITTLE INTELLIGENCE ON WEAPONS OF MASS DESTRUCTION TARGETS IN IRAQ?' THE ANSWER WAS SOMETIMES THAT WE WERE SO BUSY WITH FORCE PROTECTION… THE SPY SATELLITES OVER IRAQ BEFORE THE MARCH 2003 INVASION WERE HEAVILY COMMITTED TO KEEPING U.S. PILOTS SAFE BY WATCHING THE IRAQI RADAR AND MISSILE SITES THAT WERE A DAILY THREAT TO THE U.S. FIGHTER JETS ENFORCING IRAQ'S 'NO-FLY ZONES'… THAT MEANT THE SATELLITES COULDN'T ADEQUATELY SCRUTINIZE ALL THE SITES WHERE INTELLIGENCE OFFICIALS BELIEVED THE IRAQIS WERE MAKING OR STORING CHEMICAL OR BIOLOGICAL WEAPONS."[347]

IN MAY OF 2000, DCI GEORGE TENET "ACKNOWLEDGED THAT THE APPEALS FROM TACTICAL COMMANDERS FOR MORE INTELLIGENCE HAVE LED TO SHORTFALLS IN OTHER AREAS," SPECIFICALLY STATING THAT THE TACTICAL FOCUS HURT THE COMMUNITY'S "ABILITY TO KEEP THE NATIONAL COMMAND AUTHORITY APPRAISED ON A STRATEGIC LEVEL ABOUT WHAT IS HAPPENING."[348] SUCH MISSED

---

[347] John Diamond, "Intelligence Impasse mainly a question of control," *USA Today*, (29 November 2004): 6A.

[348] MELVIN A. GOODMAN, "IN FROM THE COLD, THE NEED FOR REFORM OF THE CIA," *FOREIGN POLICY IN FOCUS*, SPECIAL REPORT #13, (FEBRUARY 2001): N.P. ON-LINE INTERNET. AVAILABLE FROM
HTTP://WWW.FPIF.ORG/PDF/REPORTS/CIA.PDF.

STRATEGIC EVENTS ARGUABLY INCLUDE INDIA'S SURPRISE DETONATION OF A NUCLEAR WEAPON IN 1998 AND IRAN'S DEVELOPMENT OF A NUCLEAR PROGRAM THROUGHOUT THE 1990S, WHILE NEARBY US ASSETS FOCUSED ON SUPPORT TO OPERATIONS NORTHERN AND SOUTHERN WATCH IN IRAQ. MELVIN GOODMAN ARGUES THAT THE MILITARIZATION OF INTELLIGENCE IS EVEN FURTHER REACHING: "THE PENTAGON'S INCREASED CONTROL OVER THE INTELLIGENCE COMMUNITY HAS ALREADY OCCASIONED A DOWNGRADING OF THE IMPORTANT ROLE OF VERIFICATION AND MONITORING OF ARMS CONTROL AND DISARMAMENT. FOR THE FIRST TIME IN THIRTY YEARS, A DCI TESTIFIED TO CONGRESS THAT THE CIA COULD NOT MONITOR A STRATEGIC ARMS CONTROL AGREEMENT – THE COMPREHENSIVE TEST BAN TREATY – AND, AS A RESULT, THE SENATE REFUSED TO CONFIRM THE CTBT."[349]

GOODMAN FURTHER STRESSES THE DANGER OF THE MILITARY SUPPRESSING INFORMATION THAT IS COUNTER TO ITS AGENDA OR EMBARRASSING TO SENIOR OFFICIALS IF THERE IS NO INDEPENDENT CIVILIAN COUNTERWEIGHT TO PROVIDE A POLICY NEUTRAL PERSPECTIVE. IMAGERY IN OPERATION DESERT STORM INDICATED THE ERROR IN GENERAL NORMAN SCHWARZKOPF'S STATEMENT THAT BOMBS HAD DESTROYED FOUR IRAQI SCUD LAUNCHERS, BUT ANALYSTS WOULD NOT CORRECT HIM. EVEN COLIN POWELL 'CONCLUDED THAT PRESERVING SCHWARZKOPF'S 'EQUANIMITY' WAS MORE IMPORTANT THAN THE TRUTH.'"[350] WHILE THIS MAY HAVE BEEN A RELATIVELY HARMLESS OMISSION, IF THE MILITARY HAD ENOUGH CONTROL OF THE INTELLIGENCE APPARATUS TO EXPRESS ONLY ITS VIEW OF THE BOMBER OR MISSILES GAPS DURING THE 1950S OR 1960S, PARTICULARLY DURING THE VIETNAM CONFLICT, POLICYMAKING MAY HAVE SUFFERED SIGNIFICANTLY.

RECTIFYING THIS IMBALANCE IN THE IC REQUIRES AN APPRECIATION OF THE IMPORTANCE AND POTENTIAL OF INTELLIGENCE TO ALL ASPECTS OF NATIONAL POLICYMAKING. A PLAN POWERFUL ENOUGH TO OVERCOME INSTITUTIONAL OPPOSITION TO AN INDEPENDENT INTELLIGENCE DIRECTOR (WHO CONSIDERS THE INTELLIGENCE NEEDS OF *ALL* GOVERNMENT DEPARTMENTS AND, CONSISTENT WITH ADMINISTRATION GUIDANCE, PRIORITIZES AND DIRECTS THE EFFORTS OF ALL NATIONAL INTELLIGENCE ASSETS) IS NEEDED. WHILE A TRAUMATIC NATIONAL EVENT TIED TO AN INTELLIGENCE FAILURE MAY SERVE AS A CATALYST FOR REFORM, IT ALONE IS NOT SUFFICIENT TO CREATE THE MINDSET REQUIRED FOR *SUCCESSFUL* REFORM. ONCE SUCH A WILL EXISTS, MODIFYING THE STRUCTURE AND FUNCTIONS OF THE IC TO GUARD AGAINST THE FACTORS THAT HISTORICALLY DEFEAT EFFORTS TO CENTRALIZE CONTROL OVER THE COMMUNITY BECOMES POSSIBLE.

WHILE EDUCATING POLICY MAKERS IS THE PRIMARY TOOL REQUIRED TO INITIATE MEANINGFUL CHANGE, SHIFTS IN CONGRESS'S BUDGING PROCESS WILL ASSIST REFORMERS IN OVERCOMING THE OPPOSITION OF EXISTING INTELLIGENCE ORGANIZATIONS. THE ARMED SERVICES COMMITTEES SHOULD CONTINUE APPROPRIATING JOINT MILITARY INTELLIGENCE PROGRAM (JMIP) AND TACTICAL INTELLIGENCE AND RELATED ACTIVITIES (TIARA) FUNDS TO THE SECRETARY OF DEFENSE, BUT ALL NATIONAL FOREIGN INTELLIGENCE PROGRAM (NFIP) FUNDS SHOULD BE DISBURSED THROUGH THE

---

[349] Ibid.
[350] Ibid.

INTELLIGENCE OVERSIGHT COMMITTEES DIRECTLY TO THE NID. FOR SIMPLICITY SAKE, THE DEFENSE INTELLIGENCE AGENCY (DIA) SHOULD BE FUNDED SOLELY THROUGH JMIP FUNDS AND BE CONSIDERED A DEPARTMENTAL AGENCY, RATHER THAN JOINTLY FUNDED UNDER JMIP AND NFIP AS IS THE CURRENT PRACTICE.[351] GRANTING POWER OVER PURSE STRINGS TO THE INTELLIGENCE COMMITTEES WILL IN SMALL MEASURE LEVEL THE PLAYING FIELD BETWEEN THEM AND THE DEFENSE RELATED CONGRESSIONAL COMMITTEES, CONSEQUENTLY STRENGTHENING THE IC'S REPRESENTATION IN CONGRESS.

A NEWLY EMPOWERED NID SHOULD INSIST ON THE REMOVAL OF ANY RESPONSIBILITY FOR, OR AUTHORITY TO, CONDUCT COVERT OPERATIONS. ALTHOUGH THE US POPULAR IMAGINATION LINKS SUCH OPERATIONS TO THE INTELLIGENCE FIELD, NO SUCH LINK EXISTS LOGICALLY. THE CLANDESTINE COLLECTION OF INTELLIGENCE IS A LEGITIMATE IC FUNCTION, BUT WHEN THE US SEEKS TO INFLUENCE THE ACTS OF OTHER GOVERNMENTS OR PEOPLES IT SHOULD DO SO OVERTLY THROUGH THE APPROPRIATE DEPARTMENT—STATE, TREASURY, JUSTICE, OR WHICHEVER IS MOST RELEVANT TO THE MISSION. IF AN ADMINISTRATION DETERMINES THAT COVERT MILITARY ACTION IS REQUIRED, THEN THE APPROPRIATE COMBATANT COMMANDS SHOULD OVERSEE AND EXECUTE SUCH OPERATIONS. REMOVING COVERT OPERATIONS FROM THE IC WOULD FREE UP COLLECTION RESOURCES, AND WOULD ALLOW THE COMMUNITY TO REMAIN POLICY NEUTRAL, AS WELL AS AVOIDING THE DEBILITATING INVESTIGATIONS THAT INVARIABLY FOLLOW FAILED OR EXPOSED OPERATIONS.

THE PROBLEM OF ACCESS TO THE PRESIDENT BECOMES MOOT ONCE THE NID RECEIVES SUFFICIENT STATUTORY AUTHORITY TO CARRY OUT ASSIGNED RESPONSIBILITIES INDEPENDENTLY. CERTAINLY, A CLOSE WORKING RELATIONSHIP WITH THE PRESIDENT IS DESIRABLE, AND THE ADVANTAGES OF PLACING THE NID IN THE EXECUTIVE BRANCH OF AT THE POSSIBLE RISK OF POLICY DETACHMENT IS A WORTHWHILE ARGUMENT. NEGROPONTE SHOULD NOT, HOWEVER, REQUIRE THE PRESIDENT TO FORCE THE VARIOUS NATIONAL AGENCIES IN THE IC TO FOLLOW HIS PRIORITIES ANY MORE THAN ALAN GREENSPAN SHOULD REQUIRE THE PRESIDENT TO PERSUADE EACH OF THE NATION'S BANKS TO ACCEPT A NEW PRIME INTEREST RATE.

THE 2004 REFORM BILL EXACERBATED THE PROBLEM OF AGENCY PROLIFERATION AND SHOULD, IN SEVERAL INSTANCES, BE REVERSED. RATHER THAN CREATING A NEW NATIONAL INTELLIGENCE AUTHORITY (NIA), NID, AND JOINT INTELLIGENCE COMMUNITY COUNCIL (JICC) WITH CORRESPONDING STAFFS, THE EXISTING NATIONAL SECURITY COUNCI (NSC), DCI AND INTELLIGENCE COMMUNITY STAFF (ICS) SHOULD BE MADE SUFFICIENTLY ROBUST. THE ONLY NEW POSITION THAT NEEDS TO BE CREATED IS AN INDEPENDENT DIRECTOR OF THE CIA, ALLOWING THE DCI OR NID, NEITHER TITLE IS SUPERIOR (ALTHOUGH HAVING BOTH IS REDUNDANT), TO CONCENTRATE SOLELY ON COMMUNITY CONCERNS. THE CREATION OF AN INDEPENDENT NATIONAL COUNTER TERRORISM CENTER (NCTC) IS A KNEE JERK REACTION TO THE PERCEIVED CRISES OF THE MOMENT. THE CIA CAN AGAIN BECOME A TRULY CENTRAL AGENCY BY MAKING ITS COUNTER TERRORIST CENTER THE HUB OF TERRORIST RELATED INTELLIGENCE,

---

[351] Mark M. Lowenthal, *Intelligence From Secrets to Policy*, Second Edition, (Washington DC: CQ Press, 2003), 36.

AND BY CONSOLIDATING THE RESOURCES IN THE TERRORIST THREAT INTEGRATION CENTER (TTIC) AND OTHER REDUNDANT FUSION CENTERS INTO IT. OTHER NATIONAL INTELLIGENCE CENTERS (NICs) ENVISIONED BY THE 9/11 COMMISSION, IF THEY TRULY PRODUCE NATIONAL INTELLIGENCE PERTINENT TO MORE THAN ONE DEPARTMENT, SHOULD ALSO BE PLACED IN THE CIA, MAKING IT THE PREEMINENT ANALYSIS CENTER FOR ALL ASPECTS OF NATIONAL INTELLIGENCE. SUCH AN ARRANGEMENT WOULD FACILITATE CROSSTALK AND COLLABORATION BETWEEN WORKING GROUPS ON RELATED SUBJECTS. ASSIGNMENT OF PERSONNEL FROM OTHER AGENCIES TO SUCH CIA WORKING GROUPS IN THE SPIRIT OF JOINTNESS IS HIGHLY DESIRABLE.

TO REVERSE THE MILITARY'S DOMINATION OF NATIONAL INTELLIGENCE, THE NRO, NSA, AND NGA SHOULD BE REMOVED FROM THE DoD AND ESTABLISHED AS COLLECTION BRANCHES IN THE CIA, ON PAR WITH ITS CURRENT OPERATIONS BRANCH, WHICH, WITH THE REMOVAL OF COVERT RESPONSIBILITIES, BECOMES IN EFFECT A HUMAN INTELLIGENCE (HUMINT) COLLECTION ORGANIZATION. IF THE DEPARTMENT OF DEFENSE DETERMINES A REQUIREMENT FOR DEDICATED MILITARY SATELLITES OR CODE-CRACKING COMPUTERS EXISTS, IT CAN PAY FOR THEM THROUGH JMIP FUNDS AND PLACE THEM UNDER THE CONTROL OF THE DIA. SUCH DUPLICATION OF TECHNICAL INFRASTRUCTURE IS FAR MORE AFFORDABLE NOW THAN IT WAS WHEN THE NRO AND NSA WERE CREATED AS SHARED ORGANIZATIONS UNDER JMIP FUNDS. SUCH DUPLICATION SHOULD NOT, HOWEVER, BE NECESSARY. THE MILITARY'S INTELLIGENCE REQUIREMENTS ARE VALID AND WELL APPRECIATED, PARTICULARLY DURING TIMES OF CONFLICT. WHEN THE SECRETARY OF DEFENSE RELAYS LEGITIMATE INTELLIGENCE REQUIREMENTS OF THE DoD, THE NID WILL ENSURE THAT NATIONAL ASSETS ARE DEVELOPED AND USED TO MEET SUCH NEEDS, BUT NOT TO THE EXCLUSION OF OTHER DEPARTMENTAL AND ADMINISTRATION INTELLIGENCE CONSUMERS.

WITH ALL OF THE NATIONAL INTELLIGENCE ORGANIZATIONS INCORPORATED WITHIN THE CIA AND ADMINISTERED BY THE DIRECTOR OF THE CIA, THE NID CAN TURN HIS ENERGY INTO ELIMINATING THE BARRIERS THAT HAMPER THE FREE SHARING OF INTELLIGENCE AND COLLABORATION OF EFFORT BETWEEN DEPARTMENTS. THEREFORE THE NID MUST HAVE THE AUTHORITY TO DEVELOP AND COMPEL THE USE OF A SINGLE UNIFIED SYSTEM OF CLASSIFICATION THAT ADEQUATELY PROTECTS INTELLIGENCE AND SOURCES, WHILE ALLOWING APPROPRIATE MEMBERS OF THE IC AND GOVERNMENT TO ACCESS THE INTELLIGENCE. SECOND, THE NID MUST HAVE THE AUTHORITY TO DEVELOP AND COMPEL THE ADOPTION OF A COMMON COMMUNITY-WIDE NETWORK PROTOCOL FOR THE STORAGE AND TRANSMISSION OF INTELLIGENCE PRODUCTS. WHILE SUCH COMMUNITY WIDE STANDARDS REQUIRE STRONG CENTRAL CONTROL FOR IMPLEMENTATION, ONCE DEVELOPED THEY ALLOW A DECENTRALIZED EXECUTION OF MANY INTELLIGENCE FUNCTIONS. FOR EXAMPLE, DEPARTMENT OF STATE ANALYSTS IN THE BUREAU OF INTELLIGENCE AND RESEARCH (INR) AND DoD ANALYSTS IN THE DIA (OR ONE OF THE INDIVIDUAL SERVICE INTELLIGENCE ORGANIZATIONS) COULD DIRECTLY ACCESS EACH OTHER. AT THE SAME TIME, ANALYSTS COULD ACCESS CENTRAL CIA INTELLIGENCE HOLDINGS AND SHARE RELEVANT INFORMATION AND IDEAS. A NAVY COLLECTION MANAGER OR AN FBI COUNTER TERRORIST AGENT COULD MAKE

REQUESTS DIRECTLY TO THE APPROPRIATE CIA OFFICE, WHICH IN ACCORDANCE WITH PRIORITIES ESTABLISHED BY THE NID, WILL FILL THEIR REQUESTS FOR COLLECTION OR INFORMATION DIRECTLY. CAREER CIA ANALYSTS WOULD BE ENCOURAGED TO CONDUCT TOURS WITHIN ONE OF THE DEPARTMENTAL INTELLIGENCE ORGANIZATIONS TO BROADEN THEIR UNDERSTANDING OF CUSTOMER NEEDS, JUST AS DEPARTMENTAL INTELLIGENCE OFFICERS WILL BE ENCOURAGED TO SERVE A TOUR IN THE CIA TO ENSURE THE CENTRAL BODY UNDERSTANDS THEIR OWN PARTICULAR NEEDS AND PERSPECTIVES ON INTELLIGENCE.

THE 9/11 COMMISSION ENVISIONED SUCH A NETWORK BASED COLLABORATIVE INTELLIGENCE ENVIRONMENT, AND PROPOSED GIVING THE NID THE AUTHORITY TO ESTABLISH IT. THE 2004 BILL, HOWEVER, WHILE PASSING MEASURES DESIGNED TO INCREASE THE SIZE OF THE IC, DID LITTLE TO INCREASE A CENTRAL DIRECTOR'S CONTROL OVER IT, AND CORRESPONDINGLY LITTLE TO ENHANCE THE ODDS OF ACHIEVING SUCH AN ENVIRONMENT. LITTLE PROGRESS WILL BE MADE UNTIL THE PRESIDENT COMMUNICATES A CLEAR GOAL. ULTIMATELY, THE PRESIDENT IS THE DIRECTOR OF NATIONAL INTELLIGENCE AND IS RESPONSIBLE TO ENSURE THAT THE INTELLIGENCE COMMUNITY SUPPORTS NATIONAL FOREIGN POLICY AS HE OR SHE DEFINES IT. IF THAT POLICY IS A PREDOMINANTLY MILITARY ONE WITH A HEAVY COVERT EMPHASIS, THEN THERE IS NO NEED FOR FURTHER CHANGE. SUCH A MILITARY BASED FOREIGN POLICY, HOWEVER, DOES NOT APPEAL TO EVERYONE. AS THE HOUSE'S PERMANENT SELECT COMMITTEE ON INTELLIGENCE NOTES, THE CATCHPHRASE …

> "SUPPORT TO THE WARFIGHTER…SUGGESTS THAT THE PRIMARY FOCUS OF INTELLIGENCE SHOULD BE ON THE ACTUAL NEED TO USE FORCE (I.E., 'FIGHT A WAR'), WHEN WE CONTINUE TO BELIEVE THAT SUCCESSFUL FOREIGN AND NATIONAL SECURITY POLICY IS DESIGNED TO PRECLUDE SUCH AN EVENT IF AT ALL POSSIBLE. . . ALTHOUGH THE DoD MAY BE THE ACTIVE ARM OF MANY OF THE NATION'S POLICY INITIATIVES TODAY, MOST IF NOT ALL OF THESE INITIATIVES BEGAN WITH SOME LEVEL OF DIPLOMATIC EFFORT, CALLING INTO QUESTION WHETHER 'SUPPORT TO THE DIPLOMAT' MIGHT BE A MORE CRITICAL PURSUIT."[352]

IF THE UNITED STATES DESIRES A MORE PROACTIVE, LONG RANGE, STRATEGIC AND DIPLOMATIC POLICY, IT SHOULD HEED THE 9/11 COMMISSION'S RECOMMENDATIONS AND TRULY EMPOWER THE NATIONAL INTELLIGENCE DIRECTOR; TASK THAT DIRECTOR WITH STREAMLINING A BUREAUCRATICALLY OUT OF CONTROL INTELLIGENCE COMMUNITY; AND REESTABLISH THE CIA AS A CENTRAL HOME FOR ALL NATIONAL INTELLIGENCE ASSETS.

---

[352] US HOUSE. *IC21: THE INTELLIGENCE COMMUNITY IN THE 21ST CENTURY.* 104TH CONG. STAFF STUDY BY THE
PERMANENT SELECT COMMITTEE ON INTELLIGENCE, 1996. #IC21011

Appendix A – Acronyms Used

- AIA   Air Intelligence Agency
- ASD/I   Assistant Secretary of Defense for Intelligence
- BDA   Battle Damage Assessment
- CFI   Committee on Foreign Intelligence
- CFI   Committee on Foreign Intelligence
- CFR   Council on Foreign Relations
- CIA   Central Intelligence Agency
- CIG   Central Intelligence Group
- COI   Communications Intelligence
- CTBT   Comprehensive Test Ban Treaty
- CTC   Counterterrorism Center
- DCI   Director of Central Intelligence
- DIA   Defense Intelligence Agency
- DNI   Director of National Intelligence
- DoD   Department of Defense
- ELINT   Electronic Intelligence
- EO   Executive Order
- FBI   Federal Bureau of Investigation
- HEO   High Earth Orbit
- HUMINT   Human Intelligence
- IC   Intelligence Community
- IC21   Intelligence Community in the 21ST Century
- ICS   Intelligence Community Staff
- INR   Bureau of Intelligence and Research (State Department)
- INSCOM   Intelligence and Security Command
- IRAC   The Intelligence Resources Advisory Committee
- JICC   Joint Intelligence Community Council
- JTTF   Joint Terrorism Task Force
- MACV   Military Assistance Command, Vietnam
- MID   Military Intelligence Division
- NAVSECGRU   Naval Security Group Command
- NCTC   National Counter Terrorism Center
- NFIB   National Foreign Intelligence Board
- NFIP   National Foreign Intelligence Program
- NGA   National Geospatial-Intelligence Agency
- NIA   National Intelligence Authority
- NIC   National Intelligence Center
- NID   National Intelligence Director

Appendix A (continued) Acronyms Used

- NIE   National Intelligence Estimate
- NIMA   National Imagery and Mapping Agency
- NIPES   National Intelligence Programs Evaluation Staff
- NIRB   National Intelligence Resources Board
- NRO   National Reconnaissance Office

- NSA   National Security Agency
- NSC   National Security Council
- OB   Order of Battle
- OMA   Office of Military Affairs
- OMB   Office of Management and Budget
- ONE   Office of National Estimates
- ONI   Office of Naval Intelligence
- OSS   Office of Strategic Services
- OTC   Office of Technical Collection
- PFIAB   President's Foreign Intelligence Advisory Board
- SCS   Special Collection Service
- SIGINT   Signals Intelligence
- SIGINT   Signals Intelligence
- SMO   Support to Military Operations
- SNIE   Special National Intelligence Estimate
- TIARA   Tactical Intelligence and Related Activities
- TTIC   Terrorist Threat Integration Center
- USCIB   United States Communications Intelligence Board
- USIA   U.S. Information Agency
- USIB   United States Intelligence Board
- USSS   United States SIGINT System

Bibliography

BOOKS

AID, MATTHEW M. "THE TIME OF TROUBLES: THE U.S. NATIONAL SECURITY AGENCY IN THE TWENTY-FIRST CENTURY." IN *STRATEGIC INTELLIGENCE: WINDOWS INTO A SECRET WORLD,* ED. LOCH K. JOHNSON ET AL. LOS ANGELES, CALIFORNIA: ROXBURY PUBLISHING COMPANY, 2004.

ASPIN-BROWN COMMISSION. "THE EVOLUTION OF THE U.S. INTELLIGENCE COMMUNITY – AN HISTORICAL OVERVIEW." IN *STRATEGIC INTELLIGENCE: WINDOWS INTO A SECRET WORLD,* ED. LOCH K. JOHNSON ET AL. LOS ANGELES, CALIFORNIA: ROXBURY PUBLISHING COMPANY, 2004.

ANDREW, CHRISTOPHER. *FOR THE PRESIDENT'S EYES ONLY.* NEW YORK: HARPERCOLLINS PUBLISHERS: 1995

BURROWS, WILLIAM E. *DEEP BLACK.* NEW YORK: BERKLEY BOOKS, 1986.

CHU DAVID S. C. AND NURITH BERSTEIN, "DECISION MAKING FOR DEFENSE" IN *NEW CHALLENGES, NEW TOOLS FOR DEFENSE DECISION MAKING,* STUART JOHNSON, MARTIN LIBICKI, AND GREGORY F. TREVERTON, EDS., SANTA MONICA, CALIFORNIA: RAND CORPORATION, 2003.

HIGGENS, TRUMBELL. *THE PERFECT FAILURE, KENNEDY, EISENHOWER, AND THE CIA AT THE BAY OF PIGS.* NEW YORK: W.W. NORTON, 1987.

FINNEGAN, PATRICK. *MILITARY INTELLIGENCE.* WASHINGTON, DC: CENTER OF MILITARY HISTORY, UNITED STATES ARMY, 1998.

JOHNSON, LOCH K. *BOMBS, BUGS, DRUGS, AND THUGS: INTELLIGENCE AND AMERICA'S QUEST FOR SECURITY.* NEW YORK: NEW YORK UNIVERSITY PRESS, 2000.

KESSLER, RONALD. *INSIDE THE CIA, REVEALING THE SECRETS OF THE WORLDS MOST POWERFUL SPY AGENCY,* NEW YORK: POCKET BOOKS, 1992.

LOWENTHAL, MARK M. *INTELLIGENCE: FROM SECRETS TO POLICY.* WASHINGTON, DC: CQ, 2000.

LOWENTHAL, MARK M. *U.S. INTELLIGENCE EVOLUTION AND ANATOMY, SECOND EDITION.* WASHINGTON DC: CENTER FOR STRATEGIC AND INTERNATIONAL STUDIES, 1992.

MORGAN, GARETH. *IMAGES OF ORGANIZATION.* THOUSAND OAKS, CALIFORNIA: SAGE PUBLICATIONS, 1997.

RICHELSON, JEFFREY T. *THE U.S. INTELLIGENCE COMMUNITY.* BOULDER, COLORADO: WESTVIEW PRESS. 1999.

TREVERTON, GREGORY F. "INTELLIGENCE SINCE COLD WAR'S END." IN *IN FROM THE COLD.* ALLEN E. GOODMAN, GREGORY F. TREVERTON, AND PHILIP ZELIKOW. NEW YORK: THE TWENTITH

CENTRUY FUND PRESS, 1996.

TREVERTON, GREGORY F. *RESHAPING NATIONAL INTELLIGENCE FOR AN AGE OF INFORMATION.* CAMBRIDGE, UNITED KINGDOM: CAMBRIDGE UNIVERSITY PRESS, 2003.

TROY THOMAS F. *DONOVAN AND THE CIA: A HISTORY OF THE ESTABLISHMENT OF THE CENTRAL INTELLIGENCE AGENCY.* FREDERICK, MARYLAND: UNIVERSITY PUBLICATIONS OF AMERICA, INC., 1981.

TROY, THOMAS F. "THE QUAINTNESS OF THE U.S. INTELLIGENCE COMMUNITY" IN *STRATEGIC INTELLIGENCE,* ED. LOCH K. JOHNSON ET AL. LOS ANGELES, CALIFORNIA: ROXBURY PUBLISHING COMPANY, 2004.

WESTERFIELD, H BRADFORD. "INSIDE IVORY BUNKERS: CIA ANALYSTS RESIST MANGERS' PANDERING." IN *STRATEGIC INTELLIGENCE: WINDOWS INTO A SECRET WORLD,* ED. LOCH K. JOHNSON ET AL. LOS ANGELES, CALIFORNIA: ROXBURY PUBLISHING COMPANY, 2004.

WIRTZ, JAMES J. "INTELLIGENCE TO PLEASE?" IN *STRATEGIC INTELLIGENCE: WINDOWS INTO A SECRET WORLD,* ED. LOCH K. JOHNSON ET AL. LOS ANGELES, CALIFORNIA: ROXBURY PUBLISHING COMPANY, 2004.

ZEGART, AMY B. *FLAWED BY DESIGN,* STANFORD, CALIFORNIA: STANFORD UNIVERSITY PRESS, STANFORD: CALIFORNIA, 1999.

GOVERNMENT PUBLICATIONS/PUBLIC DOCUMENTS

35 YEARS, A BRIEF HISTORY. WASHINGTON DC: DIA HISTORY OFFICE,1996.

9/11 COMMISSION. *THE 9/11 COMMISSION REPORT.* NEW YORK: W.W. NORTON, 2004.

ANDREW, CHRISTOPHER "FOREWARD" IN JOHN HELGERSON. *GETTING TO KNOW THE PRESIDENT: CIA BRIEFINGS OF PRESIDENTIAL CANDIDATES, 1952-1992.* WASHINGTON, DC: CENTER FOR THE STUDY OF INTELLIGENCE, CENTRAL INTELLIGENCE AGENCY, 1995.

BEST, RICHARD A., JR. *PROPOSALS FOR INTELLIGENCE REORGANIZATION, 1949-2004.* WASHINGTON, DC: CONGRESSIONAL RESEARCH SERVICE, LIBRARY OF CONGRESS, 29 JUL. 2004.

BEST, RICHARD A. *INTELLIGENCE COMMUNITY REORGANIZATION: POTENTIAL EFFECTS ON DOD INTELLIGENCE AGENCIES.* WASHINGTON DC: CONGRESSIONAL RESEARCH SERVICE, 2004.

"THE CENTRAL INTELLIGENCE ORGANIZATION AND NATIONAL ORGANIZATION FOR INTELLIGENCE, SUMMARY." 1 JANUARY 1949. N.P. ON-LINE INTERNET, 28 JANUARY 2005. AVAILABLE FROM HTTP://WWW.STATE.GOV/WWW/ABOUT_STATE/HISTORY/INTEL/350_359.HTML.

"CONTROVERSY OVER COVERT INTELLIGENCE OPERATIONS" *CONGRESSIONAL DIGEST* 59, ISSUE 5, (MAY 1980) 131.

CUMMING, ALFRED. "THE POSITION OF DIRECTOR OF NATIONAL INTELLIGENCE: ISSUES FOR CONGRESS." CRS REPORT FOR CONGRESS, ORDER CODE RL32506. WASHINGTON DC: CONGRESSIONAL RESEARCH SERVICE, 2004.

DAGGETT, STEPHEN. *THE US INTELLIGENCE BUDGET: A BASIC OVERVIEW,* WASHINGTON, DC: CONGRESSIONAL RESEARCH SERVICE, LIBRARY OF CONGRESS, 24 SEPTEMBER 2004.

EBERSTADT, FERDINAND. *NATIONAL SECURITY ORGANIZATION,* WASHINGTON, DC: U.S. GOVERNMENT PRINTING OFFICE, 1949.

EXECUTIVE ORDER 11905. UNITED STATES FOREIGN INTELLIGENCE ACTIVITIES, 18 FEBRUARY 1976.

EXECUTIVE ORDER 12036. UNITED STATES FOREIGN INTELLIGENCE ACTIVITIES, 24 JANUARY 1978.

EXECUTIVE ORDER 12333. UNITED STATES INTELLIGENCE ACTIVITIES, 4 DECEMBER 1981.

FOREIGN AND MILITARY INTELLIGENCE. BOOK I, FINAL REPORT OF THE SELECT COMMITTEE TO STUDY GOVERNMENTAL OPERATIONS WITH RESPECT TO INTELLIGENCE ACTIVITIES. WASHINGTON, DC: U.S. GOVERNMENT PRINTING OFFICE. 1976.

PREPARING FOR THE 21ST CENTURY: AN APPRAISAL OF U.S. INTELLIGENCE. REPORT OF THE COMMISSION ON THE ROLES AND CAPABILITIES OF THE U.S. INTELLIGENCE COMMUNITY. WASHINGTON, DC: GOVERNMENT PRINTING OFFICE. 1996.

PUBLIC LAW 61-253. *NATIONAL SECURITY ACT (NSA) OF 1947.* 26 JULY 1947.

US HOUSE. *INTELLIGENCE COMMUNITY ACT.* 104TH CONG., 2ND SESS., 1996. H.R. 104-620

US HOUSE. *IC21: THE INTELLIGENCE COMMUNITY IN THE 21ST CENTURY.* 104TH CONG. STAFF STUDY BY THE PERMANENT SELECT COMMITTEE ON INTELLIGENCE, 1996. #IC21011

US HOUSE. *JOINT INQUIRY INTO INTELLIGENCE COMMUNITY ACTIVITIES BEFORE AND AFTER THE TERRORIST ATTACKS OF SEPTEMBER 11, 2001.* 107TH CONG., 2ND SESS., 2002. H.R. 107-792.

US SENATE. *A BILL, TO AMEND TITLE 10, UNITED STATES CODE, TO PROVIDE FOR THE ESTABLISHMENT OF A UNIFIED COMBATANT COMMAND FOR MILITARY INTELLIGENCE, AND FOR OTHER PURPOSES.* 109TH CONG. 1ST SESS. 2005, S. DOC. 2778.

US SENATE. *AUTHORIZING APPROPRIATIONS FOR FISCAL YEAR 1997 FOR MILITARY ACTIVITIES OF THE DEPARTMENT OF DEFENSE, FOR MILITARY CONSTRUCTION, AND FOR DEFENSE ACTIVITIES OF THE DEPARTMENT OF ENERGY, TO PRESCRIBE PERSONNEL STRENGTHS FOR SUCH FISCAL YEAR FOR THE ARMED FORCES, AND FOR OTHER PURPOSE,* 104TH CONG., 2ND SESS., 1996. S. DOC 104-278.

US SENATE. *NATIONAL INTELLIGENCE REFORM ACT OF 2004,* 108TH CONG., 2ND SESS., 2004, S.2845.

US SENATE. *SPECIAL REPORT OF THE SELECT COMMITTEE ON INTELLIGENCE,* 105TH CONG., 1ST SESS., 1997, S. DOC. 105-1.

MICHAEL WARNER, ED., *CENTRAL INTELLIGENCE: ORIGIN AND EVOLUTION,* WASHINGTON, DC: CENTER FOR THE STUDY OF INTELLIGENCE, CENTRAL INTELLIGENCE AGENCY, 2001.

PERIODICALS

BERKOWITZ, BRUCE. "INTELLIGENCE REFORM: LESS IS MORE." *HOOVER DIGEST*, NO. 2 (SPRING 2004) N.P. ON-LINE INTERNET. AVAILABLE FROM HTTP://WWW.HOOVERDIGEST.ORG/ 042/BERKOWITZ.HTML.

BETTS, RICHARD K. "THE NEW POLITICS OF INTELLIGENCE: WILL REFORMS WORK THIS TIME?"

FOREIGN AFFAIRS 83, NO. 3 (MAY-JUN. 2004): 2-8.

CANON, DAVID. "INTELLIGENCE AND ETHICS: THE CIA'S COVERT OPERATIONS." THE JOURNAL OF LIBERTARIAN STUDIES IV, NO. 2 (SPRING 1980): 197-214.

"CHAMBLISS HELPS INTRODUCE INTELLIGENCE REFORM BILL." THE CHATTANOOGAN.COM, (16 MARCH 16, 2005): N.P. ON-LINE INTERNET. AVAILABLE FROM HTTP://WWW.CHATTANOOGAN.COM/ARTICLES /ARTICLE_64105.ASP.

COOPER, MARY H. "REFORMING THE CIA." THE CQ RESEARCHER 6, NO. 5 (2 FEBRUARY 1996): 99-106.

DEUTCH, JOHN "THE SMART APPROACH TO INTELLIGENCE." THE WASHINGTON POST, (9 SEPTEMBER 2002): A17.

DIAMOND, JOHN. "INTELLIGENCE IMPASSE MAINLY A QUESTION OF CONTROL." USA TODAY, (29 NOVEMBER 2004): 6A.

DIAMOND, JOHN. "PENTAGON MULLS MILITARY COMMAND FOR INTELLIGENCE." USA TODAY, (10 JANUARY 2005): N.P. ON-LINE INTERNET. AVAILABLE FROM HTTP://WWW.USATODAY.COM/NEWS/WASHINGTON/ 2005-01-10-INTEL-POST_X.HTM.

DIAMOND, JOHN. "PENTAGON'S OBJECTIONS BLOCK OVERHAUL OF U.S. INTELLIGENCE" USA TODAY, (2 NOVEMBER 2004): 12A.

[1] DORR, ROBERT F. "A BIGGER INTELLIGENCE BUREAUCRACY DOESN'T EQUAL BETTER INTELLIGENCE." ARMY TIMES, (31 JANUARY 2005): 46.

FROMKIN, DAVID. "DARING AMATEURISM: THE CIA'S SOCIAL HISTORY." FOREIGN AFFAIRS 75, NO. 1 (JANUARY/FEBRUARY 1996): N.P. ON-LINE INTERNET. AVAILABLE FROM HTTP://WWW.FOREIGNAFFAIRS.ORG/19960101FAREVIEWESSAY4181/DAVID-FROMKIN/DARING-AMATEURISM-THE-CIA-S-SOCIAL-HISTORY.HTML.

GOODMAN, GLEN W. "INTELLIGENCE ON DEMAND AN INTERVIEW WITH STEPHEN CAMBONE, UNDERSECRETARY OF DEFENSE FOR INTELLIGENCE," THE ISR JOURNAL, (3 DECEMBER 2003): N.P. ON-LINE INTERNET. AVAILABLE FROM HTTP://WWW.DEFENSELINK.MIL/USDI/ CAMBONEINTERVIEW.HTML.

GOODMAN, MELVIN A. "9/11: THE FAILURE OF STRATEGIC INTELLIGENCE." INTELLIGENCE AND NATIONAL SECURITY 18, NO. 4 (WINTER 2003): 59-71.

HULNICK, ARTHUR S. "DOES THE U.S. INTELLIGENCE COMMUNITY NEED A DNI?" INTERNATIONAL JOURNAL OF INTELLIGENCE AND COUNTERINTELLIGENCE 17, NO. 4 (WINTER 2004-2005): 710-730.

ISIKOFF, MICHAEL AND DANIEL KLAIDMAN, "LOOK WHO'S NOT TALKING – STILL." NEWSWEEK, (4 APRIL, 2005): N.P. ON-LINE INTERNET. AVAILABLE FROM HTTP://MSNBC.MSN.COM/ID/ 7306163/SITE/NEWSWEEK

JOHNSON, LOCH K. "THE ASPIN-BROWN INTELLIGENCE INQUIRY: BEHIND THE CLOSED DOORS OF A BLUE RIBBON COMMISSION." STUDIES IN INTELLIGENCE 48, NO. 3 (2004): 1-20.

KAPLAN, DAVID E. AND KEVIN WHITELAW. "INTELLIGENCE REFORM -- AT LAST." U.S. NEWS & WORLD REPORT, (20 DEC. 2004): 31-32.

KINDSVATER, LARRY C. "THE NEED TO REORGANIZE THE INTELLIGENCE COMMUNITY." STUDIES IN INTELLIGENCE, JOURNAL OF THE AMERICAN INTELLIGENCE PROFESSIONAL 47, NO.1, (2003): 33-38.

KOHLER, ROBERT J. "ONE OFFICER'S PERSPECTIVE: THE DECLINE OF THE NATIONAL RECONNAISSANCE OFFICE." *STUDIES IN INTELLIGENCE, JOURNAL OF THE AMERICAN INTELLIGENCE PROFESSIONAL* 46, NO. 2, (2002): 13-20.

MILLER, ABRAHAM H., AND BRIAN ALEXANDER. "STRUCTURAL QUIESCENCE IN THE FAILURE OF *IC21* AND INTELLIGENCE REFORM." *INTERNATIONAL JOURNAL OF INTELLIGENCE AND COUNTERINTELLIGENCE* 14, NO. 2 (SUMMER 2001): 234-261.

MORGAN, DAVID. "NEGROPONTE TAKES INTELLIGENCE REINS." *ARIZONA DAILY STAR,* (18 FEBRUARY 2005): N.P. ON-LINE INTERNET. AVAILABLE FROM HTTP://WWW.AZSTARNET.COM/DAILYSTAR/RELATEDARTICLES/61981.PHP

NOLAN, CYNTHIA M. "SEYMOUR HERSH'S IMPACT ON THE CIA." *INTERNATIONAL JOURNAL OF INTELLIGENCE AND COUNTERINTELLIGENCE* 12, NO. 1 (SPRING 1999): 18-34.

PAPPAS, ARIS A., AND JAMES M. SIMON, JR. "THE INTELLIGENCE COMMUNITY: 2001-2015." *STUDIES IN INTELLIGENCE* 46, NO. 1 (2002): 39-47.

PINCUS, WALTER. "NATIONAL INTELLIGENCE DIRECTOR PROVES TO BE DIFFICULT POST TO FILL." *WASHINGTONPOST.COM*, (31 JANUARY 2005): A04.

PINCUS, WALTER "PRESIDENT GETS TO FILL RANKS OF NEW INTELLIGENCE SUPERSTRUCTURE." *WASHINGTONPOST.COM*, (16 DECEMBER 2004): A35,

POSNER, RICHARD A. "IMPORTANT JOB, IMPOSSIBLE POSITION." *THE NEW YORK TIMES*, (9 FEBRUARY 2005): N.P. ON-LINE INTERNET. AVAILABLE FROM HTTP://QUERY.NYTIMES.COM/GST/ABSTRACT.HTML?RES=FB0F1EF6345F0C7A8CDDAB0894DD404482.

PRADOS, JOHN. "INTELLIGENCE: NO EASY FIX." *BULLETIN OF THE ATOMIC SCIENTISTS* 60, NO. 5 (SEPTEMBER/OCTOBER 2004): 17-19

RUSSELL, RICHARD J. "TUG OF WAR: THE CIA'S UNEASY RELATIONSHIP WITH THE MILITARY." *SAIS REVIEW* 22 (SUMMER-FALL 2002): 1-17.

SMITH, JEFFREY H. AND JOHN DEUTCH "SMARTER INTELLIGENCE." *FOREIGN POLICY* (JANUARY/FEBRUARY 2002): 64-69.

"THE SPYMASTER'S MISSION: NEGROPONTE FACES HUGE CHALLENGES IN NEW JOB." *THE REGISTER-GUARD,* EUGENE, OREGON. (22 FEBRUARY 2005): N.P. ON-LINE INTERNET. AVAILABLE FROM WWW.REGISTERGUARD.COM/NEWS/2005/02/22/ED.EDIT.NEGROPONTE.PHN.0222.HTML.

TAYLOR STAN A. AND DAVID GOLDMAN, "INTELLIGENCE REFORM: WILL MORE AGENCIES, MONEY, AND PERSONNEL HELP?" *INTELLIGENCE AND NATIONAL SECURITY.*19, NO.3 (AUTUMN 2004): 416-435.

TREVERTON GREGORY F. AND PETER A. WILSON, "TRUE INTELLIGENCE REFORM IS CULTURAL, NOT JUST ORGANIZATIONAL CHART SHIFT." *THE CHRISTIAN SCIENCE MONITOR*, (13 JANUARY 2005): ON-LINE INTERNET, AVAILABLE FROM WWW.CSMONITOR.COM/2005/0113/P09S02-COOP.HTML.

TURNER, STANSFIELD "RESTRUCTURING" *WASHINGTON POST*, (1 AUGUST 2004): B01.

"TWO ISSUES STALLING INTEL OVERHAUL BILL." *NEWSMAX WIRES*. (2 DECEMBER 2004): N.P. ON-LINE INTERNET. AVAILABLE FROM HTTP://WWW.NEWSMAX.COM/ARCHIVES/ARTICLES/2004/12/2/155222.SHTML.

WATERMAN, SHAUN. "CONGRESS ALREADY TWEAKING NEW INTEL POST." *WASHINGTON TIMES.* (21 MARCH 2005): N.P. ON-LINE INTERNET. AVAILABLE FROM HTTP://WASHTIMES.COM/UPI-BREAKING/20050320-033228-9327R.HTM

OTHER

BARR, BOB. "IS IT TIME TO REFORM INTELLIGENCE REFORM?" *FINDLAW'S LEGAL COMMENTARY.* (JAN 21, 2005): ON-LINE INTERNET. AVAILABLE FROM HTTP://WRIT.NEWS.FINDLAW.COM/COMMENTARY/20050121_BARR.HTML.

CARAFANO, JAMES JAY. "THE CASE FOR INTELLIGENCE REFORM: A PRIMER ON STRATEGIC INTELLIGENCE AND TERRORISM FROM THE 1970S TO TODAY." *THE HERITAGE FOUNDATION.* LECTURE #845, (21 JULY 2004), ON-LINE INTERNET. AVAILABLE FROM HTTP://WWW.HERITAGE.ORG/RESEARCH/NATIONALSECURITY/HL845.CFM

CHAMBLISS, SAXBY. "INTELLIGENCE REFORM AND THE SAFETY OF AMERICA: HAVE WE SUCCEEDED?" *THE HERITAGE FOUNDATION*, WEBMEMO#633, 7 JANUARY 2005, ON-LINE, INTERNET, AVAILABLE FROM WWW.HERITAGE.ORG/RESEARCH/HOMELANDDEFENSE/WM633.CFM.

GREENBERG, MAURICE R. CHAIRMAN & RICHARD N. HAASS, PROJECT DIRECTOR, *MAKING INTELLIGENCE SMARTER, THE FUTURE OF US INTELLIGENCE: REPORT OF AN INDEPENDENT TASK FORCE.* THE COUNCIL ON FOREIGN RELATIONS, ON-LINE INTERNET. AVAILABLE FROM HTTP://WWW.FAS.ORG/IRP/CFR.HTML.

HELGERSON, JOHN L. *CIA BRIEFINGS OF PRESIDENTIAL CANDIDATES 1952-1992.* WASHINGTON DC: CENTER FOR THE STUDY OF INTELLIGENCE, CENTRAL INTELLIGENCE AGENCY, 1996.

KAPLAN, FRED. "WHAT NID NEEDS, BUSH'S BOLD CHOICE FOR NATIONAL INTELLIGENCE DIRECTOR?" *SLATE* 17 FEBRUARY 2005, N.P. ON-LINE INTERNET. AVAILABLE FROM HTTP://SLATE.MSN.COM/ID/2113705.

GOODMAN, MELVIN A. "IN FROM THE COLD, THE NEED FOR REFORM OF THE CIA," *FOREIGN POLICY IN FOCUS*, SPECIAL REPORT #13, FEBRUARY 2001, ON-LINE INTERNET. AVAILABLE FROM HTTP://WWW.FPIF.ORG/PDF/REPORTS/CIA.PDF.

LANDRY, ROBIN MIYOSHI. "REFORMING INTELLIGENCE: SELLING CHANGE." WASHINGTON DC: NATIONAL DEFENSE UNIVERSITY, NATIONAL WAR COLLEGE.

GOODMAN, MELVIN A. "THE ROAD TO INTELLIGENCE REFORM: PAVED WITH GOOD INTENTIONS," 1996, ON-LINE INTERNET. AVAILABLE FROM HTTP://WWW.US.NET/CIP/DIGEST.HTM.

LIEBERMAN, JOSEPH, "GOVERNMENTAL AFFAIRS COMMITTEE HEARING ON THE PRESIDENT'S PROPOSAL FOR A TERRORISM THREAT INTEGRATION CENTER." STATEMENT TO THE SENATE GOVERNMENTAL AFFAIRS COMMITTEE, 14 FEBRUARY 2003, ON-LINE INTERNET. AVAILABLE FROM HTTP://WWW.FAS.ORG/IRP/CONGRESS/2003_HR/.

LIEBERMAN, JOSEPH. "REORGANIZING AMERICA'S INTELLIGENCE COMMUNITY: A VIEW FROM THE INSIDE" STATEMENT BEFORE THE SENATE COMMITTEE ON GOVERNMENTAL AFFAIRS, AUGUST, 16 2004. ON-LINE INTERNET. AVAILABLE FROM HTTP://HSGAC.SENATE.GOV/INDEX.CFM?FUSEACTION=HEARINGS.TESTIMONY& TESTIMONYID=681&HEARINGID=197.

MARKUS, USTINA. "CIA IN DECLINE, PENTAGON ON THE RISE." *ISN SECURITY WATCH*, (24 JANUARY,

2005): N.P. ON-LINE INTERNET. AVAILABLE FROM HTTP://WWW.ISN.CH/NEWS/SW/ DETAILS.CFM?ID=10626.

"MAKING INTELLIGENCE SMARTER: THE FUTURE OF U.S. INTELLIGENCE." NEW YORK: COUNCIL ON FOREIGN RELATIONS, (1996). ON-LINE INTERNET. AVAILABLE FROM HTTP://WWW.COPI.COM/ARTICLES/INTELRPT/CFR.HTML

"NATIONAL COMMISSION ON TERRORIST ATTACKS UPON THE UNITED STATES." ON-LINE INTERNET. AVIALABLE FROM WWW.9-11COMMISSION.GOV.

PAN, ESTHER. "INTELLIGENCE LEGISLATIVE REFORM." NEW YORK: COUNCIL ON FOREIGN RELATIONS. 31MARCH 2005. ON-LINE INTERNET. AVAILABLE FROM WWW.CFR.ORG/BACKGROUND/ BACKGROUND_ INTELLIGENCE_REFORM.PHP?PRINT=1.

PRIEST, DANA. "THE CHANGING ROLES OF THE REGIONAL COMMANDERS IN CHIEF", REMARKS AVAILABLE FROM THE SECRETARY OF STATE'S OPEN FORUM. MARCH 23, 2001. ON-LINE INTERNET. AVAILABLE FROM HTTP://WWW.STATE.GOV/S/P/OF/PROC/TR/3719.HTM.

"PROFILES OF THE U.S. INTELLIGENCE COMMUNITY." TOTSE.COM. ON-LINE INTERNET. AVAILABLE FROM HTTP://WWW.TOTSE.COM/EN/POLITICS/CENTRAL_INTELLIGENCE_AGENCY/PROFUSIC.HTML.

RICHELSON JEFFERY T. ED., "FROM DIRECTOR OF CENTRAL INTELLIGENCE TO DIRECTOR OF NATIONAL INTELLIGENCE." IN *NATIONAL SECURITY ARCHIVE ELECTRONIC BRIEFING BOOK NO. 144,* 17 DECEMBER 2004, ON-LINE INTERNET. AVAILABLE FROM HTTP://WWW.GWU.EDU/ ~NSARCHIV/NSAEBB/NSAEBB144/

RICHELSON JEFFERY T. ED., "THE NATIONAL SECURITY AGENCY DECLASSIFIED." *NATIONAL SECURITY ARCHIVE ELECTRONIC BRIEFING BOOK NO. 24.* 13 JANUARY 2000. ON-LINE INTERNET. AVAILABLE FROM HTTP://WWW.GWU.EDU/~NSARCHIV/NSAEBB/NSAEBB23/INDEX2.HTML.

[1] SIOBAHN GORMAN, "FEWER, BETTER SPIES KEY TO INTELLIGENCE REFORM, FORMER OFFICIAL SAYS." *GOVEXEC,* 18 MARCH 2005, ON-LINE INTERNET. AVAILABLE FROM HTTP://WWW.GOVEXEC.COM/STORY_PAGE.CFM?ARTICLEID=30798&PRINTERFRIENDLYVERS=1&

GORMAN, SIOBHAN "FRUSTRATED INTELLIGENCE REFORMERS SEE WINDOW OF OPPORTUNITY." *GOVEXEC.COM,* 11 JUNE 2004, ON-LINE INTERNET. AVAILABLE FROM HTTP://WWW.GLOBAL SECURITY.ORG/ORG/NEWS/2004/040611-INTELL-REFORM.HTM.

SCHLESINGER, JAMES. *A REVIEW OF THE INTELLIGENCE COMMUNITY,* 10 MARCH 1971, ON-LINE INTERNET. AVAILABLE FROM HTTP://WWW.FAS.ORG/IRP/CIA/PRODUCT/REVIEW1971.PDF.

SCHLESINGER, ROBERT. "EXPANDING ROLE OF DEFENSE DEPARTMENT SPURS CONCERNS." *VETERANS FOR PEACE,* 6 AUGUST 2003. ON-LINE INTERNET. AVAILABLE FROM WWW.VETERANSFORPEACE.ORG/EXPANDING_ROLE_060803.HTM.

"SUMMARY AND ANALYSIS, 9/11 COMMISSION RECOMMENDATIONS." MILNET BRIEF, 22 JULY 2004, ON-LINE INTERNET. AVAILABLE FROM HTTP://WWW.MILNET.COM/9-11-COMMISSION/ANALYSIS1.HTML

WOOLSEY, JAMES R. IN A FORUM MODERATED BY WALTER H. PINCUS FOR THE COUNCIL ON FOREIGN RELATIONS, NEW YORK, MAY 12, 2004. TRANSCRIPT AVAILABLE ON-LINE INTERNET. AVAILABLE FROM HTTP://WWW.CFR.ORG/PUB7022/STANSFIELD_TURNER_R_JAMES_WOOLSEY_WILLIAM_H_ WEBSTER_WALTER_H_PINCUS/THE_CENTRAL_INTELLIGENCE_AGENCY.PHP.